SOPHIE TREADWELL

Sophie Treadwell.
Photo courtesy Special Collections, The University of Arizona Library.

SOPHIE TREADWELL

A Research and Production Sourcebook

JERRY DICKEY

Modern Dramatists Research and Production
Sourcebooks, Number 12 *William W. Demastes, Series Adviser*

GREENWOOD PRESS
Westport, Connecticut • London

Library of Congress Cataloging-in-Publication Data

Dickey, Jerry R. (Jerry Richard), 1956–
    Sophie Treadwell : a research and production sourcebook / Jerry
Dickey.
        p.   cm.—(Modern dramatists reasearch and production
sourcebooks, ISSN 1055–999X ; no. 12)
    Includes bibliographical references (p.   ) and index.
    ISBN 0–313–29388–0 (alk. paper)
    1. Treadwell, Sophie, 1885–1970—Criticism and interpretation.
2. Treadwell, Sophie, 1885–1970—Dramatic production.   3. Treadwell,
Sophie, 1885–1970—Stage history.   4. Treadwell, Sophie, 1885–1970—
Bibliography.   I. Title.   II. Series.
    PS3539.R342Z63   1997
    812'.52—dc20   96–43986

British Library Cataloguing in Publication Data is available.

Library of Congress Catalog Card Number: 96–43986
ISBN: 0–313–29388–0
ISSN: 1055–999X

First published in 1997

Greenwood Press, 88 Post Road West, Westport, CT 06881
An imprint of Greenwood Publishing Group, Inc.

Printed in the United States of America

∞™

The paper used in this book complies with the
Permanent Paper Standard issued by the National
Information Standards Organization (Z39.48–1984).

10 9 8 7 6 5 4 3 2 1

CONTENTS

CONTENTS

PREFACE

It is my hope that this work will stimulate interest in more serious investigation of Sophie Treadwell's work as a dramatist. So little is currently known about the career of this nearly forgotten but innovative dramatist, that such a study seems long overdue. Treadwell was an intrepid and prolific woman of the theatre; she is worthy of renewed attention and recognition.

This text, like others in its series, has been designed to be easily accessible to scholars, students and theatre artists, each of whom may bring a different reason for wishing to discover more about Treadwell's life and work. The reader will find biographical information, play summaries, critical overviews, production histories and exhaustive primary and secondary bibliographies. Descriptions of archival sources may further indicate the vast resources that await the interested theatre scholar.

More significantly, perhaps, the detailed plot descriptions may suggest something of the wide range of Treadwell's writings for the stage. The overwhelming majority of her works are unpublished and practically unknown to all but a handful of scholars. Many of these plays warrant reexamination, both in terms of scholarly assessment and as vital and stageworthy pieces of theatre.

Throughout much of her life, Treadwell was active professionally as a playwright and journalist. Since the focus of this sourcebook is on the theatre, Treadwell's accomplishments as a newspaperwoman receive only minor attention. Discussion is included, however, whenever her investigative reporting intersects with her work as a playwright. A partial list of her journalistic writings may be found in the Primary Bibliography.

ACKNOWLEDGMENTS

Many individuals deserve recognition for their support of my work on this book. I am, above all, indebted to the reference, special collections and interlibrary loan staffs at the University of Arizona Library. In particular, Roger Myers, Special Collections Manuscript Librarian, has been supportive and helpful above and beyond the call of duty. Staffs at the San Francisco Performing Arts Library and Museum and the New York Public Library for the Performing Arts have also provided much-needed assistance and materials.

I am fortunate to work with a number of stimulating colleagues and students in the Department of Theatre Arts at the University of Arizona. My department head, Al Tucci, has provided encouragement, computer equipment and travel funds to present research. I am also grateful to the Dean of the College of Fine Arts, Maurice Sevigny, for personal support and funding through research incentive grants.

Numerous individuals have taken time to share with me their memories of Sophie Treadwell. Many thanks to all of them, especially J. Emery Barker. My debt to other scholars is also very great; the early studies of Treadwell by Louise Heck-Rabi and Nancy Wynn, especially, provided insights and a point of departure. I am thankful to Naomi Sawelson-Gorse for long, illuminating conversations and for making positive things happen. Mark Fearnow provided initial encouragement for my idea for this volume.

William Demastes of Louisiana State University deserves much recognition for editing such a useful and well-planned series and for openly encouraging researchers like me to develop new volumes. Similarly, George Butler and Greenwood Press should be acknowledged for a commitment to publishing valuable works in the field of theatre and drama.

I must express my gratitude to Sophie and William Treadwell for not throwing out old manuscripts, correspondence and other materials. While sifting through the mounds of boxes at the University of Arizona archive at times felt like an overwhelming task, I was always grateful to find so much of a past life and career preserved on paper.

My most important acknowledgments, however, are very personal ones. My parents, Joe and Ethel Scramlin Dickey, continue to provide me with guidance and encouragement of the type one can never repay. The greatest thanks of all go to my wife, Deborah Dickey, for her incredible understanding and support during the past four-plus years of my Treadwell research. She always retained interest in the subject of this book, and she graciously understood why it often took over rooms in our house and hours of our time together.

A NOTE ON CODES AND NUMBERING

Extensive references in this book are arranged according to type of material and designated by a prefix and code number. Prefixes used for these listings are described below.

"A"   Treadwell's non-fiction, arranged alphabetically and annotated in the "Primary Bibliography."

"P"   Significant productions of Treadwell's plays, listed alphabetically in "Productions and Credits."

"R"   Reviews of Treadwell's plays and fiction, listed chronologically in "Annotated Secondary Bibliography: Reviews."

"S"   Secondary materials, including critical studies, biographical material and significant production information, listed chronologically in "Annotated Secondary Bibliography: Books, Articles, Sections."

CHRONOLOGY

1885   Born October 3 in Stockton, California, to Alfred B. and Nettie Fairchild Treadwell.

1890-91   Father moves to San Francisco. Along with her mother, alternately lives with and away from her father for the next several years.

1902-06   While attending the University of California at Berkeley, performs in numerous sketches and plays. Final year of college is marked by poverty and illness. Graduates with a Bachelor of Letters degree with an emphasis in French.

1906   Teaches in a one-room school at Yankee Jim's, an old mining camp in Placer County, California. Writes *Le Grand Prix*.

1907   Moves to Los Angeles and performs in vaudeville. Befriends Constance Skinner, author and former drama critic.

1908   Skinner arranges for Treadwell to type Helena Modjeska's memoirs at the actress's home in Tustin, California. With encouragement from Modjeska, markets her play, *The Right Man*, to theatrical producers in New York. Returns to San Francisco in the summer to be with her ailing mother. Hired as a journalist for the *San Francisco Bulletin*.

1910   Marries William O. McGeehan, famed sports reporter and humorist. Six months later, recuperates from a recurring nervous condition at St. Helena Sanitorium.

1912   Performs a leading role in *The Toad*, a drama of ancient Egypt, at the Forest Theatre, Carmel-by-the-Sea.

1914   Interviews celebrities, covers a sensational murder trial, and writes her first serial, "An Outcast at the Christian Door," for the *Bulletin*. McGeehan accepts a job with the *New York Evening Journal*. Completes a 150-mile march with the Lucy Stone League to deliver a petition on women's suffrage to the New York legislature.

1915   Her serial, "How I Got My Husband and How I Lost Him," adapted for the stage and produced in San Francisco under the title, *An Unwritten Chapter*. Spends four months in France writing articles on World War I for the *Bulletin* and *Harper's Weekly*. Returns to the States in August, accepting a job with the *New York American*.

1916-19   Writes several plays, acting in and producing one of them, *Claws*, as a showcase in 1918. Befriends art patrons, Walter and Louise Arensberg. Has romantic affair with the painter Maynard Dixon.

1920-21   Covers the aftermath of the Mexican Revolution, including an exclusive interview with Pancho Villa, for the *New York Tribune*.

1922   *Gringo* produced on Broadway by Guthrie McClintic.

1923   Spends the summer with a small group of theatre artists studying acting with Richard Boleslavsky.

1924   Sues John Barrymore over his failure to return her play manuscript on the life of Edgar Allan Poe.

1925   Acts in and produces her comedy, *O Nightingale*, on Broadway.

1927   Attends the murder trial of Ruth Snyder and Judd Gray.

1928   *Machinal* produced on Broadway by Arthur Hopkins.

1929   *Ladies Leave* receives a short run on Broadway. Works briefly for United Artists on script revisions and adaptations.

1930   Treadwell and McGeehan embark on the first of two lengthy trips through Europe and North Africa.

1931 *Machinal* produced in London under the title *The Life Machine*. The novel, *Lusita*, published.

1933 Visits Moscow for the production of *Machinal* by Alexander Tairov. *Lone Valley*, produced and directed by Treadwell, closes on Broadway after three performances. McGeehan dies.

1934 *For Saxophone* copyrighted. Treadwell's mother dies.

1936 *Plumes in the Dust* produced on Broadway. Travels to Egypt and the Far East.

1941 *Hope for a Harvest* produced in New York by the Theatre Guild.

1942 Spends ten months in Mexico City as correspondent for the *New York Herald Tribune*.

1944 *Highway* given a workshop production in Pasadena. Tries briefly to work as a screenwriter in Hollywood.

1949 Adopts a German baby, whom she names William. Divides her time over the next several years between Europe, Mexico, Connecticut and California.

1953 *Hope for a Harvest* aired on television's "U.S. Steel Hour," produced by the Theatre Guild.

1954 An adaptation of *Highway* televised. Sells the family ranch in Stockton.

1956-65 Based mostly in Torremolinos, Spain, turns more to writing novels. Seeks relief from a variety of debilitating ailments.

1959 Novel, *One Fierce Hour and Sweet*, published.

1960 *Machinal* revived off-Broadway at the Gate Theatre.

1965 Moves to Tucson, Arizona.

1967 *Woman with Lilies* produced at the University of Arizona under the title, *Now He Doesn't Want to Play*.

1970 Dies in Tucson, February 20.

LIFE AND CAREER

Studies of American theatre have too long omitted the accomplishments of Sophie Treadwell. Although best remembered today for only a single work, the explosive 1928 drama *Machinal*, Treadwell maintained a career in the theatre which spanned close to sixty years and included the authorship of approximately forty plays. At a time when women playwrights were growing steadily amongst the ranks of dramatists represented on Broadway, Treadwell was one of a select few of these women who also took an active role in producing and directing her own plays. She became a relentless and articulate advocate for the commercial and artistic rights afforded playwrights on Broadway and around the world. She experimented with a range of dramatic structures and styles, and often tackled timely or controversial subjects which she knew would prove unpopular with commercial producers. Perhaps above all, Treadwell continually placed female characters in subject positions of her plays and dramatized women's personal and social struggles for independence and equality. That Treadwell would eventually shun the professional theatre in America, and be shunned by it, both in terms of play production during her later years and in terms of historical and critical assessments of American drama, is an unfortunate tragedy. Only now, after highly prominent revivals of *Machinal* by the New York Shakespeare Festival in 1990 and London's Royal National Theatre in 1993, has Treadwell begun to be recognized for her original contributions to the American stage.

Sophie Anita Treadwell was born in Stockton, California on October 3, 1885. Her father, Alfred B. Treadwell, served as Justice of the Peace and City Prosecutor in Stockton. Sophie's mother, Nettie Fairchild Treadwell, grew up on a Stockton ranch her parents homesteaded beginning in 1850. Sophie would later say that her first memory of her father was that he was never present. When Sophie was about six, Alfred left his wife and daughter for San Francisco, where he practiced law and served as an elected judge. In the latter capacity, Alfred was a strict disciplinarian, rigid in his often eccentric convictions. Aware of his position as a public figure, Alfred denied his Mexican heritage (his grandmother was Mexican of Spanish descent), saying his dark skin color was the result of smallpox contracted in childhood (Pauline Jacobson, "Rough Riding as a Cure for Social Ills," *San Francisco Bulletin* 16 Mar. 1907). Even though Sophie would enjoy brief visits with her father in the city as she grew up--getting money from him, being taken to the theatre, and sometimes working in his office--she would later resent his haphazard commitment to his fatherly responsibilities. Her unreconciled relationship to her father undoubtedly formed the basis for several of her later plays, such as *A Man's Own* (1905), *John Doane* (1915-18), and *Judgment in the Morning* (1952), and individuals in many of Treadwell's plays struggle, as Alfred did, with an identity of mixed racial backgrounds.

The year before giving birth to Sophie, Nettie had a phrenological analysis of her character taken by a visiting lecturer from New York. The report identified a lack of confidence as her greatest fault, and warned her of the unhealthy consequences which may result from her current state of worry and nervousness. Nettie's later correspondence with her daughter suggests the analysis contained the essence of some truth. Nettie followed after Alfred to first San Francisco and subsequently to Sausalito. Although her parents would at times live together, the young Sophie was acutely aware of her mother's embarrassment and loneliness at frequently being left alone by her husband. Nettie's frustrations increased after 1893, when she informed Sophie she was preparing to divorce Alfred, an act upon which she was never able to follow through. Sophie watched her mother try many jobs to provide them with needed income: running a boarding house, working as an attendant in an asylum, and serving as a companion and caregiver for an invalid, the latter action dramatized by Treadwell in *Constance Darrow* (1908-09).

Treadwell excelled at her early education, but as she continued to move from place to place, she grew to dislike school and lost faith that she possessed any special aptitude. Upon graduation from a girls' high school in 1901, Treadwell's intention of pursuing a career on the stage was most likely squelched by Nettie, who could never understand her daughter's seemingly impractical career ambitions.

Instead, Treadwell enrolled at the University of California at Berkeley, where she was exposed to a wide range of new activities. While she found an outlet for her interests in theatre by regularly performing with the drama club, she also pursued training in shorthand and typing at a commercial high school. She participated on the ladies crew team, helped edit the women's edition of the college humor magazine, began writing stories and poetry, and worked as a campus correspondent for the *San Francisco Examiner*. Plagued by financial worries during her senior year, Treadwell took jobs in the circulation department of the *San Francisco Call* and at a local night school where she taught thirty foreign students. She later complained that during this time her brain got so active that she could not sleep. Fatigue and illness further disrupted her activities, as did the San Francisco earthquake in 1906. Her entire class graduated that spring in absentia, Treadwell earning a Bachelor of Letters degree with an emphasis in French.

The ensuing fall, Treadwell accepted a job teaching less than a dozen students in a one-room school at Yankee Jim's, an old mining town in the Sierra Nevadas. Winter life in the rugged and remote area afforded Treadwell much time to write, and she completed a diary-like dramatic sketch, *Wintering it at Yankee Jim's* (1906-07), and her first serious full-length play, *Le Grand Prix* (1906-07). She continued teaching the following summer as a governess to two young girls on a cattle ranch in Modoc in northeastern California, a locale which provided the setting for her comedy, *The Right Man* (1908).

In the fall of 1907, Treadwell finally decided to try her hand at the professional theatre, and she moved with her mother to Los Angeles, where she hoped to land a job in vaudeville. She attended numerous auditions before naively turning to the drama critic of the *Los Angeles Examiner*, Otheman Stevens, for help in obtaining her own accompanist. Impressed by her bravado, Stevens found her a musician and helped her get her first booking at Fischer's Theatre, where she performed as a character artist singing three songs with changes of costume. As her week's engagement progressed, however, Treadwell was overwhelmed with disgust and nausea over the squallidness of the performance conditions, and she would later describe some of her impressions with vaudeville in an unpublished short story, "Amateur Night." With her mother having returned to Stockton and her father refusing financial assistance, Treadwell decided to quit the theatre with $16 to her name.

While she had been auditioning, however, Treadwell also began circulating *Le Grand Prix* to theatre managers. By chance, a copy of the play was read by Constance Skinner, a former drama critic who was then assisting Helena Modjeska in the writing of her memoirs. Skinner befriended Treadwell, hired her as her personal typist, and upon deciding to accept a job in Chicago, arranged for Treadwell to type for Modjeska. Sensing this momentous turn of events might prove to be a career landmark, Treadwell paused to write her only autobiographical statement, an unpublished manuscript she titled "The Story of Muh Life by One Who Has None" (1908).

Treadwell's stay at Modjeska's home in Orange County did indeed prove momentous. While it appears that Treadwell, despite her later claims, did little in the way of actually helping write the memoirs, she did impress Modjeska with her passion and talent for theatre. With Madame's encouragement, Treadwell marketed *The Right Man* to an interested Jules Murry, a theatre manager in New York. When Murry subsequently demanded revisions, Modjeska encouraged Treadwell to humor Murry with slight changes, but never to sacrifice the integrity of her work. Modjeska had also encouraged Treadwell to submit the play under a male pseudonym, believing theatre producers treated women writers with less seriousness than their male counterparts (letter to Treadwell, 23 July 1908). Treadwell would use a variety of pseudonyms throughout her career, and satisfactorily accommodating producers' demands for script changes remained a difficulty for her. Treadwell had been awe-struck by Modjeska, once speaking of her time with the great actress as being akin to a religious conversion. Treadwell left Modjeska in the summer of 1908 to be with Nettie, who was ill in San Francisco, but she later paid tribute to her benefactor by performing characters modelled after Modjeska in her plays *Claws* (1918) and *O Nightingale* (1925).

While attending to her mother, Treadwell was hired as a feature writer and theatre critic for the *San Francisco Bulletin*, an event which would change her life professionally and personally. While reviewing a performance at the Valencia Theatre in October of that year, Treadwell met William O. McGeehan, a well-known sports reporter and humorist. She would marry McGeehan on January 27, 1910 in Oakland, but within six months, Treadwell experienced a sudden loss in weight, and McGeehan sent his new bride to the St. Helena Sanitarium, where doctors termed her nervous and high-strung.

The condition was a recurrence of her college illness, one which would plague her off and on throughout her life. Unquestionably, Treadwell's ailment would have been known in the early decades of this century as "neurasthenia," a nervous disorder which might have a variety of symptoms, including digestive woes, insomnia, headaches, hypochondria, and nervous prostration. It was believed to have been caused by stress due to the rapid changes in modern civilization, and it afflicted those with either extreme moral laxity or sensitivity. Neurasthenia was particularly associated with the leisure-classes, artists and intellectuals, and in some circles became a sign of social status and acceptibility. Neurasthenic characters abound in literature of the period, including Treadwell's best-known central character, the Young Woman in *Machinal*. The subject of neurasthenia would have been a frequent one in the Treadwell household as Sophie was growing up. Her father considered himself something of an expert on the disease, and believed women possessed a special susceptibility to its debilitation. He expressed his views on the illness in an interview for the *San Francisco Bulletin* on 15 April 1911, only a few months after Sophie's stay in St. Helena. Throughout her later life, Sophie would often seek relief in European sanitoriums, much like the one dramatized in her play *For Saxophone* (1934).

Details about Treadwell's marriage to McGeehan are difficult to reconstruct. Most of their correspondence which has survived dates from a period in their courtship and early marriage. It seems apparent, however, that even if McGeehan did not always understand Treadwell's demands for independence and privacy, he usually respected them. Late in 1914, though, after Treadwell had made a name for herself as a journalist and serial writer, McGeehan accepted a job with the *New York Evening Journal*. A short parable entitled "The Gift," apparently written by Treadwell at this time, suggests that McGeehan may have had difficulty living with Treadwell's increasing fame and independence. It is also possible, as Donald Hagerty suggests (S221), that Treadwell had begun an affair with the painter Maynard Dixon as early as 1911, although the earliest surviving correspondence and love poetry from Dixon in Treadwell's papers dates from early October 1916.

Whatever the reason for their separation, Treadwell made several cross country trips to visit her husband, and moved to New York in the fall of 1915, even though she maintained separate addresses from McGeehan at times. In this latter regard, Treadwell may have been encouraged by the position taken by Ruth Hale, president of the Lucy Stone League, of which Treadwell was a member. As her husband Heywood Broun's career skyrocketed, Hale entertained the idea of separate residences in order to maintain clearly her own identity, before deciding upon separate floors of the same building (Dale Kramer, *Heywood Bround: a Biographical Portrait* (New York: Current Books, 1949: 109-10)). Treadwell and "Mac," as she called her husband, made three lengthy automobile trips together, twice driving across Europe (S091) and once into Mexico. Treadwell collaborated with Mac on at least one occasion, a play about corruption in the world of boxing, *A Million Dollar Gate* (1930). The fact that Treadwell maintained a personal scrapbook on Mac's achievements and kept personal mementos of him after his death attests to the respect she felt for him throughout her life.

Treadwell's development as a professional dramatist is bound closely with her work as a professional journalist. Before McGeehan left for New York, Treadwell created a sensation in San Francisco by writing two popular serials for the *Bulletin*. The paper's editor, Fremont Older, first convinced Treadwell to do a serial related to the city's crackdown on prostitution. Treadwell was to disguise herself as a homeless prostitute and venture into charitable organizations in the city to discover what help was available to women in need. The serial gave Treadwell the opportunity to use her acting talents, and the resulting serial, "An Outcast at the Christian Door," placed Treadwell at the center of a San Francisco sensation. Another serial soon followed, the more fictionalized "How I Got My Husband and How I Lost Him," which provided the inspiration for Treadwell's first produced play, *Sympathy* (1915).

Shortly thereafter, Treadwell became perhaps the first American woman to be accredited as a foreign war correspondent as she covered World War I from various locations in France. However, denied access to front line fighting, Treadwell returned to the U.S. and took a job as a reporter with the *New York American*. These early years in New York were heady ones for Treadwell. She joined the Lucy Stone League (whose charter included the right for married women to retain their last names) and marched on the New York legislature with a petition for women's suffrage. She befriended numerous well-known journalists, and she frequently attended social gatherings of modernist artists at the home of Walter and Louise Arensberg, noted art patrons. She also wrote and marketed numerous new plays.

One of these was a biographical drama about Edgar Allan Poe. Having conceived of the title role for John Barrymore, Treadwell was delighted to learn in 1920 that the star actor loved her play and promised to perform in it (S234). Despite Barrymore's professed enthusiasm, he never offered a contract or a return of the manuscript. Nearly four years later, Treadwell learned of Barrymore's intent to act in a new play about Poe written by his wife, Michael Strange. After meeting with Barrymore, Treadwell was convinced Strange's play was pirated from her own, and she launched a celebrated lawsuit against the actor to stop production of Strange's work and to get Barrymore to return her original manuscript. Treadwell was villified in the press, and the ordeal greatly soured her views on the manner in which playwrights were treated in the commercial theatre. The play would eventually be presented in 1936, under the title *Plumes in the Dust*, in a production by Arthur Hopkins, Barrymore's former manager and director.

During the years in which Barrymore held her play, Treadwell turned more to her work as a journalist. In the spring of 1920, the *New York Herald Tribune* sent Treadwell to Mexico to cover the aftermath of the Mexican Revolution. Ten days after the assassination of President Don Venustiano Carranza, Treadwell offered detailed reconstructions of his flight from revolutionaries and the subsequent inquiries into the identities of his murderers. She followed these articles with features about international relations between the U.S. and Mexico, and in August 1921 was the only western journalist granted access to interview Pancho Villa at his sequestered headquarters near Rosario, in Chihuahua. The exclusive profile did much to acquaint Americans with a gentlemanly image of the bandit, one which Treadwell immediately furthered in her first Broadway play, *Gringo*, directed by Guthrie McClintic in 1922, as well as her first novel, *Lusita*, published in 1931.

As that play was completing its modest run, Treadwell sat in on lectures given at New York's Princess Theatre by the recently emigrated Richard Boleslavsky. Boleslavsky provided Americans with the first details about Konstantin Stanislavsky's "system" of acting, and Treadwell followed up on the lectures by joining a small group of artists who studied all aspects of theatre production under Boleslavsky's guidance in a summer retreat at Pleasantville, New York. Treadwell left Boleslavsky's summer retreat and promptly delivered lectures on playwriting at his newly formed American Laboratory Theatre. She also wrote an exuberant comedy about an innocent, aspiring actress from the midwest, titled *Loney Lee* (1923). After successful tryouts with Helen Hayes in the leading role, Treadwell picked up the option on the play and co-produced it on Broadway in 1925 as *O Nightingale*, her first and most successful venture into commercial theatre production.

New York critics had seen little evidence of innovative form or content in *Gringo* or *O Nightingale* to prepare them for Treadwell's next work, *Machinal*, produced by Arthur Hopkins. As a journalist, Treadwell was a veteran in covering sensational murder trials and deciphering meaning from small behavioral details of witnesses and defendants. For the *New York American*, Treadwell covered the heavily publicized trial of Elizabeth Mohr for plotting the murder of her husband and the maiming of his lover. Previously, she had covered for the *San Francisco Bulletin* the 1914 trial of Leah Alexander for the murder of her abusive lover. When the notorious trial began in 1927 accusing the Long Island housewife Ruth Snyder of conspiring with her lover, Judd Gray, in the murder of her husband, Treadwell attended the proceedings in an unofficial capacity. Rather than reporting on the events in the press, however, Treadwell used Snyder as a point of departure for a dramatic indictment of a society whose masculine laws and orientations stifled the emotional needs of women.

Numerous critics lauded *Machinal* as a landmark, especially for its seamless blending of European expressionism with domestic American realism. While some of Treadwell's early plays reveal an eagerness to experiment with dramatic form (*To Him Who Waits* (1915-18), *The Eye of the Beholder* (1919)), Treadwell's lectures for the American Lab, as well as the bulk of her stage writing to this point, clearly confirm her commitment to the traditional structures of the "well-made play." A study of early manuscripts of *Machinal* suggests that Treadwell employed expressionistic devices in an attempt to appeal to the subconscious minds of her audience, especially those of women. In adapting European expressionism, Treadwell may have been consciously attempting to devise a decidedly deliberate, feminist aesthetic in the theatre (S239). Critics mostly played up the unique staging elements, however, rather than the play's potentially subversive theme, and the play would prove the high point of Treadwell's dramatic career. It would also encourage subsequent experiments by Treadwell in dramatic form, especially the radically structured *For Saxophone*, a work which also reveals Treadwell's longtime interest in psychology.

Machinal also afforded Treadwell with the opportunity to continue her love for travel. She went to London for the 1931 production of the play (retitled *The Life Machine*), and to Moscow in 1933 for a production staged by Alexander Tairov. While in Moscow, Treadwell not only spent time in the homes of Stanislavsky and Mikhail Bulgakov but also visited a divorce court, abortion clinics, and a prostitution "institute." Her disdain for prevailing living conditions under Communism became the stimulus for a play she wrote upon her return to America, *Promised Land* (1933), a drama which despite its frequent didacticism remains one of Treadwell's finest works. Although the play garnished interest from several agents and producers, most feared that the play's theme was out of step with the prevailing leftist tenor of New York theatre of the mid-1930s. Treadwell's Moscow trip also included a minor triumph in that she became, at her insistence, the first western playwright to receive production royalties from the Soviet Union.

Treadwell's plays produced after *Machinal* would bring mostly disappointment and failure. Her 1929 comedy of manners, *Ladies Leave*, was improperly dismissed by most critics as insubstantial. *Lone Valley*, which Treadwell produced herself in 1933 after years of tryouts and revisions, closed on Broadway after only three performances.

These professional setbacks coincided with personal ones. McGeehan died shortly after Treadwell's return from Russia in 1933, and her mother died the following year. A few days after the Broadway opening of *Plumes in the Dust*, Treadwell left on a steamer trip to the Far East, a trip which seems designed for emotional rest and an opportunity to reassess her career. During the next eight months, Treadwell visited Egypt, Bombay, Ceylon, Hong Kong and Japan.

She returned in February 1937 and retreated to the Stockton ranch she inherited, where she continued to assess her career and her country. The result was a novel and a drama, both titled *Hope for a Harvest*. The novel would remain unpublished, but the play, set on a ranch in California's San Joaquin Valley, was produced by the Theatre Guild in 1941, starring Fredric March and his wife Florence Eldridge. Despite excellent notices in Guild tryout cities, *Harvest* was dismissed by the New York critics as well-intentioned but poorly structured. The play's call for Americans to accept the nation's growing diversity and learn again the benefits of hard work from recent immigrants was termed a naively simplistic solution to America's economic woes. Less than two weeks into its Broadway run, the Japanese attacked Pearl Harbor and the play's vision seemed a remote possibility at best.

The dismissal of *Harvest* was Treadwell's bitterest disappointment with the New York commercial theatre. From this moment on, Treadwell spent more time out of the country, and her writing often turned to revising old plays or to composing fiction. Of these later works, her best two plays are set in western America: *Highway*, televised in an adaptation in 1954, and an unproduced teleplay, *The Gorgeous Innocent* (mid-1950s). Her novel *One Fierce Hour and Sweet* was published in 1959.

In 1949, Treadwell surprisingly adopted a child, something she had been contemplating as far back as 1931. He was a German boy, whom Treadwell named William, perhaps after McGeehan. Treadwell was sixty-four years old at the time, and her diaries show that while William provided great companionship, she was ill-prepared at that age for the rigors of child-rearing. William was often sent to private boarding schools, and Treadwell relied heavily upon hired housekeepers and friends as she and William travelled between Stockton, her home in Newtown, Connecticut, Mexico, Vienna, and Torremolinos, Spain.

In 1965, Treadwell moved, presumably for health reasons, to Tucson, Arizona, a city she had visited previously, most notably to see Maynard Dixon in 1945. In Tucson, she continued rewriting a play set in Mexico, *Woman With Lilies*, which had occupied her creative energies off and on for almost twenty years. The play was eventually produced by Peter Marroney, head of the Drama Department at the University of Arizona, perhaps out of respect for Treadwell and against his better judgement. It was presented in the late summer, when most of his season subscribers were out of town seeking relief from the heat. Treadwell later termed the production "the Tucson debacle"; it would be the last production she would see of one of her plays.

Treadwell died on February 20, 1970, after her failing health had led to a nine-day stay in a Tucson hospital. She had previously made arrangements to donate her body to the University of Arizona's Department of Anatomy, and her copyrights were assigned to the Roman Catholic Diocese of Tucson. All proceeds were to benefit the education of Native American children.

Scholarly assessments of Treadwell's contributions have been slow to evolve, with mention of her largely consisting of passing references in historical texts. Shortly after her death, her papers were assigned to the University of Arizona Library Special Collections (UALSC), and these works were inventoried and made available to researchers beginning in 1975. The first dissertation on Treadwell's career was completed by Louise Heck-Rabi (S167) the following year, utilizing this archival collection. A second dissertation, completed in 1982 by Nancy Wynn (S186), provided many more biographical details about Treadwell, along with more detailed assessments of the varying manuscripts of her plays. Wynn came to Tucson as the papers were being processed by the University of Arizona, and she retained a significant amount of them, including correspondence and manuscripts, as she completed her study. These materials, along with other correspondence, diaries, scrapbooks, photographs and manuscripts, were added to the collection at Arizona in the fall of 1995. The latter materials have largely been unavailable to scholars until this time, and this study is the first to indicate the range of materials that are now available to researchers.

In the 1980s, *Machinal* began to resurface in print and in revivals. Judith Barlow's 1981 anthology, *Plays by American Women, the Early Years*, included *Machinal* and provided a brief introduction of Treadwell to a sizeable readership. The following year, Jennifer Parent (S185) offered a detailed reconstruction of Hopkins's original staging of the play. At the time of and shortly after the play's 1990 revival by the New York Shakespeare Festival, several scholarly studies appeared offering an assessment of the play (S201, S211, S225) and/or a discussion of its relationship to the Snyder-Gray trial (S214, S215, S227). The play was published separately for the first time in 1993 and again anthologized in 1995. Treadwell's gradual acceptance into the scholarly canon of American theatre may also be evidenced by the inclusion of her in introductory theatre textbooks (S222, S238) and an increasing number of reference works (see Annotated Secondary Bibliography: Books, Articles, Sections).

Treadwell's only other published play, *Hope for a Harvest*, has garnished very little scholarly attention. Olauson (S181) and Shafer (S235) examine the play's themes, while Greenfield (S183) and Marcuson (S204) draw opposite conclusions about Treadwell's personal views on diversity and immigration. *For Saxophone* was first mentioned in print by Robert Edmond Jones (S116), and was discussed later in more detail by Heck-Rabi (S179), Shafer (S235) and Dickey (S239).

Treadwell's life and career are filled with unresolved tensions. Although her works and actions were often pleas for women's rights and independence, she was acutely aware of her own contradictory yearnings for a more traditional life as wife and mother. Her plays often decry capitalism and cheer for the small, hard-working individual who is tied to the land for sustenance, yet she often preferred life in the city and was determined to succeed within the structure of commercial, Broadway theatre. Treadwell sought perfection in her art, yet the revisions of her plays were largely superficial ones and she sometimes proved a difficult collaborator in the theatre. When she turned to writing for television and film, her chosen subject matter was often unacceptable at the time for those mediums.

But the significance of Treadwell's achievements cannot be dismissed on account of these contradictions. Her plays consistently articulate the repressive and inhibiting conditions facing women in modern society. Her penchant for experimentation with dramatic style and structure led to two boldly innovative plays, *Machinal* and *For Saxophone*, which attempt to create a new feminist aesthetic in the theatre. Her tendency to raise unpopular yet important issues in her plays, such as sexual double standards and the blunting of American sensibilities due to rampant technology and commercialism, mark her as an artist of unflinching integrity. Throughout her career, she fought to improve conditions for women and playwrights, and her ability to act in, direct and produce her own plays demonstrate her attempt to realize her highly personal theatrical vision without compromise.

THE PLAYS: SUMMARIES AND CRITICAL OVERVIEWS

Treadwell often rewrote her plays over a span of many years. In writing the plot summaries, I have attempted to choose the manuscript I believed to be closest to the one produced or heavily marketed. This manuscript is not always the same as the one copyrighted. If not specified as to production or copyright, dates assigned refer to approximate dates of composition. In the "Critical Overview" section under each play are brief descriptions of manuscript variations, all of which may be found at the University of Arizona Library Special Collections (UALSC). References to a secondary source are accompanied by a parenthetical citation of the code assigned to the source in the Annotated Secondary Bibliography section of this text.

ANDREW WELLS' LADY (copyrighted 1931)

   The Characters--MRS. CLARA WELLS: a self-centered, ambitious woman in her 40s; MRS. BARBARA FIELD: warm, self-effacing; MISS JESSIE LANG: Mrs. Wells' devoted and unattached secretary; EDWARD BARNES: reporter for the *American*; ANDREW WELLS: wealthy owner of a mining industry in Mexico; THEODORA ("THEO") WELLS: stunning and spoiled young woman of 22 with excitable nerves; RICHARD KENT: about 25, intelligent and attractive; CORNELIUS ("NEAL") PIERREPONT: Theo's fiance; RICO RODRIGUEZ: graceful but degenerate young Puerto Rican dancer; DIANA MALLON ("DEAL"): about 25, ordinary, with a good heart; BEE NELSON: a common but pretty girl; MRS. MALLOY: old, Irish mother to Diana; JOHN McLOON: Diana's husband, 25.

   Plot Summary--ACT I: In the library of Andrew Wells's house in the East 60s in New York City, Mrs. Clara Wells entertains Mrs. Barbara Fields, one of the many guests attending an engagement party this evening for the Wells's daughter, Theo, to the rich Neal Pierrepont. Mrs. Fields is envious of the successful life of Clara, her old college classmate, and Clara inconsiderately tells her friend to stop mourning for her husband, who has been dead over a year now. Miss Jessie Lang, Clara's secretary, announces the arrival of a reporter from the *American*, who would like to interview Clara about her work as chairman these past six months of the Committee for Prison Betterment of the Amalgamated Clubs of America. Edward Barnes enters and queries Clara about one of her recently paroled prisoners, John McLoon, convicted of manslaughter for a killing during a hold-up in a cigar store. Clara defends the integrity and harmlessness of McLoon, and invites Barnes back to her committee meeting on Friday to get a photograph for the paper. Wells enters and reminisces with Mrs. Fields about a time when they were all young, and Mrs. Fields exits, crying at the happy memory of her husband. Wells wants to avoid the engagement party, disliking Theo's fiance, and he summons his secretary, Richard Kent, to assist him in some work. All leave when first Theo announces the arrival of Mrs. Pierrepont, then Neal urges all to watch the famous nightclub dancer, Rico Rodriguez, perform in the other room. Theo lags behind when she sees Kent enter, and he sullenly tells Theo she is still excited by his presence, even though she has toyed with him for months and turned down his offer of marriage. Theo slaps Kent, and he wishes he could have her for just one night to undo her spoiled demeanor and make a "real girl" out of her. Neal returns boasting of Rico's dancing, which Wells simply refers to as "dirty." Kent recognizes Rico's name from his days in Mexico City, where the dancer was known as a pimp and extortionist. Theo is now more excited than ever to dance with Rico, and leaves followed by Neal. Kent abruptly asks Wells if he may return to work at Wells's mining business in Mexico, but his boss wishes him to stay, seeing aspects of himself in the young secretary. After Kent goes upstairs to fetch business papers and Wells goes into an adjoining dressing room to wash up, Rico enters and makes blatant sexual advances to Theo. Wells interrupts Rico and orders him from his house; Rico departs shouting he will get revenge for such insulting treatment. Alone with her father, Theo admits she is unsure about her impending marriage, but when her mother enters, Theo claims Wells was speaking ill of Neal. Clara tells Wells he is out of date with the times, and Wells dismisses Kent for the night, saying he is going out for a bit.

ACT II: In a living room of a walk-up apartment in the West 60s, Diana Mallon arranges a makeshift lampshade. She is surprised by the arrival of her friend, Bee Nelson, who has tracked her down to her new apartment and wants to know details about the man who has been keeping her since she left her job as a dancer at the Nido nightclub. Bee also inquires to Diana, whom she refers to as "Deal," about her mother's caring for her four year-old daughter and her husband, Johnny, who is in prison serving three more years on a manslaughter sentence. The buzzer to the apartment sounds, Bee quickly asks for $50 to take care of her "usual" trouble, and Diana gives her the money while shuttling her out so she will not meet her visitor. Wells arrives, and Diana warmly kisses him, calling him "Jim." Diana happily gives Wells his set of keys to their new apartment, and she gently massages the strain around his eyes, wishing she knew more about his background. Diana's mother phones and announces she is on her way over to convey important news. Not wanting Wells to meet her mother, Diana asks him to leave for ten minutes. Rico appears, claiming to be looking for a Mr. Wilson in the apartment building, and Diana refutes his claims that he recognizes her from the Nido. As Diana goes to the door to let in her mother, Rico steals Diana's set of apartment keys. Diana ushers Rico out as Mrs. Malloy enters, saying Johnny is out of prison and looking for his wife. Mrs. Malloy leaves as Johnny arrives, the latter promising to lead a straight life if Diana will stay with him. Diana deftly evades Johnny's more and more direct questions about her activities these past months and tonight, eventually telling him she is merely fixing up a friend's apartment, and as the friend is due to return soon, he will have to wait for her tonight at a Chinese restaurant on Columbus Circle. Johnny leaves. Wells enters from within, having returned earlier and overheard much of Diana's conversation with Johnny. Although Diana has been happy with Wells, she confesses she feels obligated to return to Johnny; she admits she has a child, tells Wells her real name is Delia ("Deal"), and takes Wells's keys back, ending their relationship. Wells comforts Diana as she cries, then goes into another room to turn off the apartment lights in order to escort her to Columbus Circle. Rico enters quietly, confronts Diana, then calls out for "Andrew Wells" to come forward, Diana hearing Wells's true name for the first time. When Rico goes to fetch Wells, Diana blocks the door, struggles with him, and is shot. Rico runs off and Wells goes to the fallen Diana, uncertain for a moment about what to do, then leaves.

ACT III: Three days later, Clara returns home exhausted from a board meeting for St. Luke's Hospital, where everyone talked at length about the Diana Mallon murder. Clara dreads the impending Parole Committee meeting, fearing she will be blamed for releasing McLoon, who has emerged as the prime suspect in the murder after Mrs. Malloy's testimony placed him at the scene of the crime. Barnes arrives to update Clara on recent developments and get her statement for the paper: police are close to identifying the man who kept Diana's apartment; they have captured McLoon at Diana's funeral; and the paper plans to state that the Parole Committee's work has been ill advised. Outraged, Clara sends Barnes away. She goes upstairs to Wells, who has returned home ill from work, to ask him to call their friend William Randolph Hearst for help. Kent confirms to Theo that he will return next week to Mexico. Miss Lang returns with the afternoon papers, and Theo, Kent and Clara eagerly read the latest details of the murder. Alone with Clara, Wells admits his involvement with Diana. Clara urges him not to go to the police with what he knows, fearing scandal and no longer seeming to care too much for the welfare of McLoon. Clara tells Theo the news, and leaves her to try and reason with her father. Wells sends Kent off to call a policeman, then dictates a simple statement of admission for Kent to transcribe. After questioning her father about the details of his relationship with Diana, Theo apologizes for getting Rico involved. She comforts Wells, saying he was at least honest to Diana in loving her, if not in details about his identity. Kent returns and offers to sign the statement himself, saying his reputation in Mexico will not suffer like Wells's will here. Theo urges her father to agree and, impressed with Kent's offer of sacrifice, consents to go to Mexico with him when this affair is over. However, when Police Captain Schroeder arrives, Wells signs the statement before his family.

Critical Overview--Although the play contains a compelling premise, it ultimately suffers from overuse of melodramatic coincidence and a poorly motivated villain (Rico), the latter continuing Treadwell's use of dark-skinned menaces (see *Gringo* and *The Right Man*). Much of the second act is particularly well-written, though, with many discoveries and taut dialogue. The scenes between Diana and Wells, as well as Diana and Johnny, are especially noteworthy. Not all of the lengthy story lines introduced in Act One are adequately developed, especially that of Mrs. Fields. Treadwell re-wrote the play many years later as *Judgment in the Morning*, and then retained some of those characters for *Garry*.

THE ANSWER (c. 1918)

The Characters--LURA LAWTON: attractive, upper-middle-class young woman; JIM LAWTON: Lura's husband, a large man; JACK BONAN: strong, tall blonde man of about 30, confident and indifferent; EVELYN BALLARD: a silly and vain young woman clinging too long to the flapper age; MARY ALLEN (MISS NICHOLS): a tall, angular woman with greying, bobbed hair; HARRY ALLEN: a short, balding, overweight man.

Plot Summary--ACT I: Lura greets her beloved Jack Bonan at her New York apartment, and tells him of their impending guests this evening: Harry and Mary Allen, and Harry's flapper niece, Evelyn. Jack only wants to be alone with Lura, and begins planning ways to send the guests home early. Lura tells Jack that she is also expecting the arrival of her husband, Jim, from New Mexico, to whom she has recently written asking for a divorce now that she found Jack, her "answer" to life. The Allens and Evelyn arrive. Jack plies Harry, an alocoholic, with liquor, knowing Mary will immediately take him home to keep him from getting drunk. Evelyn flirts with Jack. Mary (who goes by her maiden name of Miss Nichols) tells Lura that she, like most American women, do not take life and women's problems seriously, including suffrage, economic independence for women and birth control. Jack stuns the party by confessing that he enlisted today for the reserve officers' camp for the war. Mary ushers her husband and niece out. Alone with Jack, Lura cries and speaks of her disappointment that Jack would not confide such an action with her. Feeling no responsibility to Lura, and claiming he is only doing his duty, Jack angrily storms out after Lura breaks off their relationship. A phone call announces Jim's arrival downstairs.

ACT II: A minute later, Jim tells Lura how disappointed he is in himself for not making her happy earlier, and that he has now returned to grant her a divorce. Lura sadly reveals that her plans have changed, but urges Jim to go on and accept a war commission rather than stay with her. Lura weakly tells Jim that she has committed an action that no longer gives her the right to ask him to stay. Jim refuses to hear the details, but tells Lura that if women demand equality, they must face life's problems with the strength of men. He leaves her alone to rest. Jack returns, incensed with jealousy after passing Jim in the elevator earlier and realizing Jim still had a right to Lura that he does not. When Lura spurns his offer to forgive her, Jack storms out, vowing to get revenge by marrying someone else.

ACT III: A year later, Lura entertains Mary while her baby boy sleeps in the next room. Harry left today after enlisting, and Mary is surprisingly relieved not to have to care for him and worry about his drinking. Lura cradles her baby, who has awoken, and speaks of finding great happiness alone with him. Mary is envious. Evelyn, having married Jack, enters with words of comfort to Mary. Jack disliked his work in the reserves. As Evelyn exits, Lura picks up her newspaper from the hallway and reads of Jim's death during a German offensive. She holds her baby in grief.

Critical Overview--The play is a disjointed effort by Treadwell. Lura lacks volition as a central character, and is too easily battered by the men in her life. Several of the characters are mostly stereotypes: Jack is little more than a villain, Jim the self-sacrificing but joyless husband, and the baby provides the ultimate "answer" to Lura's happiness. The minor characters are of much more interest: the sassy flapper, Evelyn, the muddled Harry, and the woman activist, Mary. The latter may be a caricature of a typical member of the Lucy Stone League, who insisted on maintaining her maiden name after marriage. Although Treadwell belonged to the League, she seems later to have distanced herself from formal activist organizations. The play also shows Treadwell's interest in the effects of World War I on personal relations, especially in her suspicions that men sometimes enlist not out of a sense of duty but as a convenient way of running away from commitments in their personal relationships.

LA CACHUCHA (copyrighted 1918)

The Characters--SENORITA VIVIANA YBARRA Y LA GUERRA: a Spanish dancer around 24 years of age; JOHN S. WATKINS: a middle-aged, American, short and prosperous; SENOR ALVAREDOS: a young Spaniard.

Plot Summary--In their New York apartment, the temperamental and superstitious Spanish dancer Senorita Viviana berates her lover Watkins for causing her recent fall onstage after a performance. Watkins did not count her encores and urged her back onstage for an unlucky thirteenth, clearly causing, she says, the accident. Viviana demands a vigorous rehearsal tonight to break her bad luck, and she summons Senor Alvaredos from his apartment on the floor above to come play piano for her. Watkins goes to bed, saying he is never disturbed by their music. After a brief rehearsal with Alvaredos, Viviana gets out a piano roll which continues the music while they flirt and kiss. Watkins returns unexpectedly and Alvaredos runs out. Viviana explains her behavior to Watkins: she was reluctant to live with Watkins in the first place since he was her thirteenth lover. Thus, she took on Alvaredos as a lover so Watkins could be number fourteen and their relationship would avoid bad luck. Watkins is impressed with the "sacrifice" Viviana made for him, but is surprised when Viviana announces she would like to keep on Alvaredos. Confused, Watkins agrees and gruffly calls Alvaredos back to continue the rehearsal. Alvaredos returns and plays "la cachucha." Watkins smokes a cigar and watches them rehearse.

Critical Overview--Copyrighted in 1918 but unproduced, the play has garnished no critical response. Treadwell uses Viviana's unpredictable behavior and Spanish dialect for good comic effect in this short sketch. Another version of the play, *His Luck*, depicts the Spanish dancer (here named Senorita Carlotta Blasco de Vallejo) in love with a possessive, young American named John Daniels. Carlotta rejects Daniels's marriage proposal when she discovers it is the thirteenth she has received. The accompanist is a Mr. Simpkins, a queer-looking little man Carlotta at one point calls a bug, a nothing, a grease spot. Daniels convinces Simpkins that Carlotta is in love with him, and he urges Simpkins to propose to her. After a wonderfully comic scene, Daniels returns to find Simpkins cowering in a corner, completely devastated by Carlotta's explosive reaction. Nevertheless, Daniels's plan worked: Simpkins's proposal was number fourteen and Daniels's new proposal becomes number fifteen, Carlotta's lucky number. Carlotta embraces first Simpkins then her beloved Daniels.

CONSTANCE DARROW (c. 1908-09)

The Characters--CONSTANCE DARROW: a private secretary, about 21, well-groomed; MRS. DARROW: a delicate-looking woman of 46; NAN NICOL: a 21 year-old girl, fresh, pretty; BEN COLLIER: an average-looking young man of 28; TERRANCE O'DAY: Irish-American, under 30, homely attractive; MR. JOHN MATHEWS: Constance's 60-year-old, successful boss.

Plot Summary--ACT I: Mrs. Darrow prepares dinner in the kitchenette apartment she shares with her daughter Constance in San Francisco. Mrs. Darrow asks her neighbor and Constance's co-worker, Nan, if she can borrow last Sunday's want ads. Nan gets them, then leaves, awaiting the arrival of Terrance, a handy suitor who cleans and cooks for her. Constance returns home from work, and queries her mother about the want ads. A phone call interrupts dinner and provides a job offer to Mrs. Darrow of housesitting with an invalid woman. Constance refuses to allow her mother to take the job, saying she is not trained to do anything interesting. She recounts their previous agreement that if Constance took her job as a private secretary and earned a man's wage, she should enjoy a man's freedom at home and have her mother take care of the domestic duties. Ben Collier, who also works at the same place as Constance, makes his usual nightly arrival, and Mrs. Darrow asks him about details from work, especially wondering why Constance has not developed a romantic interest in her boss, Mr. Mathews, despite the fact he is around sixty years old. Nan and Terrance drop in on their way to the movies, and Nan agrees with Mrs. Darrow that Constance is a bit slow to seize a good opportunity to marry a wealthy man. Mrs. Darrow retreats to the kitchen to review the ads further, leaving Ben alone with Constance. They discuss Mrs. Darrow's "pitiful" situation, as well as Constance's struggle to keep up with unexpected bills. Ben gives Constance the latest piece of poetry he wrote for her and proposes marriage. Constance delays accepting, feeling Ben is not able to care for both her and her mother. After Ben threatens to leave for good, Constance accepts his proposal but has mixed feelings about having to abandon her job, an act upon which Ben insists. Constance realizes he is asking her to do the same thing she is asking of her mother. They plan for a wedding in about two weeks, and speak of renting an extra room adjoining the apartment for Constance's mother. Ben exits, and Constance convinces herself that Ben needs her greatly.

ACT II: In the same apartment, about two months after the marriage, Constance prepares dinner for the family and Mr. Mathews, her former boss. Nan informs Constance that she will never marry Torrance because she does not want children or a life of poverty. She dreams of meeting a rich man at work, and is upset to learn she was not invited to dinner to meet with Mr.

Mathews. After Nan leaves, Mrs. Darrow returns home to a worried Constance, who did not know her whereabouts the whole day. Mrs. Darrow relates her experiences answering a want ad, which resulted in her selling books door-to-door to make a return on a modest investment required to join the business. Exhausted and humiliated, she cries on Constance's shoulder. Constance cheers her up with news that the old job of caring for the invalid woman has been offered again, and she thinks she should take it. Mrs. Darrow remarks on her daughter's new-found understanding and gentleness. During this exchange, the meal burns in the kitchen. Frantic, Constance borrows the dinner that Nan and Terrance are about to eat across the hall. Ben returns home with Mr. Mathews, and over dinner he proudly expounds on Constance's ability to learn domestic duties. Nan, pretending ignorance, barges in on the party wearing a fine dress, and makes such an impression on Mr. Mathews that he plans to interview her for the job as his private secretary. After all leave, Ben belittles Nan and Terrance, as well as Constance's dinner. Constance wants to share some big news with Ben, but feels suffocated by the poverty, clutter and smallness of their apartment. Ben finally guesses that Constance is pregnant. Although she feels somewhat alone, Constance wants to have the baby, but Ben cites frustration over a lack of money and his job as a "wage slave," and urges Constance to have an abortion. Constance demands to know why Ben insisted on marrying her and changing what had been her happy life.

ACT III: Eight months later, Constance sits alone in the apartment reading the want ads. Mrs. Darrow, who now has a place of her own, stops by after having gotten the evening off from her caretaker job. She is pleased with her new independence. Mrs. Darrow suspects that Constance's marriage is not going well, and is glad she and Ben have had no children. Nan enters with news that she plans to quit her job and marry Mr. Mathews. They both want Constance to return to her old job and take care of things while they go to Europe. Nan told Torrance of her plans over lunch, and now Ben is comforting him downtown. Together, Constance and Mrs. Darrow excitedly make plans about Constance's return to work. Constance soon finds herself alone with Ben and a very drunk Torrance. Ben and Constance argue vehemently over her plans to return to work. Ben threatens to leave her, and after she breaks down, he goes to her, demanding she tell Nan immediately she will not accept the job. Constance numbly calls to Nan across the hall with the news, as Torrance, dazed, rises and asks for Nan.

Critical Overview--*Constance Darrow* is one of the best of Treadwell's early plays. Several of the supporting characters are very well drawn, especially Nan, Torrance and Mrs. Darrow. Treadwell minimizes her early reliance on melodramatic techniques, preferring a rather simple and direct line of action over surprising complications. The dilemma of a young woman wrestling between an independent career and a life of domesticity runs throughout a number of Treadwell's early works. Several of the scenes contain sharp, concise dialogue, although the Ben and Constance scenes come off rather heavy-handed. The device in Act One of having Constance assume the traditional male attitudes toward work and marriage is a novel one. Nancy Wynn (S186) notes Treadwell's use of contrasting characters, and states the play was copyrighted in 1911 under the title, *The High Cost*. A note in Treadwell's hand on one of the manuscripts of the play in UALSC indicates the work was written while staying with Modjeska in 1908-09.

THE EYE OF THE BEHOLDER (copyrighted 1919)

The Characters--MRS. MARCIA WAYNE: a 30-year-old woman; WAYNE: her husband, a heavy, fleshy man of 40; MARTIN GREGG: Mrs. Wayne's lover, attractive, 24; MRS. GREGG: his mother, about 50, chic; MRS. MIDDLETON: Mrs. Wayne's mother, a large woman; SERVANT: a male butler.

Plot Summary--Through a series of short vignettes set in the living-room of a country house, the play explores the idea that individuals are known only in a fragmentary way by those around them. The character of Mrs. Wayne adopts different personas of herself as she is seen by those around her. Her husband views her as a possession, and even though she refutes his amorous intentions all he is aware of is her seductive voice and her revealing, flesh-colored negligee. Her lover, Martin Gregg, sees her as a sweet, young girl of eighteen in a pink frock, and anxiously urges her to meet his mother and discuss their engagement. Martin's mother, Mrs. Gregg, confronts Mrs. Wayne alone, viewing her as a tired woman of the world dressed in a rose dress and spoiling her son's chances at a life of optimistic bliss. After Mrs. Gregg's departure, Mrs. Wayne's heavy-set mother enters, treating her as a little girl in a short frock who does not pay enough attention to her appearance or health. Alone for a moment, as she was at the beginning of the play, Mrs. Wayne appears in a white chiffon wrap and laments that everyone in her life understands a little, but not enough, of her true self.

Critical Overview--This novel short play, first written under the title *Mrs. Wayne*, is noteworthy primarily for its experiments in characterization, costuming and dramatic form. The play is somewhat reminiscent of Alice Gerstenberg's *Overtones* (1915) in its presentation of a character's multiple personas. Treadwell's correspondence with theatrical manager, Edward Goodman, reveals her belief in the novelty of the dramatic structure of the piece and her distrust that Goodman had passed the play on to another dramatist to use as a premise for a new play. The success of *The Eye of the Beholder* is marred somewhat by superficial and flat dialogue. Heck-Rabi (S167) finds the "four-angled square" central character awkward. Although Treadwell's premise is that no one truly knows Mrs. Wayne, the audience's inability to do so hinders the piece dramatically. Nevertheless, the play significantly demonstrates Treadwell's willingness to experiment with dramatic narrative, and both Heck-Rabi and Wynn (S186) feel the play foreshadows the radically experimental *For Saxophone*.

The play may also reveal Treadwell's own frustrations with her personal relationships and the demands they placed upon her. For example, despite her marriage to McGeehan, Treadwell became romantically involved with the painter Maynard Dixon. Although Hagerty (S221) claims Treadwell ended their affair in 1917, Dixon continued to compose and send love poems to Treadwell until October 1919. It was not until the following January that Dixon acknowledged to Treadwell that they had grown too far apart in their relationship to continue.

FOR SAXOPHONE (copyrighted 1934)

The Characters--LILY LAIRD: under 20, lovely, exquisitely dressed, evoking a aura of doomed innocence; GILLY LETHE: approaching 30, unassuming; SAMUEL P. LAIRD: Lily's rich father; MILLIE and BILLIE BLYTHE: friends of Gilly's and Lily's; STANISLOS: a Russian, knife-throwing dancer who becomes Lily's lover; JOSEPH KARTNER: a Viennese author; numerous other characters, such as maids, waiters, passengers on board ship, some seen and some heard only as voices.

Plot Summary--ACT I, Scene I: "At a dance." Out of a darkened stage, servants' voices speak over the telephone of the wedding engagement of Lily Laird, only daughter to the rich Samuel P. Laird, to Gilbert Lethe. The voices fade as a pool of light reveals Lily and Gilly dancing, while voices of guests at the engagement part gossip of Lily's recent return from a convent in Paris, of her beauty and quiet demeanor, of her father's money, and of Gilly's blandness. Gilly queries the unsure Lily about her happiness, the engagement ring his mother picked out for her, and her propensity to smoke too much, while saying his mother will come to love her in time. The stage darkens.

ACT I, Scene 2: "Before a wedding." The dance music of the former scene becomes a wedding march, punctuated by sounds of doorbells, phones, typewriters, sewing machines and voices preparing the wedding arrangements. The voice of an old nurse, who used to comfort Lily when she felt lost as a child, asks to see her. A French maid arranges Lily in her wedding dress, and tells of a custom in her village of the groom removing the dress from the bride after the wedding. Lily feels she suffocates under the veil, while Samuel Laird's voice repeatedly asks if she is ready.

ACT I, Scene 3: "The wedding." A narrow shaft of light picks out Lily on the arm of her father as the wedding music grows. They cross the stage to the waiting Gilly and all go off. In the darkness, the voice of the minister speaks of marriage as being created for the procreation of children and as a means to avoid the sin of fornication. Gilly and Lily state fragments of the marriage vows.

ACT I, Scene 4: Untitled. The wedding music gives over to modern jazz music and the indistinct humming and buzzing of many voices at the wedding reception. Voices alternately congratulate the couple and deride Samuel Laird, his toast, and aspects of the wedding and the couple's planned honeymoon in Florida. Women's voices comment on how pale and strained the bride appears.

ACT I, Scene 5: "On a train." The voices dissolve into the sound of a train's wheels and lights reveal Lily and Gilly in the drawing-room of a train. Gilly's repeated question about her happiness, his boasts about his daily exercise regiment, the music from his portable victrola, and his offers of liquor from his flask all make Lily feel the room is too tight and close. A conductor takes their tickets, and leaves them in a silence underscored only by the sound of the pounding wheels. A porter enters and asks to make the bed down, but Lily asks that he return later. Gilly tries more forcefully to get Lily to take a drink, and Lily begins to cry. Gilly hopes she will not hate him after their consummation, as his mother did his father. At Lily's request, Gilly opens a window for air, but the sound of the wheels is overpowering and she asks that it be closed. Lily reluctantly agrees to take a sip of liquor from Gilly's flask.

ACT II, Scene 1: "In a hotel room." Six years later, Lily and Gilly have returned to the same hotel of their honeymoon. Lily loathes the whiny and empty sound of a saxophone playing a popular song downstairs, but marvels at the full moon shining on the ocean. She longs to lie on the sand and have the waves wash over her, and asks Gilly if she could have a child, which would at least provide "something" to her dull life. Lily draws away from Gilly's touch, and he remarks he thought she would change her mind about having a baby. Lily longs to have her comfortable but vulgar life shaken somehow. She dislikes their friends Millie and Billie, saying Billie drinks too many cocktails and Millie sits in cars and kisses men, and both of them envy Gilly and Lily's lives together.

ACT II, Scene 2: "At a dinner-dance." Over dinner, Millie and Billie dominate the conversation with talk of champagne, fashion, pay raises and desire for a Cadillac. Millie pretends to be scandalized by Lily's pleasant dream of a haystack and flowers, giving a Freudian sexual interpretation to the dream's details. Their conversation is punctuated by a performance by a knife-throwing Russian dancer named Stanislos, whose wild Cossack dance ends with a knife thrown in the direction of Lily. Lily cuts herself fingering the knife, and Stanislos dabs her finger with a handkerchief and vows to return to her some other time. More social chit-chat is punctuated by a return performance by Stanislos, who performs a wild, passionate dance with a girl in a native Cossack costume. After Lily has remained absent for several minutes to put something on her throbbing finger, Gilly worries over her whereabouts as the stage darkens.

ACT II, Scene 3: "In a hotel room." Gilly sits on the bed phoning for help in locating Lily, who has not returned. Lily enters, having been down by the sea, her dress wet, with a bruise on her cheek and a mark on her neck. To Gilly's inquiry about what happened, Lily simply replies, "Nothing."

ACT III, Scene 1: "At breakfast." Some months later, a maid remarks to Gilly that Lily has seemed restless since their return from Florida. Gilly harangues Lily for not taking care of her health, and Lily reads headlines in the newspaper which alternately speak of domestic crimes and suicide or fashion and beauty aids. Lily asks Gilly to let her go away for awhile or have a room of her own. Gilly gives Lily instructions for dinner tonight with his mother, and leaves for work. After she receives a phone call from Stanislos, Lily orders everything she owns to be sent to the cleaners and announces she is staying in all day.

ACT III, Scene 2: "Servants." Lights reveal Lily in her room listening to the radio. From the surrounding darkness comes the voices of the Maid and Cook talking of the foreigner who phones Lily. Neither feels any sympathy for the clearly unhappy Lily, who already has a good man to support her. When the Maid goes to sneak the key to the wine closet so Cook can have a nip, she notices that Lily has left her room.

ACT III, Scene 3: "In a bedroom." Lily returns in the early evening and draws a bath. Gilly, locked out of the room, calls to Lily. After Lily collapses, a string of successive voices from outside the door try to rally her: a doctor offers a litany of medical procedures and prescriptions; Gilly's mother self-righteously states that God's love will save her if she is pure; and Millie sees the locked door as a symbol of Lily's sexual repression. After sending them away, Lily finally admits Gilly and tries unsuccessfully to explain her frustrations. Lily is drawn to an interview on the radio with the author Joseph Kartner, who has written a book about a Viennese doctor who cured a woman with symptoms remarkably like Lily's. The maid delivers a gift for Lily, a bunch of white flowers and a dagger. Terrified, Lily hears on the radio that Kartner's novel will not be published in English for another year and that he plans to return to Vienna tomorrow. The interview ends, and Lily turns the dial, anxiously trying to get Kartner's voice back, only to hear a jumble of music with saxophone from every station.

ACT IV, Scene 1: Untitled. In his hotel room, Kartner admits a desperate Lily, and informs her that the incidents in his book are based on fact. Lily says she has a friend like the woman in Kartner's book, and she seeks his advice. Lily speaks to Kartner of her friend's self-deceiving life in the convent, of her marriage to a man whom she does not love enough to have a child by, of her compulsive relationship with an abusive man, the Russian dancer, which continues despite her loathing because being with him freed her of her impoverished sense of self. In response to Kartner's question about whether the woman had anyone to turn to for help, Lily begins weeping uncontrollably, not for herself but for her husband. She admits to being the "friend," a detail Kartner already knew. Lily feels remarkably comfortable confiding to Kartner, and he gives her a copy of the English manuscript of his book, with the advice that defiance is man's life-affirming answer to an overpowering feeling of destiny. Lily misreads Kartner's advice, seeing Kartner, not herself, as her salvation. The stage darkens.

ACT IV, Scene 2: "At a dock." On a dark stage, the sound is heard of a ship's orchestra playing a melody. Lily is seen standing behind the deck rail of a steamer, while a flood of voices talk of visas, destinations, room locations, goodbyes and gifts. Lily is upset when Gilly goes against his word and appears at the dock to see her off. Even though she claims not to be coming back, he refuses to tell her goodbye, saying he will be waiting for her here.

ACT IV, Scene 3: "On deck." The sound of Viennese waltzes with a saxophone underscores activity on the ship's deck. A Husband and Wife sit close together, reading and holding hands, while snatches of conversation are heard from pairs of characters: a man and a girl, a boring husband and his bored wife, a jealous wife and her husband, a stingy wife and her husband, a suspicious wife and her drinking husband, and an amorous husband and his wife. Onstage, the Husband takes a walk while his Wife speaks to Lily about Kartner's new novel she is reading in German. The Wife gives details of Kartner's personal life, including his separation from his wife and two children, and his turn to a new lover, a girl he found playing piano in a restaurant in Vienna. The Husband returns and the Wife, who seems to have found happiness in Kartner's novels, walks off arm-in-arm with him. Lily takes up the book.

ACT IV, Scene 4: "In a study." Lily arrives unexpectedly at Kartner's home and confesses that she loves him, having felt freed by his earlier advice. Kartner admits he has a lover already, a woman playing Brahms on the piano in the other room. Lily cries, saying she attempted suicide once, before she first met Kartner, but she could not die feeling as though she had never yet lived. Kartner feels responsible for Lily's state, believing he misled her at a time when she was emotionally vulnerable. Lily has broken with Stanislos, and wonders if she should return to the waiting Gilly, for whom she feels great pity.

Kartner urges her to break with what she feels is her destiny, and stay in Vienna to start a new one. Lily wonders if this new destiny will be a man, and if so how will she know when he appears. Kartner says she will know intuitively when she encounters a man who brings her happiness. Lily leaves, confused and lonely.

ACT IV, Scene 5: "Five o'clock tea." At afternoon tea at a Kur Platz, a variety of women hire waiters to dance with them or they dance with themselves. Lily sits at a table with an English woman, who speaks disgustedly of a book she is reading called *Enduring Passion*, which offers scientific advice on how to make love last a lifetime. A woman with a haggard face nearby eagerly borrows the book and turns away to read it. The English woman vehemently denounces the importance women place on sex, feeling that if a woman is unsatisfied with her husband she simply needs to lose some egoism and endure, not take a lover. Marriage, she says, at least keeps one from being lonely. The woman claims to have recovered perfectly from a dissatisfaction she once felt for her own husband, and she leaves to get treatment for a continual, deep pain in her side which baffles the doctors. Lily calls to a waitress so she can send a cable to America.

ACT IV, Scene 6: "In a cafe." The dance music from the previous scene becomes jazz music played by a small Hungarian orchestra in a dark, smoke-filled restaurant. Lily orders a martini, then dismisses a blunt man from a nearby table who tries to seduce her. Lily requests the Hungarian violinist play Brahms, then makes plans to get a taxi in one hour to catch a train departing Vienna. Kartner enters, having gotten a farewell note from Lily stating she is returning to the U.S. Kartner offers to love Lily and save her. The music changes, and Stanislos enters and begins one of his Cossack dances. Focused intently on Stanislos, Lily cannot hear Kartner's offers of love. Lily is struck by one of Stanislos's knives, and she dies looking up at the dancer.

Critical Overview--*For Saxophone* is perhaps Treadwell's most innovative and daring play. Here, Treadwell has taken much of the overall premise, central character and expressionistic use of sound in *Machinal* and added near-continual music, dance, isolated lighting and symbolic allusion (such as Gilly's last name, Lethe) in an effort to tap into the subconscious mind of the spectator. Opening stage directions suggest Treadwell hoped the fragmentary nature of the play's mise-en-scene would allow spectators to discover and "write" the play themselves, perhaps in a sort of dramaturgical extension of Arthur Hopkin's directing theory of "Unconscious Projection." The play is also noteworthy because of its lyrical, highly confessional nature, possibly growing in part out of Treadwell's own recuperative stays in European sanitoriums. The scenes between Kartner and Lily are among some of Treadwell's best, and Act One, especially, is tightly structured and highly theatrical.

Shafer (S235) compares Lily's fatal attraction to the knife thrower to Julie in Strindberg's *Miss Julie*, and believes the play prefigures Elmer Rice's *Dream Girl* and the Kurt Weill/Moss Hart musical, *Lady in the Dark*. Elsewhere, I have suggested that perhaps more than any other of her works, *For Saxophone* reveals Treadwell's beliefs on the subtle means by which modern culture maintains its hegemonic control over women's self-perception (S239).

Correspondence in the University of Arizona archive indicates great interest in the script by producers, especially Hopkins, Donald Oenslager and Robert Edmond Jones, the latter trying unsuccessfully for years to raise the money to produce it (S195). The script was rejected by Samuel Goldwyn, Inc. due to its "bizarre construction," and Treadwell's frustrations in finding a market for the play led her in August of 1937 to give up hope and recall it and other of her scripts from agent Richard Madden. Treadwell, however, returned time and again to the play, revising it as late as 1941-42 and marketing it as late as 1947. In November of the latter year, Henry Souvaine responded to the script's submission by insinuating that Agnes De Mille's 1947 production *Allegro* may have been overly influential in Treadwell's stylistic approach, a comment that undoubtedly fueled Treadwell's anger with commercial theatre producers.

In later versions of the play, Treadwell replaced Kartner with a variety of different characters, most notably a concert violinist named Hyer, whom Lily follows to Rio de Janeiro. Treadwell often changed the scene structure and ending of the play. Perhaps the most successful and stageable of the endings takes place in the Kur Platz, when a young man meets and wins over Lily's affections with his simple honesty and concern, and the two dance together (S239). The earliest title of the play was *Intimations for Saxophone*, and Treadwell's longtime friend and housekeeper, Lola Fries, completed a German translation under the title *Saxophon*.

GARRY (copyrighted 1954)

The Characters--WILMA: a small-town, 19-year-old girl from Oklahoma, in New York less than a year; plain, yet attractive; PEGGY: Garry's pretty, but cheaply made up, 23-year-old sister; GARRY: 18, handsome, well-built, graceful but restless; DAVE: a good-looking, smart, 24-year-old reporter.

Plot Summary--ACT I, Scene 1: In the basement room in an old brownstone on New York's west side, Wilma receives a visit from her sister-in-law Peggy, who has defied her brother Garry's order to stay away from his apartment. Peggy reminds Wilma of Garry's long past as a petty criminal and his days in a reformatory, and urges her to stop wasting her time trying to reform him. She urges Wilma to make some money by joining her on her "date" as a call girl, but Wilma refuses, as she has done in the past. Wilma admits she did not have sex before marriage, and that Garry is so decent he makes no sexual demands on her. Garry arrives and argues with Peggy about their mother, Peggy defending her but Garry saying she was dirty and a drunkard. Garry forces Peggy to leave after she notices blood on his sleeve. After Wilma and Garry comfort each other, Garry admits the blood on his sleeve came from a fight he had with a homosexual man who tried to seduce him. Garry tells how he met the rich man in a bar, went back to his hotel room to discuss a job, and beat him down as he tried to make advances. The man hit his head on a table as he fell, and Garry stole his money. Wilma fears Garry's probation officer will learn of the theft, but vows to lie for him if necessary. Garry dreamily speaks of the pleasure derived from choking someone to the point of death, likening the sensation to that of making love. He forces himself on the surprised Wilma.

ACT I, Scene 2: The next morning, Garry's feelings of being freed from guilt are shortlived when he reads in the newspaper that the man he beat died and that the hotel elevator boy gave a good description of Garry as a suspect. Wilma urges Garry to leave with her for Mexico, and Garry excitedly plans to steal a car and get a gun. Wilma stalls someone knocking at the door while Garry runs away. Dave Andrews, a reporter, enters and queries Wilma about Garry's involvement in the slaying. When a doorbell announces the arrival of the police. Wilma admits to Dave she knows details of the murder, but refuses to talk. Dave offers to help her in the future if she wishes.

ACT II: One night weeks later, Dave brings flowers to Wilma along with the news that police have no new leads on the still-at-large Garry. Garry sneaks in momentarily and watches them before retreating. Dave tells of the cause for his recent trip to Texas (the death of his mother), and Wilma tells of her new, more "anonymous" job in the large Macy's department store. She wonders why her life seems to repeat itself, having cared first for her father, who was imprisoned for theft, and now her criminal husband. Although touched by Dave's concern, Wilma rejects his offer to be his girl, saying she still feels tied to Garry. When Peggy knocks at the door, Wilma ushers Dave out the back way, asking him to return when he hears the radio playing loudly, a signal that all is clear. Peggy, now blonde and elegant, works for a well-known society man, who loves her and takes care of her booming "business" details. Wilma again refuses Peggy's offer to work as a prostitute, and tells how she first made love to Garry that night of the slaying. Peggy disgustedly says her brother had to kill someone in order finally to make love to a woman, and then leaves. Garry returns and questions Wilma about her visitors this night. He admits to hiding out on a ranch in Mexico, but has returned now wanting to make love to Wilma. Touchy and suspicious, Garry finally calms down and speaks of "Gooch," the rich American owner of the Mexican ranch, who returned to New York with Garry to tend to business. As Garry tenderly speaks of Gooch's love for flowers and music, Wilma realizes he is a homosexual. Garry reluctantly admits he had sex with Gooch in order to remain in the safety of the ranch. Through Gooch's teachings, Garry believes he was trying to kill a part of himself through the murder of the man in the hotel. Garry now wants to make love to Wilma to prove he is not homosexual, but after being unable to do so, he cries and says Gooch loves him. When the doorbell rings, Garry pulls his gun and tells Wilma he overheard Dave's romantic advances. Wilma weeps and gets Garry's gun after a scuffle. Garry is full of self-loathing. Wilma refuses to turn Garry over to the police, sending him off to find Gooch instead. Dave comforts Wilma, who collapses in a chair.

Critical Overview--*Garry* is an elaboration of characters and incidents from Treadwell's earlier play, *Judgment in the Morning*. Treadwell's interest in Lipot Szondi's theory of "fate analysis" is once again evident in the play's overall pessimistic predetermination that people can never really change (see *Judgment in the Morning*).

The portrait of the tormented, deviant homosexual offers nothing new beyond the dramatically familiar stereotype. The play further suffers from excessive use of exposition of Act Two, and trite dialogue for Wilma and Garry. There is no evidence the play was ever seriously circulated for production.

Under the title *Love for a Criminal*, a different version ends with Garry's threatened suicide, but Wilma stays with Dave, knowing that Garry will not kill himself now that he has found someone he loves. A version edited for television was abandoned by Treadwell prior to its completion, perhaps in the awareness that the subject matter was hopelessly ill-suited for airing in the mid-1950s. One other version, titled *In Loving Lost*, ends with Garry running out of the apartment threatening to drown himself, with Wilma running out after him.

THE GORGEOUS INNOCENT (teleplay; mid-1950s)

The Characters--PAUL LINDSTROM: a Swede rancher, about 50, strong, slow, hard-working and good; ELLA LINDSTROM: his wife, about 50, homely, but "dolled up" by the beauty shop; THEDA (TEDDY) LINDSTROM: the Lindstrom's daughter, 17, blonde and beautiful; JOHN W. LONGACRE: a nervous, New York broker of 50; JOHN W. LONGACRE, JR.: his son, 19, apathetic; MISS SARIMORE: a 40-year-old actress, the wreck of a once-pretty woman; REPORTERS; PHOTOGRAPHERS.

Plot Summary--ACT I: In the kitchen of their modest ranch house, Ella and Paul Lindstrom argue over the fate of their beautiful, seventeen-year-old daughter Teddy. Paul enjoys letting her do chores on the ranch but Ella sees her beauty as a potential way to make much-needed money. John W. Longacre, a New York stock broker, and his son, John, Jr., arrive and ask to buy the ranch in order to escape the stresses of the city. While Teddy gives son John a tour, Longacre explains that he wants the ranch in order to cure his son's apathy, caused by the death of his mother in a car accident in which John was driving too fast. Paul refuses to sell. At the river bank on the property, Teddy shows John her secret spot and talks of their farming hardships due to a dry year. As John leaves Teddy, she appears stricken by his attractiveness and social standing. Back in the kitchen, John urges his father to buy the ranch, but Paul still refuses to sell. After the visitors leave, Teddy reveals that Ella has made a secret arrangement with an agent to put the ranch on the market. Ella reveals her plan to use the money from the sale to move to Hollywood, run a court of rented bungalows, and put Teddy in charm school. Teddy suddenly wants to leave the ranch and pursue Ella's plan in order to impress John. When a letter arrives demanding payment of back taxes, Paul decides to give in and sell the ranch. It begins to rain, ruining their crop of unbaled hay.

ACT II: About a year later, in a shabby bungalow court in Hollywood, Paul works continually on maintenance problems with the apartments he bought from the ranch sale. Teddy is also reportedly unhappy, although she is now thin, glamorized and, according to Ella, bound for success after she returns from her overnight yacht excursion with film producer Gus Ringold. A drunken, middle-aged actress, Miss Sarimore, stays in Ella's bungalow while Paul goes to fix an annoying drip in hers. When Teddy returns early from the yacht trip, Miss Sarimore speaks from experience about the lustful intentions behind Ringold's excursion. Offended, Ella evicts Miss Sarimore, who leaves to pack. Teddy confides to her father that she is a failure and wants to return home to the ranch. A broke Miss Sarimore returns, waiting for her taxi to take her to stay with a male acquaintance. She tells Teddy of having failed herself to live up to her working mother's dreams for her of success and fame. After a group of reporters suddenly arrive outside, Teddy is forced to say that she fell overboard on the yacht trip, removed her nightdress to swim better, and then was rescued, naked, by a passing boat. Ella eagerly urges Teddy to meet with reporters to gain some publicity, but Teddy cries wildly. On her way out, Miss Sarimore tells the reporters how the poor, "gorgeous innocent" girl jumped, not fell, into the sea. As the reporters rush to the door of the Lindstrom's bungalow, Teddy runs away down a back alley.

ACT III: Back at the ranch, the kitchen has been modernized and John enjoys horse breeding, although Longacre's stress-related ulcers have grown worse from the worries of farming. Teddy's sudden return seems to come at the right moment, though, for a donkey has broken into the barn holding John's about-to-be sired mares, and both John and Longacre express a desire to return to the city, leaving Teddy and Paul to work the ranch on straight wages. Teddy tells John how she and her father, although broke, were happy on the ranch. Longacre brings in the morning newspapers full of stories and photos of Teddy. Paul and Ella arrive, having known Teddy would run back to the farm. Ella wants to move back, too, when she learns that Paul and Teddy will be staying. John, impressed with Teddy's resolve, not to mention her glamorized photo in the paper, changes his mind and also decides to stay. Teddy tells her father the ranch may, as he once wished, someday be hers to inherit for her children. Ella is happy the kitchen is now equipped with a modern dishwasher, as she has long wanted.

Critical Overview--*The Gorgeous Innocent* tells a naive, sentimental love story in the manner of some of Treadwell's earlier works, such as *O Nightingale* and *Highway*. The value placed on the simple, hard-working life tied to the land echoes *Hope for a Harvest*. Although the story is not original, it is touchingly presented and carefully structured. Miss Sarimore is an interesting, if slightly underdeveloped, portrait of a faded, would-be Hollywood starlet. Wynn (S186) notes that the script did not appear to be marketed much by Treadwell, even though she believes it to be "one of Treadwell's best comedies." Although conceived for television, the work is written in such a manner that it could easily be presented on stage.

LE GRAND PRIX (c. 1906-07)

The Characters--KATHERINE MORTON: a 19-year-old, high-spirited young woman; JOE MORSE: a wealthy dilletante, well-groomed man of about 30; FREEMAN RYDER: a tanned and muscular civil engineer of 28; MRS. MORTON: Katherine's mother, about 40 and fading; MRS. GREY: sister to Katherine's mother, about 45, plain and prone to headaches; MRS. CLINTON JONES: a social leader of the town; JANE TILLINGHAST: art critic for the *New York Times*; JOHN NORTHRUP: a well-known artist; CHAUNCEY JENKINS ("JENKY"): between 20-30, staff artist on the *Times*; JAMES (JIMMIE) WELLS: also a *Times* staff artist, more poised than his counterpart.

Plot Summary--ACT I: In the Morton's middle-class home, Mrs. Morton and her sister Mrs. Grey chat disapprovingly about Katherine's unreasonable pursuit of independence and painting. Although both Joe Morse, a visiting socialite from New York, and Freeman Ryder, a civil engineer, are deemed desirable mates for Katherine, Mrs. Morton fears that her daughter's headstrong behavior, reminiscent of her now-dead father's, will make her an ill match. Mrs. Clinton Jones arrives to invite Katherine to her daughters' party tonight, and informs the women that Katherine's frequent companion, Morse, is engaged to another woman in New York. Morse arrives and is treated coldly by the ladies, until they learn he plans to take Katherine to an art exhibition tomorrow in the company of the Wilsons, a young, socially elite British couple. Katherine enters and, having vowed never again to be bored at parties or socials, turns down Mrs. Jones's invitation, even though she welcomes the invitation to the exhibition. After Morse and Mrs. Jones exit, Katherine remains unperturbed by the news of Morse's engagement, and announces her plans to share a New York studio with a friend of Morse's for the upcoming year while she pursues an art career. Katherine offends first her mother, who exits tearfully, then her aunt by insisting that a mother's sole duty is to raise her children to be strong and independent. Freeman Ryder arrives, announcing he has taken a new, prestigious job with a British company that demands he move to Canada. He proposes marriage, but Katherine refuses, knowing she could not pursue her artistic career if she married him. She informs Ryder of her plans to go to New York, and he leaves believing she does not love him. Alone, Katherine exults in her independence.

ACT II: In her shared studio apartment, Katherine marvels over the accomplishments of her roommate Jane Tillinghast, a successful art critic. After reluctantly agreeing with Jane not to pass up a chance at a happy marriage for the sake of an artist's ideal, Katherine nevertheless states that she is on the verge of a breakthrough in her art. Jane exits to lie down for a bit. Katherine happily greets John Northrup, a painter whose advice helped bring about the sudden change in Katherine's work. Katherine, who never knew Northrup's full identity as a famous painter until this visit, gladly welcomes his offer to return again in a few days to see more of her work. Exuberant, Katherine wakes Jane, but only offers sketchy details about the identity of her visitor before leaving to show her latest work to her teacher of the past year. Joe Morse arrives and quickly brings up an old subject in his relationship to Jane: marriage. Jane admits she cannot marry Morse because she still loves a young man she rejected in Paris years ago to pursue her art. Katherine returns with Jimmie Wells and Chauncey Jenkins, staff artists on the *Times*, to celebrate her teacher's praise for her new work. After elaborate food and table preparations, all toast to friendship, before a phone call summons Wells and Jenkins back to work, Morse exiting with them. Katherine finally reveals the details of her artistic breakthrough, including the identity of her new advisor,

John Northrup. On hearing that Northrup will return to the apartment in a few days, Jane panics and abruptly announces her plan to accept an offer by her paper to work overseas.

ACT III: Mrs. Morton and Mrs. Grey visit Katherine in New York, where they have been buying gifts the past three days for Katherine's impending marriage to Northrup. Although Katherine is blissfully happy over the marriage, she laments the fact that Jane is still in Europe. Mrs. Morton is relieved, however, believing such a close friendship between two women to be unnatural. The ladies give Katherine presents for her trousseau, and leave to catch their train home. Northrup arrives and is disturbed to learn that Katherine no longer has a desire to pursue her art. Katherine leaves, remembering she planned to pick up a gift from a flower seller on the corner. Jane unexpectedly returns, and Northrup recognizes her immediately as his long lost "Jeanne," relating his futile efforts to find her after she ran off from the French studio they previously shared. Katherine returns with a bunch of red roses, and delightedly tells Jane about her engagement. Katherine soon discovers that Jane and Northrup still love each other. Katherine asks the two to leave, and sinks to the floor amidst her trousseau gifts, sobbing.

ACT IV: After spending five years in France, Katherine is hosting a studio reception for her work to celebrate winning the grand prize in a Parisian art competition last year. Having been invited by Katherine, Jane and Northrup feel their former friend has finally succeeded in life because her art is so accomplished and well received. Wells and Jenkins congratulate a tired and unhappy Katherine, and go off to an adjoining room to save her a seat to hear a musician play. Freeman Ryder enters, having read of Katherine's success. Katherine speaks more appreciatively than before of Ryder's work as an engineer. He speaks admiringly of a child in one of Katherine's paintings, and informs her of his own wife and son. Katherine agrees to do a sketch of the boy, and Ryder exits to find his wife. Katherine, alone, stares at one of her paintings as the music ends to applause in the other room.

Critical Overview--Cited by Treadwell as her first play, *Le Grand Prix* was written at a time when she was experiencing ongoing difficulties with her mother, who disliked her daughter's impractical ambitions and continued separations from her and her family. The play introduces a conflict which Treadwell herself was most likely struggling with, one which would emerge as a recurring theme in much of her subsequent writing: the tension between the desire for independence and the hunger for love and marriage. Here, the title proves ironic: Katherine's career has achieved international recognition but in the end the true grand prize--marriage--seems to have eluded her. Structurally, the play has many weaknesses. Not only does Treadwell rely on coincidental meetings and reunions, but Katherine's sudden reversal in her attitude toward marriage seems unmotivated. She rejects Ryder on the grounds that she does not want to give up her art simply to care for him, yet she is perfectly willing to do that very thing for Northrup. Wynn (S186) recounts details of Treadwell's attempts to market the play and get professional feedback on her writing while in Los Angeles in 1907.

GRINGO (produced 1922)

The Characters--LEONARD LIGHT: an American, about 30, a socialist and former journalist; PACO (FRANCISCO MONTES): about 20, gentle, sensitive, loyally attached to Light; BESSIE (BESITA) CHIVERS: Chivers's half-Mexican daughter, aged 16; MYRA LIGHT: married to Leornard, about 26, American, handsome and strong; DON JUAN CHIVERS: an American, about 45 but looks older, tall and thin; TITO, EL TUERTO: "the One-Eyed," Paco's brother, about 30, graceful and strong; CONCHA: the beautiful wife of Tito, now living with Chivers; STEPHEN TRENT: American, 26, big, slow-moving, untroubled; PEONS; BANDITS and their WOMEN.

Plot Summary--ACT I: The setting is a remote mine run by an American, Don Juan Chivers, in the mountains of Guerrero, Mexico. Chivers's daughter, Besita, informs an expatriate American socialist, Leonard Light, and his Mexican companion, Paco, of the death last night of General Ramon Guitierrez in a fight over a girl. Leonard tells Paco that there is only one thing men will kill each other for: possession of property, including women. Leonard and his wife, Myra, argue over his laziness, and Paco begs them both to tell him more about the riches of America. Chivers returns from the mine with his Mexican workers, having discovered what he believes to be a rich, new vein of ore deposits. Leonard dislikes Chivers's rough treatment of Mexicans, as well as his hypocrisy in maintaining a Mexican servant and lover, Concha, and fathering Besita by a Mexican woman. Myra and Leonard speak of their disillusionment after idealistically leaving the U.S. in protest of the war, only to find themselves treated as outcasts by their fellow Americans living in Mexico. Paco's bandit brother, Tito, arrives to get money from Concha, whom he abandoned shortly after their marriage but still views as his wife. When Chivers defends his rights to Concha, Tito expresses his desperation after killing Gen. Guitierrez last night and asks for 1,000 pesos ($500) in return for leaving and never coming back for Concha again. Chivers asks Leonard for a loan of the money, believing he can repay him as soon as the expected assayer arrives and confirms the ore deposit. Leonard, though, demands and gets half interest in the mine in exchange for the loan. Tito is given the money, he and Chivers sign an agreement, and Tito leaves. Steve Trent, an American assayer, arrives and gives a preliminary confirmation of gold in the mine. Tito returns and flirts with Besita, but the latter gushes excitedly about Trent's presence and their new-found riches. Talking with Paco, Tito discovers that Chivers left behind their signed agreement. Tito brazenly enlists Chivers's mine workers as his revolutionaries, promising them a horse, a gun, and free life in the mountains. They all exit, with only Paco choosing to stay with the gringos.

ACT II: Two months later, Steve and Chivers have developed a plan to smuggle out the gold to avoid troublesome banditos. For several weeks now, they have sent out mule trains loaded with gravel to confuse the bandits. Tomorrow, Steve will leave on a mule with 20,000 pesos worth of the gold in his saddlebags, while a larger, more conspicuous mule train will be sent out with sand in their bags. Besita is horribly upset when she learns of Steve's imminent departure, and she confesses to Chivers that she loves Steve, as does Myra. Alone with Concha, Besita offers her knowledge of tomorrow's plan in exchange for special herbs which the town says Concha uses to keep Chivers in love with her. Meanwhile, Myra urges Leonard to exchange places with Steve tomorrow, masking her unhappiness in their marriage in a false concern for the welfare of their gold. Besita gives Steve Concha's potient-laden coffee and, as a guitar plays in the distance, she reveals her affections for him, only to be rebuffed. When Myra enters, though, Steve instinctively rushes to her and kisses her passionately. Shots from Tito's bandits interrupt the night, and in attempting to stop the impending robbery, Steve is shot and Paco is felled by Leonard's pistol butt when he refuses to aid the Americans in shooting at his brother. Concha foils Myra's clever lie to Tito that the gold has already been smuggled out by telling him of tomorrow's plan. Concha is shocked, though, when Tito chooses to take Besita and not her away with him and the gold. Out of revenge, Concha hands Tito the saddlebags filled with sand, not gold. Tito decides to kidnap Leonard and Myra for good measure, and Chivers emerges from hiding as the bandits ride away.

ACT III: At Tito's camp in the mountains a week later, Leonard is angry at being subjected to a life on the run, Myra cooks, and Besita gets only minimal return of affection from Tito. Tito tells Leonard he must shoot him in a few days if ransom money does not arrive from Chivers, a demand he made after he learned he was tricked by Concha. It is learned that Paco and Steve have recovered from the wounds they received in the attack. Paco arrives and immediately fights with Leonard for previously beating him. During the fight, Paco confesses his love for Myra, who responds by kicking him in disgust. The fight is broken up by Tito and his men, and Leonard is tied to a tree to be shot. Chivers and Steve arrive just in time with the ransom money. Steve asks Myra if she will run away with him over the mountain. Tito freely releases the women, insisting he is not barbarous enough to hold women for ransom. He signs a formal agreement citing the receipt of money in exchange for Leonard. Paco decides to go off this time with Tito, who shakes hands with all bidding farewell. Chivers cries when Besita announces her love for Tito and departs with the bandit. Leonard supports Besita's courage to take what she wanted, but is baffled when Myra speaks of doing the same with Steve. Refusing to go back to her unhappy life, Myra leaves with Steve. Leonard slowly prepares to return to the mine with Chivers.

Critical Overview--Copyrighted and contracted to Guthrie McClintic under the title *Gringoes*, the play cleaarly grew out of Treadwell's experiences in Mexico as a journalist. Tito, the dangerous yet sometimes gentlemanly bandit, most likely is based on Pancho Villa. Treadwell tried to infuse the play with elements of local color, although not all theatre managers, especially Winthrop Ames in a letter to Treadwell, felt Broadway audiences would go see a play if they knew it was about Mexico.

Even though Treadwell deals openly at times with American racist attitudes toward Mexicans, most Mexicans in the play act in stereotypical ways, such as lying, stealing, and using a pretense of civility to mask barbarous intentions. The play further suffers from a diffuse focus: much of the play thrives on suspenseful melodrama and exotica, yet the work tries at times to engage in a serious debate on marriage. Given Treadwell's detailed journalistic writings on the subject, there is surprisingly little insight into U.S./Mexico relations in the play. Besita's altering affections for Tito and Steve are problematic.

Most critics felt the depiction of Mexico and Mexican banditry to be an authentic one, often citing Treadwell's travels and journalistic accomplishments as support (R015, R020). They are divided, however, on how the play compares to the earlier stage depiction of Mexico in Porter Emerson Browne's *The Bad Man* (R002, R008, R019).

Several critics felt the plot too diffuse (R009, R013, R025), and the ending unsatisfactory (R002). Hammond's second review (R011) cites an improved ending, changed after opening, which puts the focus on Besita and away from the Americans' love triangle. This changed ending may also be the one referred to by The Playgoer (R015), which describes Myra's unfortunate decision to stay with Leonard instead of leaving with Steve.

Generally, critics found the Mexican characters more interesting than the American ones (R006, R008). José Ruben as Tito frequently drew positive notices (R013, R017), but Edna Hibberd as Besita garnished the most praise (R006, R012, R016). John Corbin (R005) was especially interested in the character of Besita as a commentary on racial mongrelization. Treadwell's recurring interest in half-breed characters may have resulted from persistent rumors that her father was of Indian heritage. McClintic's direction was frequently applauded (R019), if not his choice of vehicle for this his second professional directing venture.

GUESS AGAIN (c. 1915-18)

The Characters--JOHN POMEROY: a handsome man of the world; SUSAN: the maid.

Plot Summary--Susan is surprised to discover Pomeroy up and about in his sitting room this spring morning. She is further startled when Pomeroy begins crying and dismisses her from the room. Sensing he is in need of some care, Susan sneaks back in the room to start the electric percolator and overhears Pomeroy reading a letter, apparently from his love, turning down his plans for a home in the country. After hearing he has lost his home, Susan tries to give Pomeroy money, but he tells her he has lost his *ideal* of a happy home, not literally lost his home financially. Pomeroy asks her about love; she replies that wanting to serve someone or letting someone serve you should be enough. Pomeroy tells Susan he seems to be seeing her for the first time, and Susan agrees, saying he usually pays her no mind even though she has noticed he works better when she is around. Susan cries, realizing her presence has meant little to Pomeroy in the past. Pomeroy appreciates her sweetness and suddenly proposes marriage to her. Surprised, Susan says she has guessed his intentions were otherwise; Pomeroy merely tells her to "guess again."

Critical Overview--The play is little more than a short, underdeveloped character sketch. Nevertheless, Susan provides an interesting study in light of Treadwell's developing themes on gender relations. Here, Treadwell seems to suggest that men see self-sacrificing women like Susan as making the perfect wives. Unlike some of Treadwell's other plays, *Guess Again* does not take a critical stance toward such an attitude.

HIGHWAY (copyrighted 1942)

The Characters--ZEPHA: a 22-year-old, pale, red-haired young woman of Okie stock; AN AMOROUS TRUCKDRIVER (LEONARD): young, strong, homely; A LOVING GIRL (MANUELA): a trashily dressed Mexican girl with a Madonna face; A DISSATISFIED WIFE (MRS. WALTER CLEMM): a small-town girl around 30; A YOUNG TEXAN (RICHARD MONIGHAN): a good-looking rancher of 24; A LUCKY MAN (BIGWELL): a middle-aged, overweight Indian; AN OLD BOOKKEEPER (CHARLES MEADOWS): small, stooped, about 60; A LONELY MAN (POP): Zepha's father, about 45, ineffectual; MRS. BIGWELL: 45, thin, stooped; AN UNLUCKY DRILLER (JEFF); A BROKE TOOL DRESSER (ART).

Plot Summary--ACT I: Around midnight in a cheap, little chili stand along a highway in Texas, Zepha dozes as she waits for customers. One of her "regulars," a Truckdriver, makes amorous advances and comments on Zepha's spotless reputation in the community. A local Mexican woman, Manuela, enjoys no such reputation, and is refused service. Zepha rejects the Truckdriver's proposal of marriage, just as she did a week ago from a man she loves, because she promised her dying mother she would marry a rich man. Mrs. Clemm enters and tells of a Packard that turned over down the road, and the Truckdriver leaves to help her husband attend to the driver of the car. Mrs. Clemm is moving to town from New Jersey with her husband, a bookkeeper newly hired by her relative, the local oilman and millionaire Billings. Richard Monighan, Zepha's love, returns after spending a week on his parents' abandoned ranch, which a recent geologist's study suggests contains valuable oil. Believing Rich will soon become wealthy, Zepha excitedly agrees to marry him, and sends him off in search of Billings to request necessary start-up funds for drilling. John Bigwell, an oil-rich, middle-aged Indian, wanders in after surviving the car crash and has Zepha phone his auto salesman to bring him a new car. Although he only learned how to drive this morning, Bigwell believes no harm can come to him as long as he carries his tribal beads and doll which provide him with good luck and protective medicine. Charlie Meadows enters and asks for the want ads, having just been fired from his long-time job as Billings's bookkeeper for making mistakes since the death of his wife some months ago. Jim Billings enters, making his usual furtive flirts with Zepha, and defending his firing of Meadows. After Billings refuses to loan Rich the needed money, Zepha calls him a bastard and a drunk, and sends him from the cafe with a brochure describing an expensive rehabilitation center in California. Zepha answers a phone call and learns that her Pop is drunk again, and Rich leaves to retrieve him. Zepha's usual optimism gives way to defeat as Bigwell wins the jackpot from a slot machine. The Auto Salesman brings Bigwell a new car, doubling its price after seeing the Indian's bankroll of big bills. Zepha is further despondent when Rich is unable to find Pop, and Bigwell leaves his lucky doll with her to help change her fortunes. Buoyed, Zepha offers Rich money from her savings to start the oil drilling, and her confidence in her new-found good fortune continues when Pop makes an unprecedented return home under his own willpower. Rich realizes Zepha had been saving the money to send Pop to the rehab clinic. When a stranger enters and reports that an Indian just smashed up a new car, Zepha is sure Bigwell's good luck has been transferred to her.

ACT II: Two months later, Zepha waits up nights expectantly and Pop has quit drinking. The Truckdriver dismisses Zepha's oil investment saying sixteen out of seventeen wildcat wells turn out to be dry. Bigwell enters on a crutch and demands his medicine doll back, the doll breaking when the Truckdriver tosses it to him. Mrs. Bigwell, a middle-aged American woman who married Bigwell after meeting him on a bus, tries to comfort her husband and mend the doll. She was on her way to Los Angeles to study with a Swami, but got off the bus with Bigwell in Texas when she learned of his oil well. His doll returned, Bigwell throws off his crutch and leaves with his wife. Two oil workers eat some of Zepha's famous hot chili to try and get over their drunken binge after their latest well turned up only water. They leave after a stunned Zepha learns that their busted well was Rich's. Mrs. Clemm arrives and orders coffee to celebrate her planned return to New Jersey, after leaving her husband. Mrs. Clemm agrees to take a desperate Zepha with her back East, but leaves the cafe after Billings arrives and tells her her Chevy has a flat tire. Billings thanks Zepha for changing his life with her surprising insult previously: his wife has divorced him and re-married and he has completed his alcoholic rehabilitation at the clinic in the brochure Zepha gave him. Zepha refuses his offer of marriage, even though she has waited a long time to marry a rich man. Billings promises to give a drunken Meadows his job back, then leaves in search of Pop, who has started another drinking binge after Zepha snapped at him. A Sailor who has just returned from sailing all over the world tells Zepha that no place compares to his native Texas. Zepha tells Mrs. Clemm she will stay in Texas after all, and a disheveled Mrs. Clemm will do the same, deciding it is better to stay with her husband who will fix flat tires for her. Zepha is confident that the sober Billings will now hire Rich to work in his oil field, and Rich promises to also work at the cafe until he can pay back Zepha's savings. He gives Zepha a present of a nightgown and matching dressing gown, and asks if he can leave with her tonight. Their departure is halted, though, when Manuela surprisingly brings the drunken Pop home. Manuela says that Pop always ends up at her house, not for sex but to listen to her sing "La Paloma," which comforts his loneliness. Zepha cries and refuses to leave with Rich. Although momentarily angered, Rich soon goes behind the counter and begins cooking an order of beans for a customer. Zepha brushes aside her vow to her mother and puns that tomorrow she may not marry wealthy but she will marry Rich. Zepha offers coffee to the customer--and to Manuela.

Critical Overview--The plot synopsis provided here is from a version of the play optioned by the Theatre Guild as the basis for a 1954 telecast on the U.S. Steel Hour series. The television adaptation for the Guild by Earl Hamner, Jr. is a shortened and more episodic version which deletes the characters of Meadows and Mrs. Billings. Treadwell began marketing a previous two-act version of the play as early as 1942, a version which included the comic characters of Pierre, a middle-aged, unsuccessful French actor, and his lover, Mimi, an English woman who promises Pierre a life of wealth in Hollywood in the first act and tries to retain him after their California bust in Act Two. A three-scene version of the play was produced by The Playbox in

Pasadena, April 16-23, 1944. In yet another version, a three-act drama written after the television broadcast and marketed by Treadwell as late as 1957, Pop is replaced by Roy, Zepha's husband, who dies after being hit by a car in Act Two. The focus of this version is primarily on Zepha's sense of guilt over her lover, Rich, and for her inability to make a happy life with Roy.

Correspondence in files with the manuscripts reveals that most producers and directors liked the mood, atmosphere and minor characterizations of the play, but cited credibility problems in some of Zepha's actions, as well as dissatisfaction with an overall lack of action. Wynn (S186) finds Zepha a mechanical, formulaic character, and summarizes some of the reactions to the play by readers such as Howard Lindsay and Elliott Nugent.

Treadwell's prefatory notes to the play suggest she conceived of the play more as a series of character studies than one built around a strong, linear unfolding of action. She relates the structure to vaudeville, where characters come on stage, do their bit, and leave. In this regard, as well as in the play's overall atmosphere and naive optimism, *Highway* resembles William Saroyan's *The Time of Your Life*.

HOPE FOR A HARVEST (produced 1941)

The Characters--MRS. MATILDA MARTIN: Elliott's mother, a vigorous lady over 70; TONIE MARTIN: Elliott's daughter, a pretty, but overly made up girl of 16; passionate and lonely; ELLIOTT MARTIN: 45, a Western rancher gone to seed; CARLOTTA (LOTTA) THATCHER: a cousin of Elliott's, possessive of a nervous intensity; NELSON POWELL: thin, dilapidated; VICTOR DeLUCCHI: 18, handsome; WILLIAM (BILLIE) JENNINGS BARNES: about 20; BERTHA BARNES: strong-looking woman in her forties; cheap and loud; JOE DeLUCCHI: over 60; a strong Italian farmer originally from Genoa; WOMAN: large, cumbersome, middle-aged.

Plot Summary--ACT I: The action takes place on a Sunday morning in early summer in the kitchen of Mrs. Matilda Martin, whose son, Elliott, operates a service station next to their house along a country highway in the San Joaquin Valley. Elliott's daughter, Tonie, complains about having to do both housework and work at the service station. Mrs. Martin, however, says it would be easier on her if she did not stay out late at night with Billie Barnes and then get up early to go flying with Al, the local duster and drunk who is giving her flying lessons. Elliott enters and upon hearing the name of Victor DeLucchi, forbids Tonie from resuming her romance with the young man because he is the son of an Italian immigrant farmer. Tonie reminds her father that she herself is of mixed descent, her recently deceased mother having been part Indian. Elliott's cousin, Lotta Thatcher, arrives, broke and tired after leaving a war-torn Paris, hoping the sun and rich land of the family ranch will rejuvenate her. Elliott stuns Lotta with news that their grandmother's ranch has now been parcelled off, having been bought by Italian and Japanese immigrants who maintain a low standard of living and let the land go to ruin. A thin man named Nelson Powell emerges from a stopped car full of Okies and asks if there is any work picking peaches from their orchard. Since Elliott no longer picks his fruit due to poor market prices, Powell leaves to go stay in one of the free camps in town. Lotta is surprised to learn that Elliott's mother has refused to give him any more land to farm, having lost all he had, including his deceased wife's, to the DeLucchis. His own parcel is the filled-in dry river bed upon which his service station is built. Since Tonie is nowhere to be found, Elliott leaves to tend to the station. Mrs. Martin reports to Lotta on news of their family: cousin Bertha is broke like everyone else; Bertha's son, Billie, collects bras from his various girlfriends and prepares to go to college; and Elliott slowly began to go to seed the day Lotta left for Europe. Mrs. Martin is unhappy her son is living with her and buying things on credit; she sees money only as a means to independence and prefers to save hers. Elliott returns, but soon calls to Victor DeLucchi when he sees him at the pump with Tonie. Elliott calls Victor's father a Dago and a cheat, but Victor defends his father as hard-working and honest. Victor reports that he is no longer planning to study to become a priest but has returned home. He then leaves. Elliott goes in to put on his best suit in preparation for lunch at cousin Bertha's, while Mrs. Martin shows Lotta her chickens. Alone with Billie, Tonie tells him she has just finished cleaning up the room they have been sleeping in together at the old ranch house, knowing Lotta will soon be going there to move in. Tonie rebuffs Billie's advances, and he leaves, suspecting she will start seeing Victor again. Tonie attends to a car at the station. Lotta enters the empty room and, stunned by the drabness of the ranch, begins crying. She tells Elliott of her fatigue from the war, her fear of poverty and loneliness after the recent death of her husband, and her desire to return home to the ranch and learn to hope again for a harvest. They prepare to leave for lunch. Lotta sees the Okie Powell fixing a flat tire, and impulsively hires him to work on her ranch amidst Elliott's protests.

ACT II: A week later, in the living room of the old ranch house, Lotta hangs a portrait of Grandma Thatcher, the pioneering matriarch who first settled the ranching community. Buoyed by Lotta's kindness, Tonie confides that she plans to marry Victor and that her father is a hypocrite, since according to rumor he is running around with an Italian himself, a woman named Rena Sanguinetti. Tonie asks Lotta how confession works and, although not religious, Lotta states her belief that one may obtain freedom of guilt through any type of confession to another. Elliott enters and sends Tonie home to take Mrs. Martin to get a long-awaited hair permanent. Elliott urges Lotta to fire the incompetent Powell, but Lotta feels responsibility for his family's welfare. Lotta vows to restore the ranch house to its former state as a landmark, but she cries when Elliott outlines the demoralizing conditions facing farmers today: many crops do not bring a fair price; one has to take out a mortgage to buy equipment and technology to remain competitive; the government pays farmers not to grow crops due to a surplus; and, finally, the ranch land they own is worn out. Cousin Bertha arrives to show off the new car for which she can barely afford payments. Elliott leaves, urging Bertha to have Billie call on Tonie, but Bertha then tells Lotta that Tonie is too fast and not wealthy enough for her son. Joe DeLucchi arrives, bringing a fruit basket for his new neighbor Lotta. He recounts with pride how he brought his first ten acres of land from Grandma Thatcher, and urges Lotta not to take out a mortgage to get her ranch started again, but to sell him a small parcel that would enable him to adjoin two separate tracts he owns. Joe claims he can return the land to prosperity through hard work and by raising a variety of crops which are in demand. Lotta agrees to the deal, clearly touched by the sincerity of his words. Lotta surprises Joe, however, by asking twice the price he anticipated, saying the land is richer than other land he has bought. Joe angrily resists, then turns vehemently on his entering son, Victor, for seeing Tonie; he claims the one ungrateful American daughter-in-law already in his family is more than enough. Joe agrees to Lotta's price, and they exit to check the boundary line. When Tonie arrives, Victor asks her to marry him in Reno tomorrow, since they are not of age to be married here without parental consent. Expecting forgiveness for her "confession," Tonie tells Victor she is pregnant by Billie even though she does not like him. Victor insists she must marry Billie, and he will return to school for the priesthood. Tonie vows to abort the child and Victor leaves. Joe returns, gives Lotta the down payment for the land, then leaves. Tonie rejects Lotta's offer to come live with her, saying before leaving that Lotta lied to her about confession. Powell enters briefly to say goodbye, stating that the work on the ranch is too hard and the wages are less than what he could get picking, even though the latter work is sporadic. When Elliott returns, he is shocked to hear of Lotta's land sale to Joe, especially since the land involved includes the slough upon which his station is built. Elliott is certain Joe will divert drainage and flood him out. Lotta realizes, though, that Elliott previously diverted the water onto Joe's land when he filled in the river bed. She stands firm on the deal, hoping Elliott will return to farming if his station is gone, but he storms out, vowing to show them all.

ACT III: A month later, numerous improvements have been made to Lotta's ranch house. A large, middle-aged widow answers Lotta's ad for a live-in worker, but loses interest when she learns Lotta has a cow to care for and no man to do outside work. Tonie returns for the first time since her outburst last month and asks if she can have the advertised job. Tonie gives Lotta an update on news of the past month: Elliott, who has refused to read Lotta's letter to him, broke off with Rena and mopes; Tonie broke off with Victor and quit her flying lessons; Victor went back to school and Tonie never sees Billie anymore. Tonie receives from Lotta a $20 advance on her job and says she will begin work after she makes a trip into the city. Joe arrives, wanting to begin work on the slough land, but he remains hesitant until Elliott responds to the plan outlined in Lotta's letter. Elliott enters and reluctantly agrees to Lotta and Joe's plan to use the DeLucchi's new $3000 tractor to install drainage pipes under the service station to avoid flooding. Joe leaves to start work. Elliott is surprised to learn Lotta will use the immigrants' approach to farming a variety of crops, and he speaks of the abuses to the land wrought by modern technology. Lotta tells Elliott that Tonie is in trouble and wants to go to the city after Victor, and Elliott blames Tonie's behavior on the blood she inherited from the Indian side of her mother's family. Lotta dismisses Elliott's explanation, and he leaves. Tonie decides to return the money to Lotta and cancel her city trip. Bertha stops in briefly with happy news that Billie has eloped to Reno with the society girl, Irma Belding, thus seemingly assuring himself of a good job in the Belding's bank. Victor enters, having decided to wait to leave for school until work on the new land is done, and Tonie tells him of Billie's marriage and then faints. When Victor refuses to allow Lotta to call a doctor, she correctly guesses that Tonie is pregnant by Billie. Victor tells Lotta he is impressed by Tonie's honesty, and when she revives he offers to marry her and raise the baby as their own. Elliott is surprised upon his return to learn of Victor's offer. As an irate Joe returns looking for his son, Victor breaks the news to him, and Joe refuses to let the couple live with him. Lotta offers her place, saying Tonie will inherit the ranch house some day. Impressed, Joe agrees to the marriage and goes to get wine to celebrate. The young couple leaves for Reno. Joe and Elliott toast their kids, and Joe offers to let them live in a house on his land. Joe and Elliott drink to each other, and Joe leaves. Elliott plans to give the couple his service station and take up Lotta on her offer to help her revive the ranch. Elliott proposes marriage, and although Lotta hesitates, it is clear they plan to build a life together.

Critical Overview--The play was adapted from Treadwell's unpublished novel of the same name, written after Treadwell's return to California from a steamer trip to the Far East in 1937. A folder marked "Source Material" kept with manuscripts of the play at the University of Arizona indicates Treadwell drew heavily from journalistic reporting on the effects of the Depression on California, farming news, federal relief, and the need for the embracing of a diversity of cultures in America. Other typed notes in the archive's files reveal Treadwell's concern for the working man's acceptance of the "new order" in Europe, and her fear that such racism and ethnic prejudice could flourish in the United States. Treadwell later wrote in the *Herald Tribune* (A23) about her personal experiences on and views about ranching and the American work ethic.

Harvest was contracted to Arthur Hopkins in 1938, but went unproduced until the Theatre Guild optioned it in 1941 as a vehicle for Fredric March and his wife Florence Eldridge. A letter to Treadwell from Hopkins a week after the opening displays his continued admiration for the play despite what he felt to be a weak performance, especially by Florence Eldridge, who he felt tried to do a star turn with Carlotta as a faded ingenue. Typed notes by Treadwell during the Guild's work on the play indicate that she, too, believed the acting to be too glib. The Guild's Theresa Helburn and, especially, Lawrence Langner demanded numerous changes throughout the rehearsal and lengthy try-out period. Wynn (S186) summarizes the nature of these changes, and offers as well a plot summary of the earliest version. Treadwell noted her difficulty in maintaining Elliott as a believable character after she merged him with a minor character from an earlier draft, a prejudiced man named Engstrom. She also felt that in the development of Lotta she deviated from her original conception of her as a deeply maternal woman who finds fulfillment through Tonie's child.

The Theatre Guild made much of the fact that *Harvest* garnished exceptional notices during tryouts but was almost universally deprecated by New York critics. They ran a large ad in New York dailies shortly after opening with excerpts from praiseworthy reviews outside of New York, while totally omitting the New York critics' responses. In subscription cities of the Theatre Guild, *Harvest* was often praised for its serious and timely subject (R238, R240, R244, R275, R280, R288), as well as for its excellent production (R265, R282, R289). Several out-of-town critics, however, pointed out the play's tendency for preachiness (R255, R264, R273, R290).

The vast majority of New York critics applauded Treadwell's attempt to tackle a serious and important subject. Most, however, such as Atkinson (R236, R237), Mantle (R271) and Lockridge (R270) felt the play was poorly crafted. Krutch (R268), Gibbs (R253) and Anderson (R235) were especially disturbed by the play's naive solution to a complicated subject. Kronenberger (R266) and Watts (R295) expressed dismay at Treadwell's lack of development as a playwright since *Machinal*, and the latter critic tackled head-on the discrepancy in responses to the play by out-of-town and New York critics. Some reviewers (R242, R262, R274) commented on the seriousness of the play's message in regard to the escalating European conflict, but only Waldorf (R292) found the play's theme more urgent after the bombing of Pearl Harbor. The entire cast was highly praised, especially the Marches and Alan Reed, the latter known as Joe Palooka on radio. Years later, Treadwell remained "awfully bitter" (S137) over the dismissal of the play by New York critics.

The play has not garnished much scholarly attention. Greenfield (S183) seems to take Elliott's racially prejudiced remarks as representing Treadwell's own, while completely ignoring the play's overall call for the embracing of diversity. Heck-Rabi (S167) finds *Harvest* a "mediocre accomplishment" plagued by "passivity of character." Because each revision of the play weakened its power, Heck-Rabi suggests that Treadwell lost sight of her purpose in trying to fit the central roles to the Marches. Wynn (S186) recounts and excerpts the reviewers' responses, concluding that there "are indications that the audience loved the play, and the critics hated it." Shafer (S235), however, believes Treadwell employed the ranch as a symbol for an America in decline, and notes the contemporary relevance of the play's three themes: "the failure of the American people, prejudice against foreigners, and improper use of the environment."

    Hope for a Harvest was given a radio broadcast by the Guild over the Treasury Hour's "Millions for Defense" show on December 23, 1941, and was aired in an adaptation on the Guild's subsequent "U.S. Steel Hour" television series on November 10, 1953. Chan (R301) found the teleplay excellent, while Crosby (R302) thought it dull.

THE ISLAND (copyrighted 1930)

    The Characters--LORETTA ANDERSON: 17, pretty, listless, with an active dream life; FELTON RINE: 40-45, a little overweight and balding, rich and domineering; REED ELIOT: an attractive but somewhat elusive man of about 28; OLOF: a Swedish masseur of 22; MRS. ANDERSON: Loretta's vigorous, hardworking mother; ANDERSON: Loretta's father, about 55, honest-looking but rather insignificant; CAPTAIN LAMBERT: master of Rine's yacht; LAURA POOLE: 22-23, beautiful, graceful.

    Plot Summary--ACT I: On the patio of the main house on "Lady's Island," off the coast of lower California, the housekeeper's daughter, Loretta Anderson, blurts out a confession of love to Felton Rine, the rich owner of the island. Loretta promises never to make a fool of Rine, the way his society-bred fiancée did when she failed to show up on the island after Rine bought it to be with her. Rine teasingly dismisses Loretta, as he hopes to renew his engagement with his girlfriend, who is due to arrive on the island today with her mother. Captain Lambert arrives and informs all that he failed to bring the young lady and her mother on his boat, as they had already left their hotel at Coronado when he arrived. Believing he has been jilted again, Rine angrily demands to be left alone. Loretta quickly returns to comfort Rine and offer herself to him, but when she hesitates to go to his room, Rine gently leaves her alone and goes inside. Moments later, Loretta, disappointed and a little angry, sneaks into Rine's room to be with him. Mrs. Anderson, the caretaker's wife, urges Rine's Swedish masseur, Olof, to watch Rine so he does not jump off a cliff in despair, as an earlier owner of the island did when her lover prepared to leave her. Laura Poole, Rine's former fiancée, arrives unannounced, her tired mother waiting in the cottage below after having hired her own boat to take them to the island, even though she is financially strapped after losing money in the stock market crash. Another guest on the island, Reed Eliot, dances around Laura's direct questions about his life and profession, claiming initially to have quit a lucrative job in L.A. as an advertising manager in order to travel the world, only to admit later that he is only on his two weeks' vacation. The philosophising Eliot tells Laura that everyone on the island but him lives on misguided illusions: the religious Olof believes that God cares especially for him; Loretta reads romance novels and believes she can find love outside her social station; Mrs. Anderson secretly years for Olof and hopes he can bring her the long-awaited excitement she desires; Anderson fails to realize his wife, for whom he gave up his life as a seaman after seeing her beautiful, golden locks, actually dyes her hair; and Rine clings to the notion that one particular girl (Laura) holds his happiness. Rine enters from his bedroom and cautiously greets Laura. Laura tells Eliot that he, too, suffers from an illusion: that he fancies himself a bum when in fact he is ambitious and yearns to become famous through his writing. Loretta emerges from Rine's room.

ACT II: A few weeks later, Loretta wildly tells Rine she will kill herself after he responds to her statements of love with offers of money. She exits crying. Laura becomes upset when she learns that Eliot is packing to sail away for good on his boat. Laura puts off Rine's marriage proposal, citing a concern for her mother's reaction, and Rine goes off to plead with Mrs. Poole. Alone with Laura, Eliot admits he is leaving because of her, and she confesses she loves him. After a prolonged kiss, Laura wants to tell Rine that their engagement is off, but Eliot says Laura would only ruin his devotion to writing and he states he will never marry. Rine returns, announcing that the wedding is set for noon tomorrow in San Diego, and Laura reluctantly agrees and goes to her mother in the cottage. Loretta becomes distraught when she overhears Rine's orders to Olof to pack all his belongings, and she tells Rine she is pregnant. Convinced she is lying, Rine brusquely dismisses her, and Loretta vows to do something to prove her devotion. Mrs. Anderson similarly panics when she learns that Olof will leave tomorrow, too. She pleads to go with Olof, saying she only married her husband because she was pregnant; she now resents Loretta for trapping her in a dull life with Anderson. Eliot enters carrying a wet and unconscious Loretta, who fell from a cliff into the ocean. He takes her inside to attend to her. Rine and Laura enter, hear the news, and Rine exits abruptly while Laura goes in to help Loretta.

ACT III: A few minutes later, Anderson tries to comfort his wife, who believes Loretta's fall is God's punishment for saying earlier she wished her daughter had never been born. Amidst the news that Loretta has revived, Mrs.

Anderson confesses she was ready to leave the island with Olof and that she dyes her hair. Laura enters with the offer that her mother would like to take Mrs. Anderson on as her maid as she travels around the world next year. Anderson, feeling he has been made a fool of by his wife, happily consents, saying he will go fishing while she is gone. Having learned Loretta is alright, Rine returns. Laura suspects Rine's involvement with Loretta and calls off their wedding. Rine admits to the affair, but pleads with Laura to stay with him. She admits she has never loved him, but Rine still offers marriage, saying their arrangement will be like a job to the economically desperate Laura. She silently consents. Loretta enters, and Rine takes her back inside to talk with her. When Eliot enters, Laura cries violently, seeing her future marriage before her. Eliot prepares to sail down the coast of Mexico. Laura fixes her makeup, recites romantic verse about the sea, and asks Eliot to take her with him. Laura agrees to sail with Eliot for three days, asking only that he leave her on the mainland afterward, so that she can go on with her marriage, buoyed by the memory of at least one romantic encounter. Rine enters and calls off his wedding to Laura, having realized that Loretta is not pregnant and must really love him if she would jump off a cliff for him. Laura tells Eliot that he is living by one other misguided illusion: that he will be able to lose her someday. They embrace.

Critical Overview--Although Laura and Eliot are bright, witty and appealing characters, the play as a whole suffers from too many character reversals and from having three women in the play who all become distraught when their men threaten to leave without them. In the end, despite some clever dialogue between Eliot and Laura, *The Island* remains underdeveloped in both theme and action. An earlier version contains a more detailed scene between Olof and Mrs. Anderson. The play received a simple production in Newtown, Connecticut in 1932 to poor critical response (R176, R180).

JOHN DOANE (c. 1915-18)

The Characters--JOHN DOANE: 45-48, rich, powerful, self-made man, inventor of the John Doane tractor; EULA: the housemaid; ALICE: Doane's private secretary of twenty years, middle-aged, unmarried, tired and nervous; TERRY: Doane's 22-year-old daughter; LAURA DE MONTEJO: a slender, fair and graceful woman of Doane's age; JANET LINDLEY: 28-30, English, Doane's mistress.

Plot Summary--In the handsome but lifeless library of the Doane house in a large midwestern city, John Doane's charismatic combination of strength and loneliness makes him an alluring focal point for the women with whom he comes in contact: Alice, his tired and possessive secretary; his wife, who is ill from his prolonged unresponsiveness; Terry, his intelligent, college-educated daughter, who he keeps at arm's length from the family business; and Janet Lindley, a married Englishwoman with whom he is having an affair. All the women lament their inability to get close to Doane, who maintains an air of self-sufficiency and indifference. Doane's old childhood friend and first love, Laura de Montejo arrives, having just returned to the city for the first time since she jilted the then-struggling Doane in favor of a sensual Argentinian. Over drinks, Laura slowly reveals the ironies and disappointments in her life: she left Doane because she felt about to be trapped in a life of commonness, but her husband took her away to Buenos Aires to live in a small apartment with his family and used her inherited money to pay off previous debts. Her husband having recently died, Laura has returned to her old home, and now pleads with Doane for help, needing someone or something to live for. Janet, Doane's latest in a string of romances, urgently innterrupts their intimacy. Laura, sensing Doane has drifted too far apart from her, leaves by a side door. Janet tells Doane that her husband has wired and will arrive back from his travels tonight. Doane abruptly breaks off their affair, still distracted by Laura's return. Terry excitedly enters and speaks of passing a woman, Laura, on the street before the house, only a moment before she ran in front of a car and was killed. After a moment's reflection, Doane goes upstairs to sit with his sick wife, while Terry manages to the affairs of the business correspondence.

Critical Overview--Although *John Doane* is one of Treadwell's best short plays, no evidence remains that she tried to market it for production. The play reveals Treadwell's early explorations of the potentials of the dramatic monologue, and several of Laura's speeches clearly prefigure those found in later Treadwell works. Although the play as a whole is slightly underdeveloped and resorts to a somewhat contrived melodramatic climax, it offers several fine character studies, especially Alice, Laura, and the destructive but desolate John Doane.

JUDGMENT IN THE MORNING (copyrighted 1952)

The Characters--ANDREW (DREW) WELLS: about 50, a man of drive and self-control; NORVAL: a middle-aged black butler; DAVID HARKNESS: a successful young reporter from the *Herald Tribune*; MARGARET WELLS: Andrew's wife, late 40s, smart-looking, efficient; WILLIAM COLTER: 50s, small, cheerful, a professional politician; FRANCES (FRAN) WELLS: 22-23, highly strung, beautiful, ill; WILMA: about 24, alternately childish and mature; DELIA: 45, Jose's mother, an over-worked, Irish cleaning woman; JOSÉ (JOEY): about 24, handsome, dark, a psychopathic criminal.

Plot Summary--ACT I: David Harkness, a reporter from the *Herald Tribune*, arrives in the study of Andrew Wells's apartment to verify a rumor that Wells is soon to run for Governor of New York as a prelude to running for the Presidency. Harkness says Senator William Colter, Wells's friend from youth, will be arriving soon from Washington, D.C. to persuade him to run. Margaret Wells enters and tells her husband that their daughter Fran is dressing to go out on this chilly night despite the fact that she suffers from one of her many colds. Wells calls a doctor in the apartment building to come see Fran, and Margaret leaves somewhat relieved, although she would prefer to get advice long distance from her close friend and spiritualist, Nellie Broker. Wells is surprised to learn that Harkness often sees Fran from afar at several nightclubs. After Sen. Colter arrives, Harkness agrees to postpone the story announcing Wells's candidacy, as he did previously for Wells during the José Campos case. During that case, Wells, as New York's District Attorney, did not prosecute Wilma Campos, then pregnant and seemingly as guilty as her convicted husband in a robbery-murder. Harkness vows to return tomorrow morning for approval to run the story. Wells confides to Colter that he is maintaining a secret affair with Wilma Campos, and he refuses to give her up even though she may cost him his political future. Wells speaks of Wilma's difficult past, including the death of her baby after José's conviction. When Margaret returns, Colter tells her of their political plans, then departs until tomorrow. Wells dislikes how Margaret never shows pleasure in anything, including their sex life. Margaret relays to Wells the doctor's diagnosis that Fran, with whom Wells has never felt particularly close, suffers from tuberculosis. When Fran enters, dressed and determined to go out, Wells informs her of her illness and scolds her for hurting her reputation by frequenting nightclubs. Wells angrily leaves. Fran weeps and confides to her mother that she is still mourning the death of a young flyer she loved, and she now drinks and parties to escape her restlessness. She is particularly sorry she never made love to the young man, and she blames Margaret for teaching her always to deny and be fearful of life. Margaret tells her daughter of Wells's plans for the Presidency, but when Wells returns Fran defiantly goes out for a night of partying. Wells tells Margaret he is going out, too, and will not be back until late. Margaret frantically tries to reach Nellie Broker on the telephone.

ACT II: That night in a cheap, westside, basement apartment, Wilma eagerly greets Wells. Wells, though, reluctantly breaks off his relationship with Wilma, although he does not explain why. Wilma refuses Wells's request to leave town, saying she must remain close to José, whom she also loves. Wells

relents, feeling he can trust Wilma to remain silent about their affair. When
José's mother, Delia, unexpectedly arrives, Wilma ushers Wells out the back
way, asking him to return when he hears her radio blaring, a signal that Delia
has gone. Delia tells Wilma that José has broken out of prison and is on his
way here. As Wilma urgently packs to leave, José enters, cursing and throwing
out Delia for ruining his surprise arrival. Wilma and José tentatively feel each
other out. He tells of one of his former prison mates, "Gooch," who helped
him escape by having him pose as a corpse as it was being removed from the
prison hospital. Wilma comforts and promises to support José, but he notices
a change in her. He insists on making love to her tonight, but she tries to get
him to leave to avoid capture. José turns on the radio for some music, and
refuses to let Wilma turn it off. Wilma hides José's gun. When José talks in
more detail about Gooch, it becomes clear to Wilma that he was José's lover
in prison, a fact to which José reluctantly admits and cites as the reason he
must now make love to Wilma, to prove his manliness. Having heard the
radio, Wells reenters, but is quickly tripped and beaten by José, who realizes
Wilma and Wells are lovers. José grabs the gun and shoots at Wells, but hits
Wilma as Wells ducks. José runs off. Wilma urges Wells not to call a doctor
so as not to be found out. She dies. Wells turns out the lights and sits beside
the body, the bars on the basement windows casting shadows like the bars of
a prison cell.

ACT III: The next morning, Wells has summoned all the press to
receive his statement, although they, like Sen. Colter and Margaret, seem more
interested in news of the Wilma Campos murder. Margaret is relieved about
Fran's health, having spoken with Nellie Broker last night. Alone, Colter and
Wells discuss the murder: Colter feels their problem is over, but Wells says he
was seen in Wilma's apartment by José, who will surely tell all once caught.
Wells will resign as D.A. Colter leaves Wells alone to break the news to his
family. Fran, having been out all night, returns just in time to hear, along with
her mother, Wells's confession. Margaret urges Wells to deny everything.
Colter enters with news that José has been found dead, having fallen or
committed suicide in the East River. When Wells still insists on resigning due
to his previous acts of cowardice, Colter leaves, asking the women to talk sense
into him. Margaret leaves, too, when Fran surprisingly comes to her father's
defense. Fran tells of her experience last night, going off to have sex with a
man she barely knew, but backing out due to the squallidness of it all. She
says she and her father are both still mourning the loss of someone they loved,
and after she goes, Wells sends Harkness to look after his daughter. Wells
takes a revolver from his desk. Margaret interrupts him, though, and he tells
her he plans to leave and not return. Margaret asks for forgiveness for her
selfishness, having moments earlier realized the importance of their love. After
Wells informs the press he will not run for Governor, Margaret realizes that
some good may emerge from all this evil: Wells may be better able to

understand and sympathize with the criminals he must prosecute, thus avoiding the hard-line attitudes about right and wrong he inherited from his minister-father. Wells plans to stay with Margaret and Fran. Their servant, Norval, cleans up the papers in the study containing Wells's statement of resignation.

Critical Overview--Written fairly late in Treadwell's career, *Judgment in the Morning* is clearly adapted from her earlier drama, *Andrew Wells' Lady*. While the characterizations are much stronger in this revised work (especially Margaret and Fran), *Judgment* still suffers from a divided focus. One plot line centers on a drama of family, politics and power, while another focuses on trying to escape the life of petty crime. Treadwell hoped to unite these disparate stories by inserting a theme based on the Hungarian-born Swiss psychiatrist Lipot Szondi's theory of "fate analysis." This theory posits that the behavior of an individual is governed by latent recessive genes stemming from the "familial unconscious" (as opposed to Freud's personal unconscious or Jung's racial unconscious). By her own estimation, however, Treadwell felt the thematic device proved unsuccessful, forcing her to rely on too much exposition. Typed notes in manuscript files further reveal that Treadwell believed she created an interesting and believable character in José Campos. She would later focus more on his story in *Garry*.

In earlier versions of the play, titled *I Was Like That* and *I Was Like That in a Way*, Wells leaves at the end to find his true self. In yet an earlier and far more interesting version, titled *Don't Leave Me*, Wells is in love with his 40-year-old secretary, a bright, capable woman named Edna Gordon. Wells tells Margaret and Fran he plans to marry Edna and reject the recent offer to become Secretary of State to the President. After Margaret leaves, Fran applauds her father's decision, saying Margaret's attraction for her spiritualist friend (here named Clare Broker) is a sexual one. Wells retorts that Fran may have the facts right about Margaret's lesbianism, but not her cheap and degrading interpretation of them. Wells relates the incidents of his wedding night with Margaret, saying his wife came to him after an idealistic "young girl intimacy" with Mrs. Broker in college, a relationship filled with poetry, music and love. Margaret's distaste for sex "in any form" was so strong, however, that she responded to Wells's advances by weeping and vomiting the entire night. Margaret, having overheard their conversation, returns. She admits her attraction to Mrs. Broker, but claims it is not a sexual one. The play ends with Wells deciding to keep going the way things are: he will maintain his affair with Edna, and Margaret will accept it. This version is worth noting in light of the homophobic theme, which would later be developed in *Garry*, as well as for the description of a woman violently reacting to sex on her wedding night, an action found in several of Treadwell's plays, including *Machinal* and *For Saxophone*.

LADIES LEAVE (produced 1929)

The Characters--DR. ARPAD JEFFER: about 35, a distinguished American-born doctor who has lived mostly in Vienna; J. BURNHAM POWERS: 38-40, a successful stuffed shirt; ZIZI POWERS: an exceedingly pretty woman of 26; PHILIP HAVENS: editor of Powers's magazine, about 28, attractive; IRMA BARRY WHITE: a short, plump, Southern woman of about 35; SERVANTS.

Plot Summary--ACT I: Dr. Arpad Jeffer, a noted women's psychologist from Vienna, joins J. Burnham Powers in his New York apartment prior to their departure for a dinner banquet. Powers runs the popular magazine, *Ladies Home Companion*, and hopes to enlist Jeffer, author of the recent popular book, *Love and Lovers*, to write a piece for the magazine after he finishes his lecture series in America. Powers believes modern American women have fallen into a moral abyss, and he is grateful to both a former romance who mothered him during his youth and Zizi, his current wife, who he sought out for her traditional, old-fashioned ways. Zizi has just finished reading Jeffer's book, though, and is now somewhat confused about her feelings. Philip Havens, the clever editor of Powers's journal, arrives, having been invited to the banquet to boost his spirits and keep him from leaving the magazine in favor of going to Paris to finish a play he is writing. Phil decides to stay with Zizi rather than go to the banquet, and Powers and Jeffer leave. Zizi is to go to the train station to meet the wife of a powerful, Southern business associate of Powers's, but Phil phones the station and tells Zizi the train will arrive late. Phil resumes the amorous advances toward Zizi which she broke off two months ago, and now she turns down Phil's offers to marry or at least become lovers, saying she does not want to hurt Powers. Mrs. White arrives at the apartment, and Zizi learns Phil lied about her train being late in order to spend time alone with her. Phil leaves, insinuating to Zizi that he will cancel his trip to Paris tomorrow if she will phone him later with an encouraging response to his advances. Mrs. White informs Zizi that she has left her husband after verging on a nervous collapse from a lack of freedom and stimulation in her life. Powers returns from the banquet, and Mrs. White is thrilled to learn that Dr. Jeffer is in town. Not only has she just finished his book, but a friend of hers recently returned from being treated by him in Vienna and promptly divorced her husband and opened a successful tea-room. Zizi agrees to accompany Mrs. White to one of Jeffer's lectures tomorrow, and Mrs. White retreats to her room to recover from such exciting news. Alone with Powers, Zizi expresses her exasperation at being asked once again to entertain some business mogul's boring wife, who plans to stay with them in New York while she writes a novel. She pleads with Powers for them to run away somewhere together, but he merely tells her to get some rest as he exits upstairs to his awaiting masseur.

ACT II: One afternoon six weeks later, Powers stops in at home from work to see Zizi. Powers is glad Jeffer is returning to Europe tonight, since he has been unable to contract him to write for his magazine. He scoffs when Zizi says she will try her hand at persuading him. Mrs. White is greatly taken by Phil's recent attentions, and wishes he would agree to collaborate with her on her novel so her life would get on track and she could divorce her husband, even though she enjoys receiving his checks in the mail. Phil arrives and wants to have it out with Zizi, having tired of maintaining appearances by entertaining the ever-present Mrs. White. He believes that now that he and Zizi are lovers, he should hold more sway over her emotions and actions. Phil expresses jealousy when he learns Zizi is about to visit Jeffer at his hotel, but she gently reminds him that she first came to Phil as a lover after attending one of Jeffer's lectures at which she redefined her sense of the word "moral." Zizi angrily discovers that Mrs. White has been eavesdropping through a keyhole all this while. She calls her guest a moral hypocrite when Mrs. White contemplates telling all to Powers, and Zizi slaps her and leaves. Mrs. White orders her trunks sent to her room. Powers returns, but innocently misreads Mrs. White's deliberate evasiveness to his questions about Zizi's whereabouts. Mrs. White finally blurts out that Zizi and Phil are lovers, then announces she is leaving, as Powers grabs his hat and exits the apartment.

ACT III: Less than an hour later, Jeffer finally arrives, followed shortly by Zizi. Jeffer is disappointed that he missed Zizi at his hotel, but Zizi does not return Jeffer's subtle, romantic advances. She offers Jeffer a reasoned argument about reconsidering the offer to write for her husband's magazine, but she is disappointed when he pulls an already signed agreement to do so from his pocket, having reached her same conclusions without her input earlier in the day. Jeffer notes the change in Zizi since his arrival, and she admits her new-found lack of concern for previous moral taboos, such as taking a lover. She views such actions as important only as a means of "coming out" and being an independent, fully realized person. Powers returns home, and Jeffer leaves to board his ship, promising to have tea with Zizi when she comes to Vienna. Powers immediately interrogates Zizi, who calmly admits the affair and says she has thoughtfully protected Powers from knowing about it before now. She says if anyone is to "blame" for her recent actions it is Powers, who drove her to her actions because he never took the time to know anything about her. While Powers remains indignant and munches on a sandwich, Zizi tells how she came to love her husband only after he ceased to be a barrier in her life. Upset that Zizi loves, in some way, both men, Powers orders her to leave, and she prepares to pack, feeling she will probably live with Phil. Phil arrives, drunk, for a show-down with Zizi about their relationship. Powers rushes at Phil, but Zizi manages to calm them to talk the matter out. Phil eavesdrops on Mrs. White, who talks upstairs on the phone to her husband and makes plans to return to him. Zizi announces she will not go with the obstinate Phil, but will go to Vienna instead. Phil pleads with her to stay, saying he is totally under her control; Powers offers to take Zizi back now that she has given up Phil. Zizi hands the signed contract with Jeffer over to a pleased Power. She leaves to pack, while Powers and Phil go in to console themselves over dinner.

Critical Overview--The majority of New York critics dismissed the play when produced as lacking substance (R146, R148, R149). Many critics repeatedly compared the play unfavorably to Treadwell's last production, the innovative and disturbing *Machinal* (R135, R137, R146, R150), Krasna finding it hard to believe that the same person wrote both plays (R136). Critical dissatisfaction seems to have been exacerbated by general overacting by most of the cast (R145, R148). Surprisingly, few reviewers seemed disturbed by Zizi's nontraditional actions, and Rathbun (R144) felt Zizi could not adequately be considered a feminist since she was so preoccupied with men. Only Robert Edmond Jones's set designs garnished widespread praise (R142), although a few critics found the play entertaining, if not original (R131, R133, R141).

Read within the context of Treadwell's entire dramatic canon, however, *Ladies Leave* is a delightful comedy, and Zizi appears a smart, witty, and forcefully independent character. Jeffer is an early prototype for the writer-psychologist in *For Saxophone*, both acting as catalysts for women making radical changes in their lives. Mrs. White is one in a string of well-drawn, comic characters playing secondary roles in the plots of Treadwell's early plays. The comedy is structurally sound, and appears much more playable than critics found it in 1929.

Heck-Rabi (S167) compares the comedy to Rachel Crothers's 1931 play, *As Husbands Go*, in their female characters' evaluation of American versus European men. Heck-Rabi concludes that "*Ladies Leave* negates the image of the American husband: *As Husbands Go* re-affirms it. The Crothers play was a success. *Ladies Leave* was a failure."

THE LAST BORDER (copyrighted 1944)

The Characters--HERCULANO: an old Mexican servant, habitually drunk; LUPE: O'Higgins's beautiful, young Indian model and lover; MRS. EVELYN HOAG: a vain American woman around 40; SINFOROSA: a thin Mexican woman of 50, dressed always in black, owner of the boarding house; DANIEL O'HIGGINS: 40s, an American painter, honest and strong; CRISTINA DE MORA: 38-40, a graceful, fair woman from Northern Spain; TONY MORA: Cristina's teenage son, handsome, intelligent; PRUDENCIO: a

musician in his mid-20s; GILDA: an attractive, passionate woman in her early
40s; HARRY BLISS: small, rich owner of a new nightclub; SARMONTE: a
strong Italian man, about 30, handsome yet somewhat vulgar; PEG: a pale,
used-up, red-haired Irish girl; A DETECTIVE: plump, vain, insecure.

Plot Summary--ACT I: An old servant, Herculano, guards
the door connecting a street to the inner courtyard of a beautiful old house in
Mexico City. Lupe, a young Indian woman, cooks a chicken in a pot. Mrs.
Evelyn Hoag, a middle-aged woman in Mexico to study art, enters and unfolds
a stream of criticisms: Herculano did not admit her musician-lover, Prudencio,
this afternoon; her husband's usual monthly check to her did not arrive in the
mail; the house has become prison-like after Sinforosa, the landlady, hired
Herculano as doorkeeper following a murder attempt on Tony Mora, teenage
son of the Spanish Cristina de Mora, who now seeks visas for the United
States; and, Lupe is suspected of having stolen and cooked her chicken. Daniel
O'Higgins, an expatriate American painter, claims he and his lover Lupe bought
the chicken, even though they have been broke for a week. O'Higgins hopes
to win a government-sponsored art contest, and expects news of the outcome
any day now. Cristina returns, unable to obtain visas, and Tony tells her he
wants to stay in Mexico City. Neurotically fearful of the effect on Tony of
another resident in the house, the forty-year-old, sexually experienced Gilda,
Cristina sobs hysterically. After being solaced by O'Higgins, Cristina relates
the story behind the recent murder attempt. Tony has been pursued for years
by a young Italian whose father was unjustly executed in Spain by Cristina's
husband, a high-ranking officer fighting against the Republic in the war.
O'Higgins gives Cristina directions to a man who will smuggle her and Tony
to the U.S., but Cristina suddenly turns on O'Higgins and calls him her enemy
after learning he fought in Spain for the Republic. After Herculano tells
O'Higgins a man called for him earlier today about a painting, O'Higgins
believes he has won the contest and dances joyously with Lupe. Harry Bliss,
the rich owner of a new nightclub, arrives and breaks the news he learned from
the radio to O'Higgins that he did not win the contest. Bliss, however, has
heard O'Higgins paints women well, and wants to commission a painting for
his nightclub of a naked, white woman lying on lilies. O'Higgins reluctantly
accepts the commission for the mural, which Bliss will call "Woman With
Lilies," in exchange for 1000 pesos in advance and another 1000 when finished.
Bliss pays, arranges an audition for Prudencio at his club, and exits. Evelyn
goes off with Prudencio, who complains he does not have a nice charro
costume for the audition. O'Higgins pays Sinforosa for another month's rental
on his room, but also demands to rent Evelyn's room and have the bothersome
woman evicted. Cristina reluctantly accepts some of O'Higgins's money for her
trip to the U.S., and after giving money to Lupe and Herculano, O'Higgins
leaves in search of a white woman to serve as his model. Tony happily greets

Gilda, back from Cuernavaca where she had supposedly gone for a divorce, but Gilda goes to her room when she hears the news of the murder attempt on Tony. Tony tells Cristina he will stay and marry Gilda now, admitting he is already her lover. Cristina will leave for the U.S. anyway, and she and Tony go to their respective rooms. Sarmonte, a strong Italian, enters through the unguarded door and confronts Gilda, jealously inquiring over her activities this past week. He gives her a plane ticket for Cuba, where they have their next job together, and says he will meet her there. Gilda suspects Sarmonte of trying to kill the innocent and decent Tony and refuses to leave. Sarmonte explains how Tony's father killed his, and Gilda agrees to leave for Cuba if Sarmonte will go with her and let Tony be. They exit. Tony bids farewell to his mother and goes to Gilda's now-empty room. He is killed by a shot from the dark hallway leading to the street.

ACT II: On a late afternoon some days later, Sinforosa admits Bliss, who tells Evelyn that Prudencio is a big hit and can be heard on the radio this afternoon. Even though Prudencio no longer visits Evelyn now that he has a job, Evelyn eagerly turns on the radio to the appropriate station. Lupe wants to think over Bliss's offer of a job as a cigarette girl at his club. O'Higgins returns after an absence of several days with a chicken on one arm and Peg, a white-skinned, Irish prostitute, on the other. Bliss angrily threatens a lawsuit and leaves after he learns that the dilapidated Peg is to serve as the model for the mural, which O'Higgins has not even started. When Sinforosa reluctantly agrees to house Peg in Tony's room, O'Higgins learns of the recent murder and of Cristina's reclusive grief. O'Higgins claims he will paint Peg's tortured body on a heap of junk, not on the lilies, as Bliss demanded. Peg is indignant and leaves, and Evelyn checks out, too, telling O'Higgins that she is just like him, a failure who has sought escape in Mexico. Cristina returns the money to O'Higgins, and he tries to comfort her despair. She explains that the police believe the escaped Gilda was a spy and aid to the murder, and they are trying to capture the Italian trigger-man before he leaves the country. Lupe abruptly abandons O'Higgins. He takes her leaving in stride, and talks with Cristina about the meaning of love, asking if they can spend the night together to fill each other's emptiness. The police phone to say they have captured Sarmonte at the airport and are bringing him over for identification. The honest Cristina is tormented, not actually having seen Sarmonte before, but O'Higgins urges her to lie and identify him, since evil must be met with evil to prevent the ruthless from taking over the world. Sarmonte arrives, escorted by a Detective. The policeman leaves, though, releasing Sarmonte after no one in the house can or will identify him. O'Higgins prevents Sarmonte from leaving by barring the door, and Herculano enters with Sarmonte's gun, which he found in the alley after Tony's murder. Cristina grabs the gun and kills Sarmonte. O'Higgins's plan to remove the body in Evelyn's trunk, which is to be sent for tomorrow, is interrupted by the return of the Detective, who was waiting outside for

Sarmonte to leave. After the Detective finds the body and hears Cristina's confession, he insinuates that Cristina and O'Higgins are lovers. While Cristina gathers her things for jail, O'Higgins deftly manipulates the Detective. He explains he is an artist on commission from Bliss, and he begins sketching the Detective for a future picture called "The Law." He shows the Detective the advance money he received from Bliss, and subtly bribes the policeman into reporting that Sarmonte was shot by the Detective as he tried to attack Cristina. He shows the completed "Law" sketch to a delighted Detective, who phones headquarters immediately with this contrived report of Sarmonte's death. O'Higgins tells a veiled and packed Cristina to continue with her plans to escape to the U.S., absolved of all guilt by the workings of the law. O'Higgins agrees to go with Cristina, after she calls him valiant and good. The Detective stands alone in the shadows of the courtyard holding his money.

Critical Overview--Wynn (S186) describes Treadwell's desire in this play to explore the justification of violence in the wake of events of World War II. Certainly Treadwell's despair over political conditions in Europe permeates the tone of *The Last Border*. Her inspiration for the storyline involving Bliss's commission of the mural seems derived from an article in the January 1944 issue of *Town & Country*, which describes Diego Rivera's paintings of nudes for a new nightclub, one of which (reproduced in the article) was a naked, white woman against a backdrop of lilies.

Although *The Last Border* is a play of high ideals (e.g. the need for and purpose of art; the justification of violence), it remains cloaked in an essentially melodramatic format. Most of the agents, actors and producers to whom Treadwell sent the play felt it was too diffuse in theme and lacked sympathetic central characters. Lawrence Langner, as usual, was more forthright with Treadwell than others and urged her not to waste any more of her time on this story of melodramatic revenge. Arthur Hopkins was one of the play's admirers and circulated the play for a time in 1945, but was unable to raise money for its production.

Treadwell reworked the play over a dozen times between the summer of 1945, which she spent in Mexico, and September 1947, the latter date being the version summarized here. A few of the characters in this latter version are composites of characters from earlier drafts, most notably O'Higgins, who is a blending of a Mexican-Irish painter (variously named Miguel O'Higgins, Miguel Ennis and Patricio Murphy), and a journalist (Alexander Constantine, Paul Thomas). One version, titled *The Watched Door*, features Aaron Mora, Cristina's husband, who kills himself after learning his wife has long loved Constantine. Mostly, though, Treadwell experimented with the removal of the villain: Sarmonte is killed alternately by the Detective, Constantine/Thomas, and Cristina on behalf of a returned and bitter Gilda. Other titles include *Borderline* and *Madrid 7* (the latter a scenario). Treadwell's long-time friend

Lola Fries completed a German translation in 1947 under the title *Die letzte Grenze*, which was circulated under one of Treadwell's pseudonyms, Alexander West. Treadwell had difficulty abandoning the play, and she reworked its setting and characters for the next twenty years into a comedy, *Woman With Lilies*.

LONE VALLEY (produced 1933)

The Characters--JOE: about 19, homely but good; LOTTIE: Grainger's 16 year-old daughter; LASLY: about 38, defeated by this life, but full of faith in another; GRAINGER: 45, the richest and most dangerous man in the valley; MARY: a frail woman between 20 and 30; ELLA: 47, Grainger's delicate sister; HARRY LYMAN: a slim and natty salesman of about 30.

Plot Summary--ACT I: On the outskirts of an isolated ranching community, Joe climbs in the window of an abandoned country cottage and begins sweeping and dusting. He tries to get rid of the pestering Lottie Grainger, who has followed him to the cottage even though her father has forbidden her to be alone with the boy. Lottie leaves as Lasly, the minister of the valley, brings gifts of flowers and a jar of wild honey to welcome the new, expected inhabitant of the cottage. Joe has been surreptitiously fixing up the cottage since the death of the kindly, reclusive old lady who lived there, leaving the cottage to her young niece in the city. Joe is defiant of the rich and powerful Grainger, who has raised him roughly after obtaining him from the orphanage to work on his land. Lottie returns, saying her angry father is on his way to the cottage, and Lasly hastily departs. Lottie explains her father's bitter disposition as a result of being forced by his father's will to pay the old lady of the cottage fifty dollars a month until her death, purportedly because she was the old man's lover. Joe teasingly chases Lottie, and catches her just as Grainger enters. Grainger's threatening advances toward Joe are interrupted by the arrival of Mary, who nearly faints from the weight of her suitcase and bags. Joe leaves to fetch her a drink. Grainger sends his daughter away, then futilely questions Mary about her past before warning her that she has moved into a decent community which he plans to uphold. Grainger leaves, and Joe returns to comfort a sobbing Mary. Joe tells her about some of the inhabitants of Lone Valley, including: Miss Ella, Grainger's sister, whose mind scattered after she was locked away by Grainger when she fell in love at thirty with an Italian farmhand; Grainger, whose money and influential positions in the community make him powerful and to be feared; and Lasly, who is honest at heart but is looked down on by the community because of his marriage to an Indian. Mary tells how she supported herself since her parents died when she was twelve, and that she did not really know her deceased aunt, whose letter about the cottage inheritance reached her while she was ill in the hospital. After Mary helps Joe roll a cigarette, he states how much he is attracted to her free and independent nature, and vows to help her in her efforts to begin ranching here. Miss Ella enters, returning the deceased aunt's caged parrot to Mary and the cottage where it lived, hoping it will begin talking again. Joe tells of his plans to attend the state agricultural college in the fall, having saved enough of his money to do so. Miss Ella leaves and Joe soon follows after agreeing to Mary's request to return after he finishes work at the desk of Grainger's hotel around nine o'clock tonight. The parrot squawks at Mary to "be a good girl."

ACT II: About two months later, the parrot repeats the same phrase to Mary as she draws a bath after hoeing onions outside in the oppressive, late afternoon heat. A drunken Grainger arrives, but his sexual advances toward Mary are interrupted by a knock at the door. Grainger leaves as Mary admits Harry Lyman, a silk stockings salesman, who recognizes her immediately. Lyman says he missed her the last time he was in the city, and one of the girls at the joint where she worked said she had a baby, a statement Mary denies at first before admitting her baby died at birth. Lyman urges Mary to leave the valley and go on the road with him, offering to serve as her pimp. When Lottie arrives, having followed Lyman, the salesman leaves under Mary's threats to remain silent about her past. Mary retreats into her bath, and Joe arrives, only to be teased by Lottie about his romantic interest in Mary. Mary emerges, wearing a kimono, and dances with an embarrassed Joe to a familiar tune on the radio, while a jealous Lottie departs. Mary is exuberantly happy with her independence and with "adopting" Joe as her baby, but a distracted Joe merely admits he has given up studying for his college entrance exams. Grainger interrupts their dancing by throwing Joe's bank book on the table and accusing Mary of leading Joe along in order to get his money. Although she insists she has merely borrowed the money from Joe, Mary is visibly shaken with Grainger's news of how one year of the valley's frequent droughts can break a farmer, and that the only way her deceased aunt was able to live here independently was because she was his father's lover. Mary asks if Grainger will buy the place from her now so she can pay back Joe, but Joe vehemently claims he does not want the money returned. When Grainger shares Lottie's news that Joe has been seen coming to the cottage at nights, Joe tries to fight Grainger, but wilts under his own sense of impotence. Grainger laughs and exits. Shamed and feeling dirty, Joe looks in on Mary in her bedroom as she dresses. Mary returns, angry and crying over the fact that the Joe she thought was innocently caring for her has been snooping around at night, lustily spying on her. Joe rushes out, and Mary cries that he need not return. After reflection, Mary begins packing her suitcase. Lyman returns, and Mary agrees to his earlier business proposition. Lyman leaves, vowing to pick Mary up in twenty minutes at the crossroads nearby. Joe becomes desperate when a packed

Mary leaves the cottage. He prays to God for forgiveness and not to let Mary go. Mary returns with a request for someone to care for the parrot, but Joe sees her reappearance as a sign from God. He pitifully asks to touch her, then Mary comforts him in an embrace as she cries and takes off her hat. ACT III: Around midnight that night, Mary emerges from the bedroom, puts on her kimono and calls to wake Joe, saying it is time for him to go home. While coyotes cry in the distance, Joe rouses and dresses, vowing to take Mary riding with him sometime by moonlight. When Mary refuses his offer of marriage, Joe believes she made love to him only out of a sense of pity and is crushed. Mary, however, offers to accompany Joe as he goes to college, taking a menial job to support them and perhaps marrying him after college. Joe feels freed by Mary of his longtime sense of sexual shame. The drunken Grainger bursts in and begins to relate how Lyman told everyone at the hotel about Mary's past. She cuts him short, agreeing to leave town and wait for Joe to join her. Grainger, though, blurts out Mary's past as a prostitute, as well as her recent baby, and Joe goes to comfort Mary when she admits all and tells how her baby died. Joe attacks the belligerent Grainger, but Mary, unashamed of her past, separates them, then exits to the bedroom to dress. Miss Ella enters with news that Lottie ran away with Lyman over an hour ago, and Grainger weeps over his tormented life. Lasly enters and, on behalf of Grainger's wife, summons him to the house. Lasly refuses to marry Joe to Mary, saying he heard about her past at the hotel and Joe would be doomed to a life without respect, as he himself as been. Mary rejects Joe's offer to leave the valley with her, believing he will always be plagued by her past. She leaves, saying Joe is at least free now from his sense of guilty inhibitions about sex. Lasly believes Mary's departure is God's will, but Joe climbs out the window to go with Mary, asking if Lasly's wife will take care of the parrot.

Critical Overview--Wynn (S186) outlines the play's lengthy revision and tryout process, which culminated in Treadwell's bitterly disappointing three-performance run on Broadway in 1933, a production she directed and produced.   Surviving manuscripts reveal that Treadwell experimented with many different characterizations and endings. In a version completed after a tryout in Nyack, New York in 1932, Lasly begins to marry Joe and Mary in the third act despite Grainger's protests. When Grainger angrily reacts to reading a note from the runaway Lottie, he grabs his gun and shoots Mary in an ensuing struggle, and she dies comforted by Joe's words that God sees and forgives all.   In an odd version titled *Bound*, written after a Baltimore tryout in October 1927, a harsher, cruder Mary ends the play by selling herself as a wife for $500 to a stereotypical, amoral Chinaman who peddles vegetables in the valley. She repays the money to Joe, who picks up Mary's suitcase and leaves. The version which played Baltimore (titled *Wild Honey* and subsequently revised after opening as *Set Free*) ends with Miss Ella giving to Mary (named May here) her dying father's last note in which he admits that Mary's aunt gave him the only happiness he ever knew. Joe (named Henry) feels that Mary has done the same for him and outfits her in a bridal wreath he gave her as a gift at the beginning of Act Three. In a version titled *Deliverance* (unproduced), Lasly has lengthy speeches about his attraction to the young Indian girl who would become his wife, and Mary (May) is a former club dancer and entertainer who has had previous lovers. The earliest versions, titled *Better to Marry* (produced at the Lakewood Theatre in Skowhegan, Maine in June 1927) and *Inheritance* (copyrighted 1926), end with the couple's union, and minimizes Lasly's role in the plot (he is named Hanson and is no longer married to an Indian but to a middle-aged white woman who serves as a witness to the wedding in one version).

Crosby Gaige produced the versions which played in Lakewood and Baltimore. Most likely, Treadwell decided to produce the Broadway production herself after being unable to secure the interest of other producers. In an undated letter in the manuscript files, Katherine Hepburn graciously defers interest in performing the play, believing the role of Mary not to be her type, although she states an affinity for Treadwell's ideas and writing style ever since she sat in awe at the opening at *Machinal*.

Tall (R063) and the critic for the *Baltimore News* (R065) are typical of the brutal reviews of the play's tryout in Baltimore, singling out both Gaige's cheap production values and Treadwell's poor direction. Five years later, Garland (R177), the *Nyack Daily News* (R178) and the *Rockland County Evening Journal* (R179) praised the show highly, and the enthusiastic audience response probably convinced Treadwell of the play's potential on Broadway.

Unfortunately, New York critics almost universally panned the show. Pollack (R191), Gabriel (R182), and Atkinson (R181) all unfavorably compare the play to *Machinal*, and Sobel (R194) and Waldorf (R195) note that the plot, with its attack on small town America's sexual double standard, is far too familiar. Lockridge (R184) remarks that the play was lacking in sufficient complications to sustain audience interest. A few critics simply were offended by the sight of a young girl in a slip or the frequent swearing by the characters (R060, R062). Marguerite Borough as Mary received mixed notices, and only Alan Baxter garnished widespread praise for his avoidance of stage tricks in his portrayal of Joe (R193).

THE LOVE LADY (produced 1925)

The Characters--NANETTE (NANA) TRUMBULL: a tall, thin woman of over 40; ZACHARY ALTON: early 20s, sensitive and earnest; KATHERINE TRUMBULL: an average American girl of about 17-18; RITA

ALVAREZ: a vital and graceful woman of about 40; speaks English with a hint of a Spanish accent; ALVIN KENT: a well-born, sure man of 40; WILLIAM BARNES: 46-50, thick-set, heavy-jowled; EULALIE: a middle-aged French maid, married to Constant; CONSTANT: a French valet who also serves as cook; CHAUFFEUR; MAID; BOY.

Plot Summary--ACT I: The action revolves around three women: Rita Alvarez (the "love lady" of the title); her sister Nana; and Rita's daughter, Katherine, whom Nana has raised from childhood. Nana shares a rented house in a small town with Katherine, who is attending college and dating Zachary Alton, a new graduate who plans to go to New York to pursue a career as a writer. Rita unexpectedly arrives for a visit, having been temporarily left alone by her lover, William Barnes, a powerful publisher who appears to have taken on a new, younger mistress. Nana is envious of Rita's exciting past life as a stage performer and frequent lover, but Rita confesses that the men in her life have never truly loved her, only themselves. Alvin Kent, the landlord of Nana and Katherine's house and friend of Barnes, learns of Rita's visit and comes by to proposition Rita, having just been abandoned by his wife. Rita refuses Kent, but deftly arranges for Zachary to return with her to New York with the promise of a job in Barnes's publishing company.

ACT II: In a New York apartment four months later, Rita's relationship with Barnes is on the rocks. The infatuated Zachary proposes marriage to Rita, having forgotten all about Katherine. Barnes returns unexpectedly from work and witnesses the romantic advances of Zachary and Rita. Barnes angrily brings up all of Rita's old lovers, and Zachary, sickened and disillusioned, runs off. Rita breaks off her relationship with Barnes.

ACT III: A few days later, Katherine and Nana receive a desperate telegram from Rita. Nana departs immediately for New York, but Katherine, still upset over her mother's theft of Zachary, refuses to leave. Having just returned from New York, Zachary visits Katherine and is moved by her confession of love for him. Emotionally confused, he proposes an immediate marriage to Katherine, who agrees once she receives another telegram saying Rita will arrive soon. Rita arrives as Katherine packs, and she immediately tries to stop the marriage, sensing Katherine will abandon her education and lose her independence. Rita relents, though, when she sees that Katherine is determined, having lost interest in everything except Zachary. After the young couple leaves to be married, Rita feels alone and unwanted, and calls Alvin Kent to accept his proposition.

Critical Overview--The play was performed twice as a showcase for Treadwell's writing and acting, once in 1925 and in 1918 under the title, *Claws*. Neither production received any critical reviews.

Treadwell appeared in the "love lady" role in both productions, billing herself under the pseudonym Ana Montes for the 1925 production. A few months after the *Love Lady* production, Treadwell again appeared onstage under a pseudonym, acting under the name Constance Eliot in her comedy *O Nightingale*.

Intended as a portrait of a woman's loneliness and disillusionment with love, *The Love Lady* suffers from a plot based on coincidence, sudden complications and character reversals, and sometimes trite dialogue. Wynn (S186) notes the difficulty in sustaining sympathy for any of the characters, although there are occasional moments of insight and genuine emotion, as when Rita gently spurns Zachary's confession of love by telling him that in her experience men only say "love" when they really mean "want."

Earlier versions of the play (*Claws*, 1918; *The Tigress*, copyrighted 1918; *Old Rose*, c. 1921) possess the same basic structure and action, but contain different character details: Rita (named Mme. Alla Xares in these versions) is of Polish descent and currently maintains her stage career; Nana works typing Madame's memoirs (a detail borrowed from Treadwell's work for Helena Modjeska); Katherine (Allison) rehearses in Act One to appear in the school play, *Paolo and Francesca* (a play Treadwell was cast in at the University of California); Zachary, also cast in the play, wants to be an aspiring actor instead of a writer; William Barnes is replaced by William Beck, a boorish theatre producer who forces Madame to appear in a new, commercial play, *The Tigress*, to meet her past debts; and Alvin Kent is absent. These versions reveal that Treadwell experimented with different endings. In *Claws*, Madame returns to find that Allison and Zachary have spent the night together. She claims Zachary as belonging to her and Allison shoots herself and falls between her mother and her lover. In *Old Rose*, Madame resigns herself to the young couple's marriage and even gives Zachary money for their honeymoon and early life together, not wanting Allison to have any of the cheap and ugly experiences to life that she has had.

MACHINAL (produced 1928)

The Characters--YOUNG WOMAN [HELEN JONES]: an ordinary young woman, not homely or pretty, ages from 23 to 29 during the course of the play; TELEPHONE GIRL: "young, cheap and amorous"; STENOGRAPHER: faded, efficient, "drying, dried"; FILING CLERK: a boy of "callow adolescence"; ADDING CLERK: a male counterpart to the Stenographer; MOTHER: the Young Woman's mother; HUSBAND [GEORGE H. JONES]: heavy, with fat hands; BELLBOY; NURSE; DOCTOR; YOUNG MAN: ordinary; GIRL: ordinary; MAN: middle-aged, homosexual; BOY: young, "untouched"; MAN [RICHARD ROE]: "pleasant, common, vigorous," with "coarse wavy hair"; ANOTHER MAN [HARRY]: "an ordinary salesman type"; WAITER; JUDGE; LAWYER FOR DEFENSE: verbose, yet eloquent; LAWYER FOR PROSECUTION; COURT REPORTER; BAILIFF; REPORTER; SECOND REPORTER; THIRD REPORTER; JAILER; MATRON; PRIEST.

Plot Summary--EPISODE I: "To Business." Against a backdrop of noises from their machines in the office of George H. Jones, the Telephone Girl, Stenographer, Adding Clerk and Filing Clerk note that Miss A (the Young Woman) is late to work again. After the Young Woman arrives and goes into Jones's office to receive dictation, the office workers speculate on the Young Woman's prospect of marriage to the boss. The Young Woman returns and turns down the Telephone Girl's offer to double date, citing her need to care for her mother instead. At her desk, the Young Woman flinches when Jones touches her shoulder. After her co-workers tell her about how her marriage to the boss would lead to a life of luxury, the Young Woman utters a monologue in which she ponders marriage; her repulsion over the thought of Jones's fat hands and the expectation of having babies merges with the memory of her near-suffocation this morning on the crowded subway, and she pleads with her mother, with "something--somebody," for advice.

EPISODE II: "At Home." Over dinner, the Young Woman interrupts her Mother's nagging with news that a man has proposed marriage. The Mother is immediately interested when she learns that the man is the Vice-President of a company. The Young Woman feels disgust for the man, yet yearns to marry someone since she feels she can no longer continue supporting her mother on her own. The Mother calls her crazy, and the Young Woman says she will kill her if she says that again. The Mother cries, the radio plays a sentimental song, and the Young Woman repents. The Young Woman puts on rubber gloves to do the dishes, saying her pretty hands are what have landed her her future husband. Throughout the scene, the women's conversation is punctuated by snatches of dialogue coming across the courtyard of their apartment building: a mother bosses her child; a baby cries; lovers make a rendezvous; a man leaves his wife at home again; and a wife spurns her husband's sexual advances.

EPISODE III: "Honeymoon." In a resort hotel bedroom with a dancing casino opposite through the window, the Husband (Jones) admonishes the Young Woman for continually raising the window shade and for not undressing. She stops his physical advances and coarse jokes. The Young Woman finally goes into the bathroom to undress, and the Husband speaks of future pleasure trips and a more relaxed life for himself now, while hurrying her on. In the darkened room, the Young Woman enters, crying and calling for her mother.

EPISODE IV: "Maternal." The Young Woman recuperates in a

hospital room after giving birth to a baby girl. Riveting sounds come through the open window as the hospital builds a new, large maternity wing. The Young Woman refuses to eat, speak, and, since she is not yet lactating, nurse. The Husband enters with flowers, urges the Young Woman to "brace up," but leaves when she begins gagging. The doctor dismisses the Young Woman as "neurotic," and gives orders that she be given solid food and her baby to nurse. Alone, the Young Woman's mind races: she speaks of a dog, Vixen, who crawled off under the bed after her puppies were born dead; of long stairs to heaven with children coming down to be born and dead ones going up; of religious images--the weight of the book of judgement pressing heavy on her, of God's fat hands, of Mary (not God) giving birth--and finally of herself not submitting anymore.

EPISODE V: "Prohibited." The action alternates between three separate tables in a speakeasy. At one, a man and woman discuss the necessity of having an abortion, the woman ultimately convinced to do so in order to keep her job. At another table, a middle-aged homosexual man plies a young, virgin male with amontillado and convinces him to go back to his room with him. At the third table, two men await the arrival of their dates. The 2nd Man, Harry, wants the 1st Man, Richard Roe, to preoccupy one of the women so he can leave with his date for a sexual encounter and still make it home to his wife by six o'clock, as promised. The women arrive: the Telephone Girl from the first episode teams with Harry, a traveling salesman, while the Young Woman (whose name we finally learn is Helen) interests Roe with her restless desire "to keep moving." Harry leaves on "business" with the Telephone Girl. Roe recounts how he killed two banditos in Mexico who had kidnapped him by striking them with a bottle filled with stones. Impressed by Roe's ability to win his freedom, as well as by his flattery, the Young Woman somewhat hesitantly goes off with him to his apartment.

EPISODE VI: "Intimate." Outside Roe's basement apartment, a hand organ plays "Cielito Lindo" ("Little Heaven") in the street. Inside, the Young Woman and Roe talk intimately after sex of their future together, but Roe says truthfully he will be leaving again sometime to go back to Mexico where he feels free. A street light comes on outside, and the Young Woman hurriedly dresses, knowing she is late returning home. Roe talks of his early, easy life riding horseback outside San Francisco, and the Young Woman, feeling purified, wishes she could join him someday. They kiss, and tearfully the Young Woman takes a potted lily from his room as a memento.

EPISODE VII: "Domestic." The Young Woman and her Husband sit on opposite ends of a divan in their sitting room reading newspapers to themselves, she of headlines of domestic unhappiness and escape and he of business profits. A phone call brings the Husband news that his purchase of a new piece of property has been completed. The Husband says the Young Woman is also his property, and she flinches at his touch. She reads of domestic murder in the headlines; the Husband feels a cold draft. He calms his anxious wife, then reads of another revolution below the Rio Grande. Roe's voice is heard recounting his fight to freedom with the bottle, and the voice blends with that of a huckster selling stones in the street. The Young Woman starts in terror from her chair.

EPISODE VIII: "The Law." The action occurs in a courtroom during the continuing trial of the Young Woman for the murder of her husband, killed by a blow from a bottle filled with stones. All members of the proceedings, except the Young Woman, behave in a mechanical manner. Lawyers squabble over protocol, and reporters reach opposite conclusions about the unfolding events. On the witness stand, the Young Woman denies killing her husband. Under cross examination, though, the Lawyer for the Prosecution brings out a string of incriminating details, including: the Young Woman's delay in calling for a doctor after the murder; her return to wearing rubber gloves to bed every night since the past spring to protect her hands, even though her Husband objected (thus explaining why no fingerprints were found on the murder weapon); her washing-out of her blood-soaked nightgown before phoning the police; the stones used to fill the bottle were the same type of stones found in the topsoil of the now-dead lily plant; and especially Roe's affidavit from Mexico admitting to his almost daily intimate relations with the Young Woman from the spring until his departure in the fall. The Young Woman interrupts the reading of this affidavit with a sudden confession. Reporters hurriedly compose their lead-ins.

EPISODE IX: "A Machine." In a prison room, a Priest offers a prayer for the Young Woman, but she draws greater solace from a negro singing a spiritual off in another part of the prison. Barbers shave a patch of hair from the Young Woman in preparation for the electric chair. A plane flies overhead and casts a shadow across the room. The Young Woman speaks of her one moment of freedom and wonders how it could be determined sinful. When she is greeted by her Mother, the Young Woman first rejects her as a stranger, then embraces her and asks her to look after her daughter and "tell her." Darkness engulfs the stage as she is led toward her execution. The voice of the praying Priest alternates with that of reporters describing the Young Woman moving her lips and arranging her hair. The Young Woman cries out to "somebody," as the Priest prays for mercy.

Critical Overview--A manuscript at the University of Arizona which pre-dates the original 1928 production clearly indicates the play was suggested by the sensational murder trial of Ruth Snyder the preceding year. The same manuscript also reveals that Treadwell hoped the play's expressionsitic devices would appeal directly to the unconscious mind of the spectator, especially the female spectator (S211, S239). Helen's monologues in this early version are also much longer than those in the production and published versions, most notably that in "Maternal." That more overt version has the Young Woman saying her baby reminds her of Jones, that she wanted to get rid of it, that she would like to leave Jones but thinks of her mother, and wondering why her mother did not tell her what having a baby meant. Monologues for this version were also intended, but not yet written, for the ends of the speakeasy and courtroom scenes. Wynn (S211) suggests director Arthur Hopkins may have been influential in editing many of these monologues. Another noteworthy variant in this early version appears in "Intimate," where the Young Woman refutes Roe by saying that she was the initiator in their romantic relationship, not vice versa, and that she will do something about her husband in order to keep them together. Lastly, the "Domestic" episode is absent.

In a folder of "Fragments" at UALSC, additional scenes and monologues not present in any version may be found, including monologues after the "At Home" and "Intimate" episodes, as well as a scene in which Helen returns to her husband in their bedroom after her encounter with Roe. In this latter scene, Jones wants to watch Helen undress, and then tries clumsily to make love to her before she throws him off, opens a window and sees a burning building opposite.

Although there are several different versions of the play which have survived, most retain the same basic arrangement of scenes and action. Some contain variant titles for the individual episodes, and the 1928 production manuscript includes a stage direction of the Robert Edmond Jones/George Schaff lighting effect. A brief rewrite for the 1960 production adds specific references to Helen's Long Island home, as well as "two hoodlums" to the scene in the speakeasy (here referred to as a "dive") who speak disgustedly about the older man's homosexuality and who leave following him in order to rough him up.

Arthur Hopkins kept the subject of *Machinal* a secret until just before its September 1928 opening, after which time numerous critics discussed its relationship to the Snyder-Gray murder case. Some, such as Winchell (R127, R128), Mantle (R101), Locke (R097) and Lockridge (R098) felt the play closely mirrored the events relating to Snyder. Others, such as Atkinson (R069), Hammond (R088) Pollack (RR114), and Littell (R094), felt the resemblance merely superficial.

An equal amount of time was spent by the New York critics comparing *Machinal* to other expressionistic plays (R096, R119, R126). Elmer Rice's *The Adding Machine* drew the most comparisons (R068, R083, R085, R101, R114, R116), but Kaiser's *From Morn to Midnight* (R068, R123), O'Neill's *The Hairy Ape* (R106), *The Emperor Jones* and *Strange Interlude* (R121) drew others, as did the works of Capek (R117), Toller and Brecht (R109). The character of George H. Jones was frequently cited as reminiscent of the hero of Sinclair Lewis's *Babbitt* (R083, R085, R094, R113, R116).

More importantly, several critics noted Treadwell's unique fusion of European expressionism with domestic American realism (R079, R094, R097, R113). Sayler (R121) believed *Machinal* the first American expressionist play to combine successfully form with content.

Treadwell's writing drew praise for its simple beauty and subtle use of suggestion and allusion (R068, R094, R096, R151). The scene in Roe's apartment was noted for its sensitive treatment of adultery (R084, R091). Ruhl (R118) found the writing particularly feminine and Winchell (R127) thought the play would have a special appeal to women in the audience. Surprisingly, almost no mention is made by the critics of the subjects of homosexuality and abortion in the "Prohibited" scene or the damning indictment of motherhood found in "Maternal." Several, though, thought he male characters too superficial and Treadwell's sympathies disproportionately weighted toward the Young Woman (R075, R107, R110, R123).

Arthur Hopkins's direction was frequently praised for its casting and subtle, unobtrusive staging (R066, R091, R092, R113). Anderson (R066) praised Robert Edmond Jones's set design, which allowed for quick changes between scenes, and the final scene of the play was singled out by many reviewers for its powerful lighting and design elements (R066, R079, R090, R091, R092, R101, R103, R124). Similarly, George Stillwell as the Husband and Zita Johann, in her first major role, as the Young Woman were repeatedly praised (R066, R068, R083, R085). As Richard Roe, Clark Gable also received commendation for his performance, although the playbill's listing of characters by type not name created some confusion about who actually played this role. Some critics credited Hal K. Dawson (listed as "A Man" in the playbill) with this role, a mistake which led numerous critics and scholars subsequently to state that Hal K. Dawson was actually Gable's stage name (S188).

There was a flurry of interest after the premiere production to stage the play in Europe. Henri Duvernois originally received Treadwell's permission to adapt the play for production at the Grand Guignol in Paris during the 1929-30 season. Duvernois abandoned the project, however, when Treadwell expressed concerns over the nature of the adaptation. At approximately the same time, Hans Bartsch did a German adaptation of the play, but apparently was undermined in his efforts to market it to several state theatres due to a pirated translation which preceded his in circulation.

London critics, reviewing the play in 1931, frequently referred to the overly graphic nature of the play's content (R154, R158, R160, R169, R170, R173). Of particular concern were the honeymoon and speakeasy scenes, the frankness of which led to the play being banned by the Lord Chamberlain (R160). Similarly, reviewers noted the play's morbidity or overall inappropriateness of theme (R152, R153, R156, R170). Often, critics felt the Young Woman was upset over nothing of consequence (R154, R155, R162, R169). Still others disliked expressionism as a dramatic style (R152, R161,

R173). Nevertheless, Mary Grew garnished kudos as Helen (R152, R157, R158, R160, R161, R169, R173), as did David Horne as her Husband (R159, R162, R169). Critics for the *Evening News* (R158) and *Daily Mail* (R157) were alone in finding the play a moving tragedy.

Alexander Tairov's 1933 production received few reviews in English. Watts (R196), Leyda (R197) and the *Variety* critic (R188) all commented on Tairov's staging effects, but Watts found it less sympathetic to the Young Woman than Hopkins's version. The production's anti-capitalist message is discussed in scholarly studies by Torda (S172) and Worrall (S200).

An attempt was made in the early 1950s to adapt *Machinal* into a musical drama in the manner of Gian Carlo Menotti's *The Consul*. Abby Mann worked on the adaptation, Lawrence Chaikin the music and Carol Gluck the lyrics. Treadwell gave permission, and its progress stopped a planned production of the play by the Equity Library Theatre in 1955. Production of the musical treatment never materialized, however.

When revived off-Broadway in 1960, several critics noted their dislike for Treadwell's melodramatic or imitative script (R319, R321, R326, R327, R328, R329, R330). Others praised Gene Frankel's stylized staging (R317, R319, R329), while Hayes (R324) and Lewis (R326) found the expressionist form an apt one in evoking a tragic response.

In reviewing the 1990 New York Shakespeare Festival revival, critics were divided on the play's merits. Some hailed it as a lost treasure (R338, R344, R348), while others felt it a dated work with a victim for a central character (R339, R342, R343, R347). The play again drew comparison to modern writers, such as Elmer Rice (R338, R340, R346, R348), Georg Buchner (R346, R348), Kaiser (R348), James Joyce (R338), Henry Adams, Theodore Dreiser and Eugene O'Neill (R338, R344). Some critics, though, felt the play anticipated the dialogue sructures found in David Mamet's work (R344, R348). Director Michael Grief and actress Jodie Markell drew much praise (R338, R344, R346, R347, R348). The playbill for this production featured an infamous photo of Ruth Snyder's execution, taken covertly by a reporter for the *New York Daily News*.

As staged by the Royal National Theatre in London in 1993, *Machinal* again divided the critics on its merits. Several applauded the play's rediscovery (R353, R356, R373, R377, R379), while others liked the staging better than the script (R360, R366, R367, R381, R386). Many reviewers cited the lack of sufficient justification for Helen's extreme reactions (R360, R372, R376, R378, R381, R384). Director Stephen Daldry and designer Ian MacNeil drew much praise for their extreme conceptual approach (R355, R356, R361, R369, R370, R373, R382), and several critics also remarked on their innovative use of the traditionally designed Lyttleton Theatre (R357, R365, R368, R376). Unlike the 1931 London production, reviews for this production are filled with descriptions of specific staging moments, especially the effective execution scene (R356,

R357, R370, R376, R378). A few reviewers, though, thought the extensive use of theatrical machinery overwhelmed the play's content (R353, R359, R362, R375, R386). Program notes compared Treadwell's dialogue to that of contemporary playwrights, such as Mamet, Harold Pinter and Samuel Beckett, and numerous critics echoed this sentiment (R353, R354, R357, R379, R380, R381). Fiona Shaw's performance as Helen was often termed exceptional (R353, R356, R359, R362, R363, R364, R370, R373, R374, R379, R381).

Whenever *Machinal* has been produced, playbills and reviews often offer explanation as to the meaning and pronunciation of the play's title. The latter point, especially, offers numerous explications. For the 1928 production, "MAK-i-nal" appeared in some of the Plymouth Theatre playbills, a pronunciation deemed acceptable, along with "ma-SHIN-al" by the critic for the *New Yorker* (S082) and Warren (R151). Burns Mantle offered "MA-shin-al" (R102). In his article on the 1960 revival, Morgenstern (S142) corrected director Gene Frankel's pronunciation ("mackinal"), saying the "ch" of the title is soft. In the 1990s, Rich (R344) and Watt and Richardson (S237) proclaimed "mock-en-AHL" the proper pronunciation, and the Royal National Theatre's 1993 playbill listed "MAK-in-al" [long A]. The result is much confusion. In speculating why the finely staged 1960 revival lacked sufficient box office sales, Morgenstern even suggested that audiences are reluctant to go see a play they cannot pronounce. In discussions with those who knew Treadwell, it appears she preferred "MA-shin-al." In a similar vein, the word is not a neologism as Strand (S215) asserts, but was taken from a word in French usage meaning "mechanical," "automatic," or "involuntary."

A brief overview of the scholarly assessment of the play may be found in the "Life and Career" section of this book.

Treadwell's decision to withhold the name of the Young Woman until late in the play seems clearly tied to thematic, rather than stylistic, concerns. The slogan of the Lucy Stone League, of which Treadwell was a member, was: "My name is the symbol for my identity and must not be lost" (Dale Kramer, *Heywood Broun: a Biographical Potrait* (New York: Current Books, 1949: 9)). This idea is echoed in the play as the Young Woman's name only becomes apparent once she begins to gain her identity as an independent being.

MADAME BLUFF (copyrighted 1918)

The Characters--MADAME SIMONE DE BYNG: a fashionably dressed young woman in her early 20s; CAMILLE JONES: a former "sob sister" journalist, about 38; MRS. MILLIE BOONE: small and dainty in appearance but rough in manners and speech; JOHN TRELLYNE: an attractive airplane pilot; WILLIAM T. LOOMIS: a short, thick-set millionaire gambler of about 60; MR. FARNSWORTH FISH: of the *New York Earth*; TOM BOONE: motion picture director; GRANTVILLE LeROY: a beautiful but vapid leading man in films; JOHNNY WATTS: motion picture technical director; HIS ASSISTANT; A CAMERAMAN (WATSON); BENNIE: an assistant camerman; REPORTERS; A SHIP STEWARD; A COLLECTOR; A HOTEL CLERK.

Plot Summary--ACT I: A French steamer sits anchored in the lower Hudson River for a night before docking in New York City. Camille Jones, a former journalist-turned-screenwriter, has failed to contract a famous French film actress for her new movie, and is anxious about breaking the news to her boss, the film's director, Tom Boone. The New York press descends on Camille and William T. Loomis, a millionaire gambler, looking for an exclusive story of the rich and famous. They introduce the press to Madame Simone de Byne, who is coming to America to receive recognition for her courageous, young husband, a poet, who was killed fighting at World War I's front lines, leaving only a few poems behind. John Trellyne, an ace fighter pilot during the war, is more interested in another manuscript Simone has brought with her, a treatise by her university professor father which claims to have discovered the Egyptian secret of manufacturing the durable and lightweight cloth used to wrap mummies. Alone with Simone, Camille correctly guesses that the story of the poet-soldier was made up just to gain publicity and media interest for her manuscripts. Sensing Simone wants money, Camille persuades her to pass herself off as a countess and to consent to act in the upcoming movie, hopefully appealing to the fawning Loomis for financial backing. During a French lesson over a poker game, Loomis teaches Simone how to bluff believably. Moments later, Camille and Simone easily persuade Boone to accept Simone as an actress and Loomis to provide funds. Millie Boone, Tom's overbearing wife, is jealous of Camille, but is placated by Tom with the promise of a new car. Alone with Simone, Trellyne makes plans to visit her in New York as soon as he finishes his work in Washington, D.C.: treating cotton to make light wings for airplanes. Simone is awed as the beautiful lights of New York shine from across the harbor.

ACT II: On the set of a motion picture studio in New York, technicians prepare for the filming of one retake which will complete Boone's picture. Simone, deply in debt due to six months' worth of expenses, conspires with Camille to drum up more publicity--this time pretending her dead husband recites new poetry to her from the grave via a ouiji board. Boone arrives for the filming, and has to resort to showing physically the inept leading man, Grantville LeRoy, how to play his love scene with Simone. Millie sees Simone in the arms of Boone, and runs off to sabotage the picture. Trellyne lands his plane on the roof of the studio, and informs Simone he has adapted her father's discovery to the manufacture of light, durable airplane wings. Simone tries to gain Trellyne's affections, even going so far as to self-inflict an injury on her ankle to draw out his affections. Panic ensues when the cast and crew learn that Millie has stolen the print of the film and dumped it, along with her car, off the Madison Bridge.

ACT III: In her apartment at the Ritz Hotel the next morning, Simone lies in bed with a broken foot and fears financial destitution. Camille urges her to court Loomis for more money. While Simone entertains Trellyne, Camille meets with LeRoy in the lobby, returning moments later to borrow money and clothes. Loomis arrives and engages Trellyne with the proposition of a business partnership concerning his invention, and Simone steals Trellyne's wallet as he prepares to leave to meet Loomis's lawyer. Alone with Loomis, Simone accepts his marriage proposal but admits all her "bluffs" about her identity and past. Lomis accepts them all until he learns she has never really been married, then withdraws his proposal, fearing that Simone will leave him once she truly falls in love. After Loomis leaves for good, Simone instructs Boone to be more forceful with his misbehaving wife, and after Boone spanks her, Millie apologizes to all. Camille returns, newly married to LeRoy. Trellyne returns and learns of Loomis's proposal and Simone's bluffs. No longer feeling obliged to hide his affections in deference to Simone's dead husband, Trellyne proposes to Simone. She accepts his proposal, and Boone returns with the news that Millie did not destroy their movie after all.

Critical Overview--*Madame Bluff* is one of Treadwell's best early plays. The work is neatly crafted and filled with a playful sense of comedy. Written during Treadwell's first year in New York after her return from Europe during the first World War, the play reflects an energetic Treadwell's varying interests at the time: the return to life after the war; the use of comic dialects; the power of media to manufacture interest in personalities; parapsychology; and filmmaking (S230). Act Two's parody of early filmmaking seems among the earliest to appear in drama, prefiguring Kaufman and Connelly's *Merton of the Movies* and others. Treadwell juggles the large cast of characters with ease. Simone is a great vehicle for a comic actress, and Loomis emerges as a likeable and practical entrepeneur who bumbled his way into money and readily admits his own follies.

The manuscript files at UALSC contain a scenario Treadwell wrote for a musical comedy version of the play. The scenario retains the basic structure, plot and characters from the play, the one notable exception being the replacement of Millie with Vaska Vara, head of the Vampire's Union #21. Vara leads a group of vamps who are angry that they cannot find film work because non-union actresses like Simone are continually being hired. They steal the finished picture, only to return it in the final act after converting to Salvation Army lasses, a group decidedly more in demand for casting on Broadway. The third act setting is also relocated to the roof of the movie studio, and ends with Trellyne and Simone flying off together.

This scenario contains no dialogue, and has lyrics to only one of the play's seventeen planned songs. Perhaps the most remarkable feature of the scenario includes the suggestion that songs will be used to advance story, an innovative concept for the late 1910s. Of special note is a dance sequence in Act Two between Trellyne and Simone, in which a shadowy figure (Trellyne's imagined persona of Simone's dead husband) darts in and out between them. The moment is conceptually similar to the famous dream ballet which would appear in *Oklahoma* some twenty years later.

On a more minor note, Treadwell conceived of reporters in this musical as a sort of "dance team," dressed alike and making simultaneous gestures. Alexander Tairov would employ the same tactic for the journalists in his 1933 production of *Machinal*. Since Treadwell was in rehearsals for Tairov's production, she may have suggested the effect.

A MAN'S OWN (c. 1905)

The Characters--JOHN CURTIS: head of Curtis & Co., a Chicago department store; about 50; quiet, self-centered; MARTIN: 40 year-old manager of the store; GIRL: one of a thousand such girls hired at the store for between $6-8 a week.

Plot Summary--Martin enters Curtis's private office in the store to gain signatures on the weekly payrolls. Martin informs Curtis that Mrs. Skiddles, of the Women's Improvement Club is at the store again trying to organize the young women workers into realizing the need for recreation and the beauty and uplift in life. The men chuckle over a frank worker who refuted Mrs. Skiddles, saying she sounded like the whistle on a peanut stand. After Martin leaves with the checks, Curtis ruminates on Martin's thought that it's "a man's own" family that counts in life, and he takes out a picture from his desk drawer and studies it. Curtis exits to an inner room. A pretty girl of eighteen sneaks into the office and begins going through Curtis's desk drawers. Upon returning and questioning the girl, Curtis learns that she was the pert worker who told off Mrs. Skiddles. The girl further reveals that she has worked in men's furnishings for two years at $6 an week. When she approached Martin last week asking for a needed raise, Martin urged her to find a "gentleman friend" to help support her. The girl snuck into the office with the intent of stealing the money she felt was her due. She wishes Curtis would call the police and have her jailed, since the only options for young and poor women such as her are to marry, teach school or turn to prostitution. She recounts her lack of education, the death of her mother, and her fantasies of her benevolent father, who ran away when she was very young. As the girl imitates the advice of her mother to be pretty and loved, Curtis recognizes the woman's foreign dialect and phrasing. He pulls out the photo once again from his desk and shows the girl her mother. The girl sobs and Martin returns, threatening to throw the girl out. Curtis weakly stops Martin as the girl sidles up to her father and asks that he tell Martin to raise her salary by the previously requested dollar a week.

Critical Overview--This short play, written while Treadwell was still in college, raises many of the preoccupations found in Treadwell's early dramas: the options available to young, impoverished women to improve their station in life; the inability of family to provide assistance or love; and the young woman who rebels against mistreatment in the worlds of business and sex. Undoubtedly, the play captures many of Treadwell's own concerns during her later years in college. Treadwell took a variety of odd jobs due to financial hardships, and grew more and more to resent her father's abandonment of the family.

A MILLION DOLLAR GATE, with William O. McGeehan (copyrighted 1930)

The Characters--DION O'DONNELL: a quiet, determined, perfectly conditioned athlete; POP DIME: Dion's trainer, about 60; WILLIAM (WHISPERING) WALLER: Dion's manager, about 45, affable; MATT (MUSH) MULLINS: "The Senator"; a bully of about 45; SAMMY PEARLSTEIN: "The Fox," a sharp dresser, about 35; PIETRO TORTURICI: "The Torch," 40, swarthy and savage; HANK CLARK: a respected sportswriter; COCKY COCHRAN: Torch's "yes man"; GOOFY CANNON: a once-popular fighter, now old and down-and-out; LESTER: a black cook; A CAMP VISITOR: a nondescript hick, the Mayor of Canojaharie; AN ADVERTISING MAN; A MOTION PICTURE MAN; CAPTAIN OF THE BELL BOYS; NORA KELLY: a dancer at the Golden Slipper nightclub; 28 but looks and acts like 16; LINDA HILLS: about 24, charmingly attractive.

Plot Summary--ACT I: In the private office of Pietro "The Torch" Torturici's nightclub, "The Golden Slipper," Cocky Cochran, Sammy Pearlstein and Senator Mullins are waiting impatiently for the arrival of Dion O'Donnell, challenger for the heavyweight boxing championship. Together the men outline the various percentages they hope to gain from the million dollar gate if Mullins can get the boxing commissioner to agree to hold the fight in New York and if Dion signs their contracts. William Waller, Dion's manager, arrives, and says his fighter is wising up to the excessive greediness of the men, due in part to the continued influence of his trainer, Pop Dime. Dion now believes he can defeat the champion Kilbane without any fixing on their part. Torch enters and angrily sends the men to fetch the reluctant Dion. Torch calls Pop at his hotel and threatens to either kill him or turn him over to the Mowbray gang, of which Pop was a member before turning one of the mob in to the Federal District Attorney. Nora Kelly, a dancer at the club, enters at Torch's summons. It was Torch's idea to give Nora, who is really Swedish, an Irish name and innocent reputation in order to appeal to Dion, and now he asks her to help them convince Dion to sign the contracts. Cocky shows in Hank Clark, a noted sports writer, and Linda Hills, his colleague and star trial reporter, who will do a feature on Dion from a woman's perspective. The gangsters return with Dion, and Linda is impressed with him immediately. Dion agrees to an exclusive contract with their powerful newspaper and Linda will go to Dion's training camp for background material while Clark will go to Kilbane's. Dion promises a championship to the departing reporters. The men try to convince Dion of the necessity of his signing on for their "services," but Dion still balks. Nora enters and, after the men leave, easily soothes Dion's anger. Dion is attracted to Nora, believing they are "mates" due to their Irish names and the way they are dismissed by others because of their respective lines of work. Pop arrives, having changed his mind after Torch's phone call, and now tells Dion he should not anger Torch. Dion finally agrees to sign after Pop tells him to merely pretend to go along with the men's plans. He signs agreements with Mullins and Pearlstein, but again balks at signing with Torch, who claims sole responsibility for making him a winner. Torch vows for revenge against Dion, who exits quickly.

ACT II: The afternoon before the fight at Dion's training camp, Pop confides to Mullins that Dion has been unable to sleep. Lester, the camp cook, wants to get paid today, believing Dion will lose the fight tomorrow. Linda arrives, having been summoned by Dion to work on the story to relax him, and delivers Dion's mail, which consists of both fan accolades and anonymous threats. After failing to win approval by New York's conservative boxing commissioner, Waller enters and confesses that he altered the deal with the new New Jersey fight promoter to accept a $100,000 guarantee rather than 20% of the gate, fearing that the Jersey location would mean a smaller draw. Mullins is angry at this financial snafu since the gate in Jersey is still approaching a million dollars. Pop steams open a letter to Dion from Nora, in which she writes of anxiously waiting for any word from the silent Dion. Pearlstein arives with the news that he has been unable to buy off the fight promoters; someone else already having beaten him to the punch. Dion enters and all lie that the fight details on their end are set. Alone briefly with Linda, Dion confesses his anxiety about the fight. Clark arrives and privately tells Linda the paper is taking her off the story due to the receipt of several obscene, insinuating letters which may reflect poorly on her reputation. Clark reports to

Linda of the criminal aspect of Kilbane's camp, with Torch and Pearlstein present and looking to harm Dion. Linda tells Dion she will not fly down with him for the fight, citing something else of importance she must do. She confesses to Dion that she loves him. Nora arrives, despite Dion's orders to say away during training, and tells Dion that the betting at five-to-one against him. Nora erupts after Dion agonizingly tells her he does not love her anymore, and she blames Linda, who ran off when she arrived. Nora tells Dion she never cared for him at all, and was only playing him along for Torch's sake. She says if Dion wins the fight, she and Torch will use Dion's letters proposing marriage as grounds for getting a large chunk of his prize money. Dion tells her to inform Torch that he plans to win the fight--for now he will take a nap, relieved that he and Nora are through.

ACT III: The morning after the fight in Dion's expensive hotel suite, Pearlstein fields phone calls for the new "Champ" and Mullins reads the newspapers' accounts of the fight. Waller and Mullins order a dozen quarts of wine in anticipation of Dion greeting the press and politicians. Clark arrives and Waller recounts highlights of the fight. Clark toasts Dion, who has just entered, but Dion is disappointed that Linda did not come for the post-fight exclusive interview. During the interview, Dion's "associates" steer him away from talking about tabloid reports of his plans to marry. Dion has Pop call Linda to come over, and after she agrees Dion chases everyone out. Nora unexpectedly arrives after drinking all night. She claims to truly having fallen in love with Dion during the fight, and offers to return Dion's love letters if he will have her back. Dion refuses. Torch arrives, and he and Nora demand $40,000 in exchange for the letters, or they will give them over to the press and ruin Dion's reputation. When the men return, Dion orders Waller to pay Torch and Nora the money so he can be rid of them, but Waller explains at length how Dion himself does not have that much money, having only cleared thirteen-and-a-third percent of their $100,000 portion of the gate. After Linda arrrives, Nora shows her the signed agreements in an attempt to prove that Dion is not an innocent man, but knew fully that the fight was being rigged. Linda takes the agreements and, along with files she has brought with her, begins to analyze them. Linda systematically refutes their claims by coercing and blackmailing them: Torch has no legal claim to Dion, only his associates; Waller signed a second, secret deal with the fight promoter and pocketed the extra money; the Senator's voting public would surely be interested in knowing how he tried to bribe an honest boxing commissioner; Pop had double-crossed Dion from the beginning; and Pearlstein gives up his share before hearing Linda's summary of his misdeeds. Only Pop receives a portion of his money, at Dion's insistence. Finally, Linda reveals that Nora had previously used love letters to similarly extort money from another men, and Linda plans to work out details with the newspaper's lawyer waiting in the lobby to be rid legally of her and all Dion's "associates." Dion gratefully embraces Linda.

Critical Overview--The play was clearly the product of Treadwell's collaboration with her husband, William O. McGeehan, a well-known sports reporter with a special interest in boxing. This collaboration accounts for subject matter, characterizations and smart, tough, slang-filled dialogue unlike those found in any of Treadwell's other plays. Surviving manuscripts cloud the authorship picture somewhat: some give joint credit to Treadwell and McGeehan, some cite only Treadwell, and one cites only McGeehan. McGeehan dabbled in playwriting, as is evidenced by some of his surviving manuscripts at UALSC. Treadwell's role in the collaboration is clear, though, in the role of Linda, particularly in an early draft where Linda's helpless love for Dion in Act Two is very reminiscent of heroines in several of her previous plays. Wynn (S186) believes Treadwell previously collaborated with McGehan on early versions of *Plumes in the Dust*.

A Million Dollar Gate (or *The Million Dollar Gate*, as stated on some manuscripts, including the copyrighted version) is noteworthy as an early stage indictment of the criminal underworld of boxing, pre-dating Odets's exposé on the subject, *Golden Boy*. Wynn (S186) discusses the play's incorporation of filmed montages between acts, and correspondence in the manuscript archives indicates the script was marketed for both theatre and film between 1930-37 (McGeehan died in 1933). Theatre managers either disliked the subject or were afraid of it, and as a story for film the script was rejected by MGM, Paramount, RKO, Twentieth Century, Columbia, Warner Brothers and Universal. McGeehan's sports columns often attacked the integrity of the boxing profession, but the subject still seemed unfit for most commercial theatre markets at this time, despite its successful treatment.

Treadwell and/or McGeehan experimented with alternate endings of the play. In one version, Dion is much more active in getting himself out of trouble with the gangsters, along with a little help from Linda. This version includes an ending where Dion, who has carried around a fake, one-volume edition of Shakespeare filled with a bottle of explosive nitroglycerine for protection, blows up Torch and his henchmen on the balcony of the hotel. In another version, the character of Benjamin Stern, Linda's boss, patron and former lawyer, dispenses justice for Dion in Act Three.

A Million Dollar Gate is a well-crafted and entertaining play, although the subject matter might cause it to be viewed as a period piece by modern audiences.

O NIGHTINGALE (produced 1925)

The Characters--RICHARD WARRINGTON: about 25, slow-moving; MME. VERA ISTOMINA: about 60; a former Russian dancer who possesses a dilapidated air of grandeur; DOT NORTON: an actress preparing for vaudeville; good-natured, but lazy; 30 but says she is 22; APPOLONIA (LONEY) LEE: a small, homely girl of 16 from Kansas; LE MARQUIS DE SEVERAC: a distinguished Frenchman of about 65; A WAITER; LAWRENCE GORMONT: a successful New York theatre manager; FLORA ST. JOHN: a pretty, but affected actress.

Plot Summary--ACT I: Richard Warrington, an artist, refuses a phone invitation from the Marquis de Severac to go on a two-week cruise vacation to Cuba, preferring instead to remain in his New York studio apartment and work. Mme. Vera Istomina, a former great dancer in Russia, enters and prepares to give her weekly dance lessons in the studio, having an on-going rental agreement with Warrington. He is anxious for Madame to end her lesson on time, as he expects a visit from the Marquis which may lead to a commission, and he is unhappy with the continual disorderly state of the apartment. Disgusted by the tardiness and naive theatrical ambitions of her pupils, Dot Norton and especially Appolonia (Loney) Lee, Madame departs. Loney confides her desperate situation to Dot: she has no money, she cannot find a job performing, and she has no family to return to in her midwestern hometown except a father whose life has been ruined by alcoholism after he abandoned his dream of becoming a poet. Loney wants to apply for a job as a domestic after overhearing Madame say that Warrington needs one for this studio. Dot urges her to find a man, as that is the only way for a woman to succeed in the world. The Marquis agrees to commission Warrington to do his bust, but only if he will accompany him on the Cuban cruise and entertain his daughter. Touched by Loney's heartbreaking story of her troubles, including her recent eviction from her apartment, the Marquis successfully pleads her case with Warrington to stay in his studio while they are gone. The Marquis confides to Loney that he will return to her shortly and introduce her to his influential male friends in the theatre.

ACT II: A week later, the Marquis has bought Loney expensive clothes and has dined with her everyday since abandoning Warrington as the cruise ship sailed. Although their relationship has remained innocent, Loney is aware of the Marquis's true intentions to seduce her, but is grateful to him nevertheless. This evening, Loney and the Marquis, along with a hired waiter, prepare for the arrival of their dinner guests, Lawrence Gormont, a successful theatre producer, and his actress-companion, Flora St. John. While Loney takes a quick bath, Madame enters and she and the Marquis tersely discuss their former romantic relationship in Europe years ago. The cruise cut short, Warrington unexpectedly returns and demands to know why the Marquis abandoned him. The Marquis exits quickly to get home before his wife discovers the receipts for Loney's expensive clothes he bought. Madame also leaves. Loney emerges from the bath wearing Warrington's robe, and

Warrington, angered over how she has changed the state of his apartment, orders her to leave. Desperately believing that tonight may be her one big break as an actress, Loney refuses to leave. So does Warrington. Fearing the Marquis may not return, Loney plans to enlist Warrington's help in rounding out the party and keeping the conversation lively.

ACT III: After a brief scene in which a nervous Loney fills Dot in on the events of the past week, the guests arrive. Warrington makes a quick escape when the Marquis returns. Most of the conversation involves Gormont and St. John bickering. The Marquis urges Gormont to appraise Loney's talents, but Gormont merely dismisses her based on her physical type. Loney freezes when she tries to recite the Shakespearean lines of Juliet, lines which have served as her inspiration in the difficult times since she played that role in her high school play. Gormont encourages her to find a man to help her build an act, and he and St. John leave. The Marquis comforts the devastated and tearful Loney, and eventually tells her to abandon the theatre, a business which will coarsen her and destroy her naive charm. As he did in his relationship with Madame years ago, the Marquis suddenly leaves rather than get embroiled in an emotional scene. Having entered unnoticed moments earlier, Warrington overhears Loney recite lines of Juliet's as she begins to undress. Loney hears Warrington as he tries to sneak out, and he holds her trembling, crying body while reciting softly poetry about Philomel, verses which Loney's father used to speak to her as a child. Loney and Warrington tenderly kiss.

Critical Overview--Written at a time when Treadwell had just experienced rejuvenating summer study with Richard Boleslavsky in 1923, *O Nightingale* is one of Treadwell's simplest and most pleasing comedies. Loney is a charming portrait of youthful innocence, and the role was a fine vehicle for the young Helen Hayes in Broadway tryouts produced by George C. Tyler. All of the characters are well drawn, including Madame Vera Istomina, a "grand dame" character type perhaps modelled after Modjeska. As an actress, Treadwell had performed a similar type role in her play *The Love Lady*, so it is not too surprising to find that Treadwell performed the role of Mme. Istomina in her own production on Broadway, under the pseudonym Constance Eliot. As a playwright, Treadwell gets a lot of comic mileage out of Gormont and St. John while poking fun at theatre practices and personalities.

Overall, the play still echoes some of Treadwell's earlier concerns, most notably the belief that society will not allow a woman to make it on her own withouot the aid of a successful man. Here, Loney is crushed by a selfish, uncaring theatre world, abandoned by a self-serving parasite, and ultimately comforted by the love of a caring young man.

During the play's tryout performances under an earlier title, *Loney Lee*, Helen Hayes garnished most of the critical attention for her engaging performance in the leading role. When subsequently produced on Broadway, many critics again felt the play was carried by exceptionally strong performances, especially by Martha Bryan-Allen as Loney and Ernest Lawford as the Marquis. Numerous reviewers were also captivated by the innocence and charm of Treadwell's script (R033, R039, R045, R051, R052). Others, however, such as Mantle (R040), Dudley (R036) and Pollack (R053), grew impatient with Loney's incredible naiveté. Smith (R028) and Gillette (R038) thought the love story between Loney and Warrington needed further development.

The script for *Loney Lee* includes the characters of the Marquis's wife and her daughter, the latter a flapper. The action is also broader: Act Two ends with the kiss of the young lovers and a final act features their hesitant union, as well as a confrontation scene between the Marquis and Mme. Istomina and a scene of jealous pursuit by the Marquise and daughter Sally. A subsequent version, titled *Philomel*, is structurally very similar to *O Nightingale* but contains an expanded scene between Loney and Warrington to end Act Two. All in all, the final *O Nightingale* version has a structural tightness and simplicity that works well with the play's straightforward theme.

The play seems to have its origins in a play copyrighted in 1915 under the title *Sauce and the Goose*. A film scenario based on the play survives in UALSC. Although the setting of *Sauce and the Goose* begins in Arizona, its action parallels that of *O Nightingale* in that its central character is a naive, young western girl who goes to New York to be an actress, falls in love with an artist, is wooed by a Count who arranges a meeting with an influential theatre manager, and is finally united with the artist at the end.

PLUMES IN THE DUST (produced 1936)

The Characters--MRS. FRANCES (FANNY) ALLAN: Poe's foster mother, about 50, timid, nervous; MIRANDA: a black servant of the Allans; LIZZIE: an old black woman; JOHN ALLAN: Poe's foster father, about 46, thick-set, lame; ROSALIE POE: Poe's sister, about 15, small, thin; EBENEZAR BURLING: Poe's boyhood friend, about 20; EDGAR ALLAN POE: beautiful, sad, quiet; MONCURE HARRISON: the son of a Roanoke planter, tall and fashionably good-looking; ELMIRA ROYSTER SHELTON: Poe's boyhood sweetheart, a frail girl of 16; MRS. MARIA CLEMM: Poe's aunt, a large and motherly woman of 45; VIRGINIA CLEMM: Poe's 13-year-old cousin, frail, thin; MISS McNAB: a buxom young woman of 20; JOHN P. KENNEDY: a prominent citizen in his mid-30s; MISS ANN LYNCH: a literary hostess, 30; MRS. SARAH ANNE LEWIS: a plump poetess of 40; MR. LEWIS: her husband; N.P. WILLIS: editor of the *Mirror*; MRS.

ELIZABETH FRIES ELLET: a novelist, short, stout, over 40; MISS MARGARET FULLER: a critic and literary editor of the *Tribune*; MRS. FRANCES SARGENT OSGOOD: a poetess, usually pale; DR. RUFUS GRISWOLD: a 31-year-old writer and editor, infatuated with Mrs. Osgood; MRS. SUTHERLAND: an overbearing English lady; LOU: Elmira's black servant; HOSPITAL ATTENDANTS; DR. MORAN; MATRON.

Plot Summary--ACT I, Scene 1: The setting is December 1826, Christmas eve, in the sitting room of the Richmond home of John Allan, a wealthy Scotch merchant. Mrs. Fanny Allan, Poe's foster mother, expects Edgar's return this evening from the university in Charlottesville, and goes to the back door to retrieve letters for Edgar from a Yankee pedlar. A servant, Lizzie, tells John Allan of the birth of a baby boy to his mistress, two blocks away. Mrs. Allan confronts her husband about the rumored pregnancy, then cries when he dismisses her. Rosalie, Edgar's sister, displays an ugly, patchwork sofa cushion she has made for her brother for Christmas. Orphaned like her brother at a young age, Rosalie has been raised by Mrs. McKenzie, while Edgar was housed by the rich Allans. The young girl exits when Allan rants that the letters which arrived were actually Edgar's bills for fine clothing and a lost book from the university. Allan denounces the bad blood the two youths inherited from their hard-drinking parents, the now-deceased Poes of Baltimore, but Mrs. Allan reminds her husband that he so admired their mother when she came to town as an actress on tour that he instigated the adoption of Edgar upon her death. Allan says that was before he learned of her immoral past, including her admission that she did not know the identity of Rosalie's father. The eighteen-year-old Edgar arrives, accompanied by his drunk schoolmate, Moncure Harrison, son of a rich planter. After Edgar escorts his faintly mother from the room, Harrison tells Allan how he and Edgar lost a great deal of money playing cards. Harrison then leaves, escorted by Allan, who is on his way to visit his mistress. Elmira Royster enters looking for Mrs. Allan, and is shocked to see her former love, Edgar. Having never received any of his many letters, Elmira tearfully admits she has recently married the grocer, Mr. Shelton. She claims their parents told her Edgar did not love her, and after Edgar denounces the moral hypocrisy of his foster-father, Allan shows him a letter from his mother revealing the Poe family's dishonorable past. Elmira departs. An angry Edgar promises to pay Allan back the $1,000 gambling debt, a debt he incurred only in a desperate effort to pay his university bills. Allan and his wife angrily leave the room. When Edgar's boyhood friend, Ebeneezer Burling arrives with news of a new schooner on the river, Edgar grabs his bag, drinks, recites some of his poetry, and leaves to go sailing with his friend.

ACT I, Scene 2: Seven years later in Baltimore, Edgar lives in the attic lodgings of his aunt, Mrs. Clemm, and her thirteen-year-old, sickly daughter, Virginia. The young girl tells her mother that Edgar is still sleeping in the next room, having stayed out past four o'clock last night. John P. Kennedy arrives to present something to Edgar, but vows to return after Edgar has risen. Mrs. Clemm rouses Edgar, who is despondent after learning last night that he lost *The Saturday Visitor* prize for poetry to a man who is one of the publication's editors. Edgar has lost all faith in his writing and plans to leave today for "anywhere." Virginia, who is in love with her cousin, swoons. Mrs. Clemm tells Edgar she fears for her daughter's health; Virginia nearly died from self-imposed starvation and strained, weak arteries the last time he went away. Kennedy returns with news that Edgar was the winner of the magazine's fiction, not poetry, contest. Edgar is outraged, though, to learn that the judges also thought his poetry to be the best submitted, but they did not want one author to win both prizes. Kennedy awards the $50 prize money, arranges for Edgar to take a job in Richmond as a critic and editor of a new weekly, then leaves after urging Edgar to curb his inclination toward brutal honesty in his criticism. Edgar refuses to allow his relatives to go with him to Richmond, but falls on his knees over the beauty of the fainted Virginia.

ACT II, Scene 1: Fourteen years later, Edgar writes a series on famous writers in his impoverished room in Fordham. His consumptive wife Virginia hopes her mother will return with some money from selling Edgar's series in order to buy cough medicine. Virginia urges Edgar to attend Miss Anne Lynch's Valentine's party tonight, where the literary elite will exchange anagrams to each other. Edgar reads from his fanciful story about Eleanora, based on Virginia, and he comforts his wife when she asks how long she has to live. Mrs. Clemm returns with news that no editor was interested in purchasing Edgar's current series. While attending to Virginia, who had a momentary seizure, Edgar discovers a magazine proof sheet in Mrs. Clemm's bag which describes Poe's current state of destitution and urges friends to help. Outraged, Edgar prepares to leave in search of the magazine's editor to stop the article's publication, but he vows to return to Virginia tonight on a late train.

ACT II, Scene 2: That evening in New York, Miss Lynch entertains a group of elite literati: poet Sarah Anne Lewis and her lawyer husband; editor N.P. Willis; novelist Elizabeth Fries Ellett; critic and editor Margaret Fuller; poet Frances Sargent Osgood, and writer and editor Dr. Rufus Griswold. Mrs. Sutherland, an overbearing English woman, arrives and demands to meet Poe, whom England considers America's finest critic. Several guests drop innuendoes of Poe's drunkenness, debt and pursuit of other women. Edgar enters, drunk, and overhears assaults on his moral character by Griswold. Edgar falls in trying to attack Griswold, and all the women leave the room. Mr. Lewis bribes Edgar to praise in print his wife's writings, and Edgar reluctantly agrees. Mrs. Sutherland and Mrs. Osgood return, and Edgar begins reciting "The Raven" upon request. Mrs. Clemm enters and announces Virginia's death. She collects Edgar to take him home and he sobs violently.

ACT III, Scene 1: In the sitting room of Elmira Shelton's Richmond home two years later, Edgar visits his old sweetheart after a public lecture. Both are surprised to learn that each still loves the other, but Elmira weeps and says their love cannot be realized due to Edgar's drunkenness. Edgar agrees to Elmira's request to sign a temperance pledge. When Elmira asks if he will go into business of some kind, Edgar says that with her aid he could start his long dreamed of magazine, the *Stylus*. Anonymous letters had warned Elmira of Poe's immoral character and debt, and she now fears he merely seeks her money. Sensing they have grown too far apart, Edgar leaves.

ACT III, Scene 2: A couple of weeks later in a hospital in Baltimore, two attendants carry in an unconscious Poe, accompanied by Kennedy, who found the poet in this state. Edgar mutters in delirium of his former life and of impending darkness. Dr. Moran confirms the severity of his condition, a weak heart complicated by excessive drinking. He offers Poe some medicine to drink, but the poet speaks excitedly of visions, such as the one which serves as the play's title. While a matron reads passages about "many mansions" from the Bible, Edgar calls for his mother, then for God to rest his soul, and dies.

Critical Overview--While some critics of the play's tryout performances felt Treadwell had offered an insightful explanation of Poe's life (R218, R219), most New York critics felt she was not up to the difficult challenge of interpreting the contradictions within the poet (R204, R209, R220, R221, R228). Some felt that biographical drama as a genre was generally uninteresting (R200, R212, R213, R214), while others blamed Treadwell's excessively episodic structure for the lack of a clear point of view (R198, R206, R207). Watts (R229) was one of the few New York critics to praise Treadwell's treatment, and only Mantle (R222) recalled the play's turgid association with John Barrymore. Henry Hull's performance as Poe was frequently celebrated.

Elsewhere (S234), I have outlined the evolution of the script in terms of Treadwell's evolving career, including details surrounding her lawsuit against Barrymore, which contended that he knew his wife, Michael Strange, had plagiarized her manuscript.

Stage directions in the play suggest Treadwell tried to remain as faithful as possible to her biographical research into Poe's life, and this fact may account for the relatively minor changes in the various manuscripts, even though they range in dates from 1920 (when first copyrighted) to 1936. Treadwell even enlisted the advice of the psychiatrist, Elmer Ernest Southard, in detailing Poe's alcoholism.

The version given to Barrymore in 1920, titled *Edgar Allan Poe*, is probably the one that best gives play to Poe's genius and sympathetic characteristics. In this version, the Valentine's Day party scene precedes the one in Poe's Fordham apartment during which Virginia dies. At the party, Poe (not drunk) has a lengthy scene with Mrs. Osgood in which he confesses his love for her, saying he loves his wife as he would a child. In the subsequent scene, Mrs. Lewis arrives to have Poe rewrite her poetry (a service provided for by her husband's payment to Poe), Mrs. Ellet appears to offer a handout to the destitute poet, and Miss Fuller arrives to retrieve Mrs. Osgood's love letters. The scene ends dramatically after Poe chases the meddling women from his lodging, and dictates a vehement letter to the editor who published the article on his impoverished state, while Virginia quietly dies. This version also contains one other noticeable scene variation: at Elmira's house in Richmond, Poe meets her sixteen-year-old daughter Lenora, has already taken the temperance pledge for Elmira, and leaves with an understanding that he and his former sweetheart will resume their lives together upon his return.

In versions between *Edgar Allan Poe* and *Plumes in the Dust* (variously titled *Poe, Edgar Allan Poe* and *Nepenthe*), Elmira's role is greatly diminished as her scene with Edgar late in the play is omitted. In the most radically different version, copyrighted in 1925 under the title *Many Mansions*, Treadwell has retained some of the principal characterizations and scenes, but has placed them in a modern setting and removed any reference to Poe. The central character is now named Jack Poer (a sort of cross between Jack London and the young, seafaring Eugene O'Neill), but little of the poet's genius remains. Poer is egotistical, pompous and morbid in his attitudes toward women. In losing the historical framework for the action, much of the dialogue has become overly sentimental and self-conscious.

PROMISED LAND (copyrighted 1933)

The Characters--MME. MILIUTINA: a gentle old lady of about 60, works in an office; MASHA: a new peasant, about 30, strong, works in a museum; TANIA: Masha's pretty, 14-year-old daughter; VASSILI: a factory worker, 35-40; VITYA: Mme. Sukotina's son, about 10; SUKOTIN: a playwright, about 35, sensitive-looking; PELAGEIA: the worker's wife, short, thick, about 40; PARASHA: Nikolai's wife; XENIA (NADIA): attractive, about 30; MME. MAKLAKOVA: a very ill woman, about 40; PRINCE VIASENSKY: a tall old man, dressed in traditional clothes of a Russian droshky driver; MAKLAKOV: a former revolutionist, about 45, with a short, black beard and a look of Mephistopheles; MME. SUKOTINA: a dancer, young, rather coquettish; ANTON VOLKOV: a strong Georgian of 40, possessive of physical swiftness and brooding silence; BORIS: Volkov's henchman; A PEDDLER; BATES: an American reporter, 35-40; TWO G.P.U. AGENTS; A PEASANT GIRL.

Plot Summary--ACT I: In the kitchen of a shared house in Moscow, inhabitants occupy themselves before their stoves on "rest day": Mme. Miliutina mends; Masha irons; Tania reads; Nikolai drinks tea; Vassili plays his accordion; Vitya plays in the courtyard; and Sukotin periodically emerges from his room to see if his tardy wife has returned after completing her matinee ballet performance. Pelageia returns from a long day at the factory and bread line and curses her husband Vassili's laziness. Masha, who works in an anti-religious museum, is angered by Nikolai's repeated references to God, and by his wife Parasha, who returns from having sneaked off to church. Tania reads *Anna Karenina*, which was given to her by her teacher Nadia (Xenia), even though Tolstoy is banned. Masha condemns the decadent morals of the book, as well as those of the older generation, such as Mme. Miliutina, who left her husband to live with another man and still wears a ring to remind her of her former love. Xenia arrives in search of Volkov, who had promised her the use of his room during his absence if she needed it. No one is sure where the enigmatic but powerful Volkov is or what he does, but he has left a G.P.U. seal over his door to prohibit entry. Xenia leaves. The very ill Mme. Maklakova enters, hopeful of getting an exit visa approved today, now that her husband's new boss, an American reporter named Bates, has taken up her cause. Prince Viasensky, a former aristocrat, returns from his job as a droshky driver, bringing white bread and butter to his friends. Mme. Maklakova despairs over her and her husband's sacrifices for the revolution, which has now deserted them because they are "intellectuals." After Mme. Sukotina finally returns home from the ballet, her son Vitya tries to blackmail her for butter by saying he will tell Sukotin that a man escorted her to the corner. Sukotin dismisses his wife's criticisms of not caring adequately for Vitya, saying he has ben too hard at work on a play commissioned by the Party designed to liquidate the bourgeois notions of love and jealousy. Sukotin becomes jealous himself, however, when he learns that the man who escorted her home is the master of the ballet company. Xenia returns, claiming agents have evicted her from her nearby room and confiscated her furniture. She confides to Mme. Miliutina that she has lied about her proletarian background in order to get her job as a teacher; her identity papers belonged to her former maid, Nadia, who was killed by the Red Army along with her husband, an aristocratic officer in the Tsar's Cossack guard. Volkov returns and speaks of his recent job in the Caucasus, where he turned 40,000 people out of their homes and liquidated entire impoverished villages like Mosdok, Masha's hometown. Volkov offers to share his room with Xenia, who reluctantly accepts, knowing that while she is attracted to Volkov, he does not love her. She leaves with Boris to fetch her remaining belongings. Bates arrives and awkwardly tells Mme. Maklakova that her visa was denied. Angered, Maklakov pleads with Volkov for help in getting his wife abroad and to a decent hospital, but Volkov refuses, finally admitting the Party does not want intellectuals painting a bad picture of Soviet

Russia abroad. Two G.P.U. agents appear to collect valuables. Vitya tells that Parasha has hidden an illegal religious icon in her room. The agents collect it, along with Mme. Miliutina, who refuses to part with her ring. Bates emerges from the bathroom, scared by a rat that jumped out of the toilet, and quickly departs in his chauffeur-driven Ford. Mme. Maklakova requests and receives Maklakov's revolver and leaves for her room. Maklakov exits the house, and all debate whether or not to go to Mme. Maklakova. Masha enters with packed bundles, and tells Tania to stay and take her job in the museum while she leaves for the destroyed Mosdok in search of her aged father. Xenia returns with her belongings and agrees to marry Volkov, who celebrates by leading all except a moody Xenia in a rapid Cossack dance. Mme. Maklakova calls for her husband and a shot is heard. Xenia rushes toward her room.

ACT II: In their room, Xenia comments to Volkov, now her husband, on the disrepair of everything in the city, and doubts that Volkov's beloved proletariat possesses the invention and drive to maintain the marvels of modern civilization. Volkov casually questions Xenia on details of her job as a translator and guide for an American, using her as an unwitting spy for the secret police. After Xenia leaves to take a bath, Volkov receives orders to go to the Kuban to perform a job similar to the last one in the Caucasus. Volkov becomes angry when Xenia seems pleased at the news that he will be gone all winter. Tania confidentially tells Xenia of her worries: her mother has not returned from Mosdok or written, and she fells degraded after being pressured by a sense of duty to give herself sexually to a boy. Volkov overhears Xenia say that she is pregnant, and he enters, chasing Tania off. Volkov dismisses Xenia's request to allow Tania to search for her mother, but promises to obtain a larger room to accommodate their new baby. Prince Viasensky worries over Mme. Miliutina, who appears to have stood in line all night to obtain her passport before today's deadline. Volkov explains that everyone in Moscow must now have a passport or leave to at least 100 miles from the city. Boris has obtained Xenia's passport for her, and when Xenia asks if Boris might do the same for Mme. Miliutina, Volkov hands his henchman a written order. Mme. Sukotina, with Vitya, says goodbye before leaving for the Divorce Bureau to divorce Sukotin, fed up with his refusals to make censor-mandated changes to his play. She leaves Vitya with her husband, and vows to marry the ballet master, Petroff, who has the luxury of two rooms in which to live. Maklakov introduces Xenia to his new wife, a heavy peasant girl who works as Bates's cook, and Xenia recognizes that his marriage is one of convenience, allowing him continued access to fine dining. Mme. Miliutina returns, her passport denied, and Prince Viasensky comfortingly takes the weakened woman to her room. Volkov confirms Maklakov's suspicions that he arranged for the denial of Madame's passport in order to obtain her room for his new baby. Volkov also admits unashamedly to putting Xenia out of her room previously because he desired her. Xenia erupts, saying she will not give birth to a brutal peasant child and admitting her former marriage to an aristocrat. Volkov reveals he was about to be named Head of the G.P.U., and Xenia's background threatens to make him a laughing-stock. He leaves, vowing to divorce her.

ACT III: Xenia returns the next day and tells Volkov she spent the night in the abortion hospital, although she left this morning without going through with the procedure due to the hospital's grimy, overcrowded conditions and overwhelming presence of death. While sitting alone in the old garden under the Kremlin, she felt a great pity for Volkov and his blind devotion to one way of thinking. Xenia offers to start a new life with her husband, but Volkov plans to go through with the divorce (although he still plans to live with her) in case the facts of her birth come to light. She defends her lineage as honorable and tolerant, but Volkov shows her welts on his body he, like countless others, received at the hands of Russian noblemen. Bates arrives and asks to go with Volkov to the provinces to confirm firsthand rumors of widespread famine outside Moscow. Volkov evades Bates's request, and gives Xenia a letter from Tania, saying she has gone in search of her mother. Masha, dressed in rags and weary, returns, having been unable to find any of her people, who have been transported to Siberia. Masha confirms the famine, but Bates says he must see it for himself before reporting to his skeptical readership. After Bates departs, Mme. Miliutina and Prince Viasensky offer their farewells, the Prince offering to escort the Madame to her exile south of the city in his carriage. As the old couple depart as gaily as possible, Xenia is upset that Masha and Maklakov did not do something to warn them of the famine they will face outside the city. Masha goes to her room to rest, unaware that Tania is gone. The Sukotins return, having gotten back together after Mme. Sukotina's brief marriage to Petroff ended when she discovered he only had one room after all and was about to lose his job at the ballet. Sukotin, feeling suddenly empowered, shakes the bratty Vitya until he cries and runs off, followed by his parents. Maklakov offers the Sukotins to Xenia as the answer to her question about why he failed to help others: there are only petty people left in Moscow who are unworthy of assistance. After Xenia defends humanity as kind and courageous, Maklakov wonders why she does not help others, especially being married to the influential Volkov. Maklakov admits he lacked the courage to kill himself this morning, and he leaves his revolver with Xenia. After Volkov returns and refuses to leave the G.P.U., Xenia points the gun at him, then drops it, weeping. Volkov calls Xenia weak, then lifts the gun to himself, saying Xenia has managed to undermine his convictions and his work. Xenia goes to him, takes the gun, and embraces him, saying she and her son need him to help make a better world.

Critical Overview--The play emerged from Treadwell's own experiences in 1933 when she visited Moscow for Alexander Tairov's production of *Machinal*. During her visit, Treadwell kept sketchy notes about her activities and the people with whom she came in contact. The notes reveal she visited an abortion clinic, divorce bureaus and a "prostitution institute," and was cognizant of the dreariness of life in the Soviet city. One of the play's subplots involving Sukotin's drama is a very entertaining critique on the absurdities of Stalin's "Back to Ostrovsky" doctrine which paved the way for socialist realism.

Treadwell's correspondence with her agent Harold Freeman reveals that a number of producers and actors either disliked or feared the point of view taken toward the Soviet Union. The play was finally contracted, however, in an earlier version with the copyrighted title *The Last Are First*, to Thomas Mitchell, who wished Treadwell to revise the work to minimize its propaganda and to strengthen the love story between Volkov and Xenia. Treadwell seems to have been reluctant, urging Mitchell to read the newly published *Escape from the Soviets* by Tatiana Tchernavin to compare how mildly she had depicted conditions in her play. Treadwell also resisted for a while Mitchell's urgings to come to New York from her ranch in Stockton for revisions, feeling exhausted after the deaths of McGeehan and her mother within the preceding year and already at work on her next play, *For Saxophone*. In addition, Treadwell expressed dismay when she learned her contract with Mitchell interfered with inquiries by Fischer Verlag about the German production rights to the play.

Subsequent correspondence with Barrett H. Clark, who began marketing the script in 1935 after Mitchell failed to produce it, indicate the play was out-of-step with the theatrical times. Influential, liberal theatre producers such as the Group Theatre and the Theatre Union often advocated a pro-Soviet bias.

The earlier version of the play includes a thrilling Prologue in which Xenia and her aristocratic husband are pursued by the Red Army. *Promised Land* reveals that Treadwell tried to improve the love story between Volkov and Xenia, mostly by providing Volkov with a finely written monologue on the brutalities of Russian aristocrats under the Tsar.

Despite whatever "propaganda" dominates, *Promised Land* is an expertly crafted play, clearly one of Treadwell's finest. Her tapestry of characters struggling to deal with life in Soviet Russia is deftly woven, with all but one of the play's many characters introduced by the end of the first act.

THE RIGHT MAN (copyrighted 1908)

The Characters--BERTHA ("BERT") ROGERS: a sophomore; JANICE STUART: a freshman; CONSUELA BROWNE: a senior; appears bored with everything; PHOEBE VAN ORDEN: a senior who, like Bertha, Janice and Consuela, is a member of Alpha Zeta Sorority; President of the Associated Women Students; handsome and well-groomed; MRS. SHEFFIELD: the sorority chaperone; HARRY EDWARDS: a freshman, dating Janice; CAPT. STUART: Janice's father; NED TOBIN: a senior; IM: an Indian woman, about 40; NETTIE: Im's half-breed daughter; TEX WHARTON: buccaroo boss of the XX Ranch, handsome, about 25; ROY MILES: a buccaroo on the ranch, about 20, tall and awkward; DOROTHY WEST: 17-18, youngest granddaughter of old man West, who owns the ranch; IRMA WEST: Dorothy's older sister; TIM HARDING: a ranch buccaroo, prone to drunkenness; SAUNDERS: an old buccaroo and fiddler.

Plot Summary--ACT I: In Phoebe van Orden's sorority room, Bertha, Consuela and Janice are preparing for their last exam of the year and their future time away from college. Janice, the freshman, is reprimanded for her poor study habits, but still gains her upperclassmen's approval to go to a dance tonight. Phoebe has shocked the campus community with her plans to take a job as a governess at a remote cattle ranch upon graduation. She rejects a marriage proposal from the rich but lazy Ned Tobin, her friend since childhood. The four sorority sisters share an elaboate, last meal together, and Phoebe gains their approval to keep her sorority room as a future headquarters and hospitality center. Ned leads a group of his college chums in a serenade outside their window.

ACT II: Five months later, all the hired cowboys on a ranch in Modoc, California are in love with Phoebe, especially the handsome buccaroo boss Tex Wharton. Tex's former love interest, a half-breed Indian girl named Nettie, is jealous over Phoebe's presence. Phoebe returns with her two pupils, Dot and Irene West, after a day of adventurous horseback riding. Nettie overhears Tex and Phoebe discuss their newly agreed upon plan to marry, and runs off after Tex reads a letter from the ranch owner, Mr. West, making him the ranch superintendent. Army soldiers led by Janice's father, Capt. Stuart, arrive days ahead of schedule to buy horses for their cavalry, and Phoebe is surprised by their unexpected travelling companions, Janice, Consuela, Ned and Harry. Phoebe, in turn, surprises the visiting party by announcing her engagement to Tex. Nettie ominously returns with her face blackened, rejecting her previous attempts at passing for a white woman.

ACT III: Three days later, a dance is being held in the school house on the ranch. An often drunk cowboy, Tim, is once again out of control; Nettie still wears pitch on her face and stares menacingly at Phoebe; Consuela tries to romance Capt. Stuart; and Consuela and Ned doubt that Phoebe will really enjoy a marriage to Tex and life in the country. Phoebe tells Tex of her uneasiness tonight, due to Nettie's presence and word that Tex and Tim argued during the dance. During a quadrille, Ned intervenes and saves Phoebe from a knife attack by Nettie. Phoebe learns from Nettie that Tex used to be her lover before she arrived. Tim enters to shoot Tex, but Nettie throws herself in front of him and is killed.

ACT IV: Back at college six months later, the sorority house is in disarray on this the third day of fires after the San Francisco earthquake. Over a dozen homeless people are finding refuge within the sorority, and the entire city is frantic to communicate with loved ones. Phoebe has left Tex without a word, and helps out during the city's disaster as a nurse in a makeshift hospital. Janice supervises the homeless in the sorority, Harry works as a civilian relief officer, and Ned has displayed leadership and heroism in providing emergency aid, even though his family has lost its entire fortune in the fires. Janice agrees to marry Harry. All marvel at how their college peers have shown bravery and courage. An exhausted Phoebe wonders if Ned would still like to marry her. She has lost a lot of grit and independence and now seeks the love of another. They vow to stay in the city, doing whatever work they can to help the city rebuild.

Critical Overview--The play was written while Treadwell worked as a typist for Helena Modjeska and was sent, under Modjeska's sponsorship, to New York agent Jules Murry. Murry liked the play, but requested alterations. Taking Modjeska's advice not to sacrifice her vision as an artist to anyone, Treadwell resisted the alterations and Murry immediately lost interest.

Like many of Treadwell's early plays, *The Right Man* is based on personal experiences. Treadwell worked as a governess for two young girls, Irma and Irene Williams, on a cattle ranch in Modoc the summer before moving to Los Angeles and gaining employment from Modjeska. Treadwell also had her final college days interrupted by the San Francisco earthquake. Through the character of Phoebe, Treadwell displays her restlessness upon finishing college, and her boredom with formal study and the polite social life of her peers. The ending shows Treadwell wrestling with the idea of women's independence, here ultimately tempering such desire with the need for the support and love of a man.

The threatening characters of Tim and Nettie are poorly drawn, especially Nettie, who emerges as a half-literate, noble savage stereotype. Despite an early lighthearted tone, Act Three degenerates into poorly motivated melodrama, and the final act seems an entirely different play in terms of action and mood.

RIGHTS (copyrighted 1921)

The Characters--MARY WOLLSTONECRAFT: the noted

women's rights activist and author; 32 years old; MRS. ELIZA BISHOP: Mary's younger sister; MRS. FUSELI: wife of the artist; an affected English woman; ROSE LACOMBE: Mary's neighbor; young, intense, tubercular; THOMAS PAINE: Mary's friend; over 50; CAPTAIN GILBERT IMLAY: a tall, dashing American of about 35; WILLIAM GODWIN: the philosopher; self-absorbed and contemplative; A SMALL MOB OF REVOLUTIONISTS, WITH THEIR LEADER.

Plot Summary--ACT I: Mary Wollstonecraft urges her sister Eliza to use their time in Paris during the French Revolution to continue her education and gain independence from her brutish husband back in England. Eliza, however, chastizes Mary for her continual studying and writing. Mary and Eliza's neighbor, the prostitute Rose Lacombe, delivers a letter from their brother, Charles, and speaks of her lack of hope that the Revolution will bring equality for women. Alone with her sister, Eliza reads Charles's news of receiving an offer for Mary's hand in marriage from the rich but drunkenly Squire Melford. Mary's disgust for the offer reflects her low opinion of the marital state, an opinion forged while watching her mother patiently endure her spouse's drunken abuse. The revolutionary idealist, Tom Paine, arrives with his friend, Captain Gilbert Imlay, to seek refuge while the king passes by outside en route to his execution. Imlay impresses Mary with descriptions of the vast resources of frontier America, and Paine celebrates the triumph of the rights of man by showing Mary the key to the Bastile, given to him to convey to General Washington. The philosopher, William Godwin, arrives, not wanting to depart from his visit to Paris without meeting Mary, whose writings he has admired. A philosophical discussion ensues, which includes: Paine's vision of a free and equal world republic; Imlay's defense of bloodshed in the name of revolution; Godwin's belief in the power of education and free thought; and the subject of Mary's latest book, *A Vindication of the Rights of Woman*, which argues that women will impede the progress of men unless they become their true and equal partners. The debate turns to issues of sex, marriage and conventional morality, with Mary and Godwin in virtual agreement on most points. After Paine and Godwin depart, the latter returning for England, Mary, despite her philosophy, surprises herself by enjoying and returning Imlay's romantic advances.

ACT II: Months later, Rose excitedly tells Mary of the fall from power of Robespierre and the Girondins. After Mary confesses her love for Imlay and relates her dreams for their carefree future together, Imlay announces his departure this evening for The Havre on matters concerning his new lumber business. Paine, drunken and ill from witnessing the execution of his friends, vainly urges Mary to return to England for her own safety. Eliza frantically returns from market, pursued by an irrational mob of revolutionaries intent on imprisoning her because of her English heritage. Rose is able to thwart the mob, however, when she presents a cachet of safe conduct signed by Danton. Mary still defends the French populace, maintaining more faith in what they may become than what they currently are. Alone with Mary, Eliza is shocked to learn that her sister considers herself married to Imlay without benefit of a formal ceremony. When Imlay returns, Mary recognizes she cannot reason away her passions, and begins to cry over her impending loneliness after Imlay's departure. Imlay leaves his pistol with Mary for protection, and Mary sends Eliza away when her sister is outraged to learn of Mary's pregnancy.

ACT III: Over a year later, a dispirited Mary welcomes Imlay home after another of his lengthy business trips to The Hague. Unable to find a reliable nurse, Mary is worn from trying to care for her baby and continue her writing, realizing that this double-strain is the historical reason why men have subjugated women to the domestic realm. Mary expresses her fear that she is no longer a part of Imlay's affections, and he casually promises not to leave her alone again. When Mary leaves to get food for them, Rose enters, having followed Imlay back from The Havre where they have been continuing a lengthy affair. Mary returns, overhears their conversation, then asks Rose if she may be alone with Imlay. Now knowing she is not viewed by Imlay with the same devotion and passions she has for him, Mary refuses to let Imlay stay or offer financial support out of a sense of responsibility to her. After she bids Imlay farewell, Mary takes the pistol from a drawer, contemplates it for a moment, and then puts it away in favor of caring for the needs of her daughter in the next room.

Critical Overview--With *Rights*, Treadwell continued her interest in biographical drama, which began with a work completed the previous year, *Poe*. As with *Poe*, Treadwell continued to revise this play over a span of many years.

In Mary Wollstonecraft, Treadwell discovered the perfect embodiment of her own dilemma: the desire for independence as a woman countered with the need to find fulfillment in the love of a man. Treadwell focused on historical events surrounding Wollstonecraft's authorship of *A Vindication of the Rights of Woman* and tormented affair with the abusive Imlay. The play recognizes the contradictions in Wollstonecraft's ideals and personal actions, and posits the belief that reason and passion sometimes produce such conflicts. Unlike many of Treadwell's other early heroines, however, Mary emerges from her need for male companionship with resolve and without a sacrifice of her principles.

As suggested by Wynn (S186), Treadwell most likely conceived the play to coincide with a major success of the American women's rights movement--winning the right to vote. The title refers not only to the legal rights a man has over his wife, but, set against the backdrop of the French Revolution, also suggests the discrepancy between the newly won rights of men in France and those still withheld from women.

Numerous versions of the play survive in manuscript form. Variant texts under the titles of *Rights* and *The King Passes* include characters such as Mary's servant, Thatcher, her brother Charles, and her publisher and confidant Mr. Johnson. Throughout these early versions, Treadwell strengthened the character of Rose and experimented with the placement of a scene between Mary and Godwin in the overall plot sequencing. In one version, this scene appears at the end of the play, as Godwin interrupts Mary's contemplation of suicide, and through reason and honest concern for her welfare restores her desire to live. Although the scene creates an awkward and sudden reversal for Mary, it presents Treadwell's ideal that a male-female relationship be founded first upon friendship, mutual respect and intellectual partnership.

In the late 1930s, Treadwell returned to revisions on the play. Perhaps sensing that America's interest in women's rights had waned, Treadwell altered the text to disguise Wollstonecraft as its subject, changing character names, providing an obligatory happy ending, and suggesting in stage directions that the play was based in part on the life of the English novelist, Fanny Burney. Under the titles *Mary Beaton, by Mrs. Beaton, Love and Principle* and finally *Rights*, the character of Godwin is eliminated and Mary and Imlay's confrontation scene ends with Imlay's realization that he really does love Mary after all. In a couple of versions, Mary (now called Ellen) actually calls after the departing Imlay (now Rogers), and the play ends in their embrace. The revisions show Treadwell's desperation in trying to get her works produced during the lean years of the late 1930s. Treadwell even began billing the play as a comedy.

THE SETTLEMENT (copyrighted 1911)

The Characters--STANISLAUS BENDA: a waiter from Poland; ordinary-looking; 25-40; JOHN P. MULCAHEY: a brawny police detective; MISS EDNA (EDDIE) KEMSEN: a rangy society girl; MR. DWIGHT DWINELLE: a man about town; from an influential family; BETH AHLMER: a slight, pretty reporter for the *Morning Sun*; LAURA BRIGHTON: a typical, newly rich society girl; JAMES CRERY: an attractive man of about 30; runs a welfare agency, the "People's Place"; BELLE PALMER: a handsomely dressed woman of about 35.

Plot Summary--ACT I: Police security is tight for the wedding reception at the Brighton home, especially since Laura Brighton's continual need to be in the limelight has led her to wear a priceless, one-of-a-kind jeweled necklace, effectively upstaging her brother's wedding. Miss Eddie

Remsen tells her fellow socialite, Dwight Dwinelle, that Laura came by the necklace last summer as an engagement present before jilting her fiancé, Count Morosini. Dwight blabs the details of the necklace's past to a young reporter, Beth Ahlmer, who dares not print the story since the Brightons are major advertisers with her paper. Alone with James Crery, the director of a welfare shelter, Laura gushes enthusiastically about her new-found interest in trying to uplift the destitute, including Beth's notorious sister, Belle. Upset at Laura's hypocrisy and snooping, Beth dismisses Crery's proposal of marriage, refusing to put aside her pursuit of a career. In the confusion surrounding the departure of the newlyweds, Laura's valuable necklace turns up missing. She promptly accuses a Polish waiter, Benda, and has him arrested. Alone, Laura pulls the necklace from the front of her dress and hides it.

ACT II: At the "People's Place" welfare home a week later, Benda despairs over the loss of his job and his failure to find work, both as a result of his wrongful arrest. Upset by his presence, Laura orders Crery to send the waiter away, then proceeds to write a check to help with his welfare. After Crery and Laura quarrel over their relationship and goals, Laura confronts Belle, a prosperous madame, concerning the whereabouts of a missing young woman from the shelter. Belle bluntly dismisses Laura's philanthropy, saying money and men rule society, not morality and uplift efforts in social activity and etiquette. After the women leave, Beth enters, fired from her job and excessively fatigued. Crery now turns down Beth's proposal to resume their former relationship. Having overheard Beth's despair, Belle returns and warns her sister about the dangers of life on the streets. Detective Mulcahey arrives to arrest Beth on suspicion of theft in connection with Laura's necklace, and Crery decides to abandon Laura to accompany Beth to the police station.

ACT III: At the settlement house two hours later, Crery returns with Beth, having managed to convince Belle to post bail. Laura has waited for their return, and soon breaks under Crery's suspicions to reveal that the necklace theft was actually an accident. Laura was simply too embarrassed to reveal the necklace had fallen down her dress. This afternoon, however, Laura was truly robbed of all her jewels and is too afraid to tell the police the truth about her former accusations. Benda returns briefly to say goodbye, and Crery discovers Laura's jewels in his valise. Crery believes that Laura's initial accusations were responsible for turning the honest Benda into a desperate thief, and he demands she phone the police and clear Benda's reputation. After Laura confesses to the police, Crery announces his resignation from the shelter in order to work in Laura's employ with Beth as his partner. Benda happily serves everyone coffee.

Critical Overview--The play further reveals Treadwell's concern in her early writing with the disparity between rich and poor, especially as it impacts women. Belle's speech about using prostitution to control men and money stands out as one of the play's highlights. The character of Belle may have been inspired by a young woman Treadwell and her editor, Fremont Older, befriended while working at the *San Francisco Bulletin* (S074). The play also reveals Treadwell's general distrust of charitable organizations, a sentiment she would use to good advantage in her first serial for the *Bulletin*, "An Outcast at the Christian Door."

As with many of Treadwell's early heroines, Beth's thirst for independence and a career gives way to fatigue and a return to dependence on men, a characteristic which probably echoes Treadwell's own interrupted starts in career jobs due to recurring bouts with illness during these early years. Despite some strong characterizations and a promising situation, the play often resorts to the devices of melodrama: eavesdropping, climactic curtain scenes, a whodunit suspense formula, and a pat ending. Beth has many good moments as a smart-talking journalist, but Treadwell's theme of the power of media to make and break reputations is largely underdeveloped. Treadwell entered *The Settlement* in a play competition sponsored by Winthrop Ames, but the play did not win, nor did it lead to any real sign of encouragement from Ames.

Treadwell revised the play under the title *Limelight*, and sometimes marketed it under the pseudonyms John Marn and Laure Reska. These versions attempt to clarify the protagonist by having Crery arrested for the necklace theft and making Beth the principal agent of the action who breaks down Laura's lies. In a late version, Dwight and Edna are eliminated and Laura's old fiancé, Count Ernesto Bozelli is added. Bozelli drives the early action as the villain of the piece, using Laura's old love letters as blackmail to set up the fake robbery of the necklace for his own monetary gain. This change serves to soften the character of Laura, making her more of a victim. This version also changes the cause of Belle's notoriety, here making her a chorus girl who has shot a millionaire, a piece of exposition which is not well integrated into the action.

THE SIREN (copyrighted 1953)

The Characters--FRED MILLER: early 30s, strong, heavy-set; ANNE BRANDT: 30s, attractive, feminine, not clever but full of common sense; HALLETT (HAL) BRANDT: Anne's husband, mid-40s, lame from a twisted leg, frustrated; HELENA OPID: a slender, beautifully tragic-looking Polish woman of about 40.

Plot Summary--ACT I: Fred Miller listens to the radio and waits in his newly rented slum apartment outside Seattle. Anne Brandt enters, nervous and tired from having driven her husband, Hal, non-stop from New

Mexico, even though he has remained secretive about the purpose for their trip. After Fred leaves to fetch Hal, who is waiting in the car, Helena Opid, a Polish immigrant, enters, thinking Anne and Fred are her new neighbors. Helena tells of her son, who is proudly fighting for America in the Korean War. Fred returns and chases off Helena, angry at Anne for admitting her. Hal soon arrives. Fred tells the Brandts of his background as a Russian pilot and agent and leaves to hide their car. Anne demands an explanation from Hal, who removes first a gun from his briefcase and then plans for a new, powerful bomb. Hal reveals his idealistic faith in Communism and the Soviet Union. Anne calls his actions treasonous but refuses to leave her husband because she loves him. Helena returns, upset by a recent air raid siren, and tells of her husband, a Polish soldier killed by the Russians. Helena again leaves when Fred enters, contemptuously speaking of Americans' false sense of security. The radio brings news of the anticipated executions of Ethel and Julius Rosenberg, as well as the spy conviction of Dr. Klaus Fuchs, before blaring "The Lone Ranger" show.

ACT II: Weeks later, at night, Anne nervously watches the moon, unable to stay confined with the restless Hal in their small, inner room. Hal is concerned by the lack of their departure for Russia and fears investigation. Alone with Fred, Anne pleads for information and help for Hal. Fred surmises that Anne merely loves Hal as a helpless child, not as a lover, and he gives her sleeping powder to help calm Hal before leaving without explanation. Helena enters, briefly needing to share with someone a vision she had of her son in Korea, in which he told her he was alright even though something bad happened. When Hal defends the actions of the treacherous Stalinist Frank Jackson, as reported on the radio, Anne says her husband has become a different, morally lost person. Anne goes to her room as Fred returns with packages and a bottle of vodka, telling Hal they will steal an American plane and fly to Russia when they get word tomorrow. Fred offers a toast to Stalin, whom he calls the greatest and most cunning world leader, but Hal gets sick from the vodka and vomits. Anne takes Hal to bed, then returns with her hat and coat ready to leave on her own. Alarmed, Fred plays on her vulnerability, caressing her and telling her how a strong man makes love to a woman. Anne admits she would like to sleep with Fred, and he touches her sensually and leads her, trembling, to his room.

ACT III: The next morning, Fred abruptly leaves without eating the breakfast Anne cooked for him. Helena enters with a telegram announcing that her son was killed two weeks ago. A radiant Anne urges Helena not to despair, saying life continually changes and her sorrow will pass. Helena leaves and Hal comes to Anne to ask for her forgiveness. He now realizes the danger the Soviet Union poses to the world as long as it is led by power-hungry, morally bankrupt men like himself. Anne confesses she slept with Fred and wants to leave with him, hoping she is pregnant with his child. Fred returns, saying they must leave immediately. Hal refuses and goes to his room. Fred tells Anne he planned all along to leave her behind and only slept with her to keep her in the house, silent. A siren announces the arrival of Russian planes, which will serve as a distraction while Fred steals a plane. He gets a knife and goes to Hal's room, followed by Anne, who has picked up a revolver. After shots are heard, Anne returns and tends to Hal's cut hand. Fred has been killed. Amidst the sirens, Hal confesses he has previously helped Russia obtain a big bomb. He gives Anne his briefcase of plans and asks her to turn it over to the authorities while he waits here for the Russians. Searching Fred's suitcase, Hal finds only clothes for a little boy, probably his son. Anne weeps bitterly, then tells Hal she loves him more than ever. She reluctantly leaves. The sirens continue, and Helena enters and meets Hal. They hold hands, expecting to die in the raid. Helena remembers a child abandoned by its mother during an air raid in Poland, and she leaves in search of a child who may need her. Hal goes to the window to await his fate.

Critical Overview--Wynn (S186) suggests the play was intended for television, and like Treadwell's other TV plays, *The Siren* did not undergo lengthy revisions. The play reveals Treadwell's continued disillusionment with the Soviet Union, as seen in her earlier work, *Promised Land*, as well as her growing fears of global conflict during the Cold War. *The Siren* never attracted much positive response from readers at the time, and it ranks as one of Treadwell's weaker dramas. Talk replaces action, Hal's third act reversal is poorly motivated, and Anne is exceptionally deferring to the men in the play, most unbelievably to Fred at the end of Act Two.

A STRING OF PEARLS (1950)

The Characters--EDITH PRENTISS: a small, frail woman of 42; LANGLEY PRENTISS: Edith's older brother, tall, a little stooped; JOHN SIDNEY: the Prentiss's good-looking, English secretary; 30-40; A MAID; ERICH ERDMANN: a German man in his 40s; KATHERINE (KATE) ASHTON: Langley's late wife's 17-year-old daughter; MRS. MEEKER: a middle-aged English nurse; MR. HATHAWAY: the Prentiss family lawyer, about 65.

Plot Summary--ACT I: The invalid Edith Prentiss sits in her wheelchair reading and listening to music in the library of the family home she shares with her unfeeling brother, Langley. Langley fears Edith's growing intimacy with their secretary, John Sidney, a man she hired without a sufficient reference check. Sidney enters with flowers and the mail, including a letter to

Edith from her friend Jean, a doctor in Mexico, containing an invitation to winter with her in her village. Edith plans to go despite Langley's protests. Langley sees a letter fall from Sidney's back pocket, a letter from the secretary of his former employer, a Mr. Neville of London, to whom Langley had written for information. Edith privately tells her brother he pries too much in other people's lives, just as he did with his deceased wife Kitty's. Langley retorts that Kitty flaunted her so-called rosary at him, a string of valuable pearls, each of which was given to her by a former lover. Langley reads to Edith the contents of the letter from London: Sidney is the illegitimate son of a wealthy Englishman and an Indian woman; he was well educated in India, but later disowned by his father. Fearing Sidney, Langley asks his sister to fire him, then leaves the room. Edith confronts Sidney, who is embittered over both how his mixed ancestry made him a social outcast in England and how Mrs. Neville made his previous job intolerable. Sidney announces his love for Edith, and Edith is attracted to his Eastern beliefs and seeming sincerity, even though she is hesitant about their future together as she is unable to bear children. After Edith tells Langley that Sidney will be staying, Langley tells the visiting Erich Erdmann, an authority on antique furniture, of his book, which outlines a plan for a new world order synthesizing the ideas of Marx and the West. After Edith agrees to purchase an antique desk from Erdmann, Kate Ashton, Kitty's teenage daughter, is heard coming in the back way after unexpectedly leaving college. Erdmann sees much of her mother in Kate, having met Kitty the day she died as she tried to sell him her string of pearls, which disappeared after her death. Kate weeps wildly, and Edith, Langley and Erdmann exit to allow her to compose herself. Alone with Sidney, Kate admits she came back to marry him, hoping to continue their affair from the summer, but she suspects Sidney has found someone else when he tells her to return to college. After Sidney exits, Kate surprises Edith by announcing she knows her mother's apparently accidental death was a suicide. Kate tells Edith she is going to have a baby, but she refuses to name the father, not wanting to be married out of pity. Kate wants an abortion, but Edith urges her to have the child and give it to her as her own. They plan to go to Mexico and have Jean deliver the baby secretly. Kate runs out as Sidney returns, but when she comes back in for her coat, she watches as Sidney carries Edith to her room.

ACT II: The following spring, Edith and Kate are just returning from Mexico, with a baby girl and a new English nurse, Mrs. Meeker, in tow. Langley does not believe the child is Edith's, even after she shows him the Mexican birth certificate listing her as the mother. Alone with Kate, Sidney tells her she will never be able to get over longing for him, the first man to make love to her. Edith returns and agrees to marry Sidney soon, saying the baby is theirs and she is getting stronger every day and closer to walking again. After Sidney leaves, Kate urges Edith to send Sidney away. When Edith announces, however, that Kate will be leaving and going back to college, Kate admits that Sidney is the baby's father. Edith insists that Kate must leave, and she retrieves Kitty's pearls from a box secretly hidden in the bookcase and gives them to Kate to use as she needs. Erdmann arrives, eager to retrieve the desk he sold Edith, having found out it was not a genuine antique. Kate takes Erdmann up on his previous offer of a job, and gives him the pearls to hold until she has learned the trade and can justify a salary. They leave together, and Edith clings to Sidney, saying she has done an evil thing.

ACT III, Scene 1: On a chilly, late afternoon in the fall, Mrs. Meeker tries unsuccessfully to comfort a relapsed and sickly Edith. Kate enters, telling Edith of her plans to marry Erdmann and getting her to agree never to tell him the truth about the baby. Edith urges a departing Kate to bring Erdmann to the house at tea-time to cheer Langley, who is despondent after having his book rejected by publishers. Sidney returns after completing his daily prayer session for Edith's recovery at an East Indian temple. Edith becomes suspicious when the family lawyer, Mr. Hathaway, arrives and meets with Langley. Edith shows Sidney her new will, naming him the guardian of the baby and leaving all she has to the two of them. She returns the will to hiding as Hathaway enters with Langley, the latter having learned of the new will. The lawyer fears Edith made out the will under duress, and has hired detectives to follow Sidney. Their report says he goes each afternoon to an East Indian house of prostitution, not a temple, and maintains a Syrian girl there. Hurt, Edith dismisses Hathaway and reprimands Langley for destroying her longing to be loved and to walk again. Edith suffers a deep pain in her side, but rejects Sidney's offer to carry her to bed, reaching out to a re-entering Kate instead before dying.

ACT III, Scene 2: Shortly afterward, a guilt-ridden Langley emerges briefly from the room containing Edith's body to learn from Mrs. Meeker that Sidney is gone and has been locked out. Langley tells Kate of the new will giving Sidney custody of the child. Kate dispels Langley's suspicions about Erdmann's motives, saying she is living off her mother's pawned pearls, not Erdmann's money. When Erdmann enters, Langley immediately asks that the pearls be returned, and Erdmann agrees, saying the appraisal he ordered for Kitty years ago showed all the pearls to be fake. Kate cries, now knowing that her mother committed suicide from shame and disappointment. Kate wants no such illusions in her life, and she tells Langley of her marriage plans. After the men leave to see the lawyer, Kate retrieves the will, but hides it elsewhere as Sidney breaks through the terrace door. Langley enters and tells Sidney that Edith knew of his whoring, but Sidney demands what is legally his, even though he cannot find Edith's will. Langley and Sidney leave to settle all with the lawyer. After Erdmann tells Kate that one must always live with the consequences of one's actions, she confides to Langley that the baby is hers. Kate will tell the truth to Erdmann without shame or fear. Left alone, Kate burns Edith's will, then leaves to face the men in the other room.

Critical Overview--Wynn (S186) discusses the biographical details leading up to the play: Treadwell's return to Germany in November 1949, her adoption of an infant boy she would name William, and her nervous collapse leading up to a two-month stay in a Viennese sanitorium. The play was completed in April 1950 and, although marketed with agents through December 1953, never copyrighted. Several readers found the play well-crafted, but a bit dated in terms of subject and style. Sidney and Edith's relationship is a complex and ambiguous one; he is not merely an adventurer, but genuinely seems to care for her and works to maintain her illusions.

A String of Pearls echoes many of the themes found in earlier plays by Treadwell: the social mystique surrounding an individual of mixed descent; the necessity of illusions to maintain hope; and, the longing of a childless woman who steps into a surrogate maternal role (an action Treadwell had just completed herself).

In the earliest draft of the play, the setting is Riverdale, England during World War II. Ben Moses, a Chippendale expert, replaces the German Erdmann. In the most significant difference, however, Sidney has a prolonged affair with a French cook in the Prentiss household, and it is Mrs. Meeker, not Mr. Hathaway (who is not present onstage as a character) who breaks the news to first Langley and then Edith. In a subsequent version, the setting is New York at the turn of the century. Erdmann is an American; John Sidney becomes Sidney Radcliffe, a psychic originally employed by Langley to explain Kitty's suicide and find the pearls, and Mr. Hathaway brings the news in Act Three of Sidney's East Indian heritage.

SYMPATHY (produced 1915)

The Characters--A MAN: wealthy, fashionable; HIS MAN; JEAN TRAIG: a young, inexperienced woman.

Plot Summary--The setting is a fancy apartment where a man and his servant have prepared an exquisite cold dinner. The Man is anxious for the arrival of his date. The young woman, Jean Traig, arrives in shabby clothes. The Man persuades her to put on a fancy dinner dress he bought. She scarfs down the food while he tries to seduce her. She quickly goes from the table, changes back into her old clothes, and readies to leave. Angered that she would take advantage of the food without returning his sexual advances, the Man turns on her threateningly. Jean shoots him in the arm and leaves, as the servant calls a doctor.

Critical Overview--This very short play is the first of Treadwell's dramas to have been produced. The play was written to capitalize on Treadwell's sensational serial for the *San Francisco Bulletin*, "How I Got My Husband and How I Lost Him: the Story of Jean Traig." Wynn (S186) reports how the model used for photographs of the supposedly real "Jean Traig" continued her fictional impersonation onstage as "herself" in the cast of this play. Playbills and reviews refer to the title, *An Unwritten Chapter*, but the only surviving manuscript, a prompt copy, bears the title *Sympathy*.

Although the play is little more than a sketch, it articulates a couple of Treadwell's concerns: the belief that a man can buy possession of a woman, and the sexual double standard in society concerning reputation. The play also prefigures the action of a young woman taking violent recourse to ward off the unwanted advances of a man, as seen in later plays such as *Machinal*.

THREE (copyrighted 1936)

The Characters--KATHERINE (KIT) CLAIR: a successful commercial artist, exceptionally attractive, strong and sure; about 28; MARY: Kit's young, good-looking black maid; IAN REITH: about 38, very good-looking, secure; a doctor; RICHARDS (DICK) CLAIR: Kit's 30-year-old brother; DOROTHY (DO) CLAIR: a young matron of 26, full of self-importance; Richards's wife; MATTHEW BROOKS: 29-30, intelligent, somewhat detached; MISS WILLIAMS: a trained nurse.

Plot Summary--ACT I: Kit Clair is settling in to a late dinner in her New York apartment. She is interrupted, though, by the arrival of Dr. Ian Reith, a neighbor who Kit met and impressed earlier this morning as they flew back to New York from Mexico on the same plane. Kit tells Reith about her job as an artist for her brother's advertising agency, which specializes in promoting resort locations and real estate, including their newly secured job working for the Mexican government to attract tourists. Kit's brother Dick and his wife Do arrive as planned to discuss this project, but Dick is worried because the young writer he secured to write the ad copy missed their dinner engagement this evening and may fail to show up tonight as well. The Mexican government would not agree to the project unless this writer, Matthew Brooks, was hired, but Do believes he is drunken and untrustworthy. Dick and Do learn excitedly that Kit's guest is the famous Dr. Reith, who made recent headlines with his proven theory that women have three chemically based drives that generate their emotions: the need to eat, to have a baby, and to take a lover. Do asks Kit briefly about Gordon, her former lover who has taken a job in China, then she and Dick give up on Matthew and leave to take in a movie. Reith confesses he is drawn to Kit and asks to be her lover. A phone call from Reith's house summons him home, and Kit agrees to his request to return later that night. Matthew Brooks arrives after all, saying he missed his dinner engagement with Dick because he never agreed to the Mexican project. Kit and Matt intimately share their views on America and Mexico, and when Matt admits he cannot seem to get started on his novel, Kit urges him to take this advertising job. Matt remains hesitant, having previously taken many such jobs to support his dependent mother, now dead. Matt shares with Kit the subject of his novel, which clearly seems based on Matt's father, who escaped a despairing marriage to a stern, religious woman by intermittent encounters with a sad Mexican prostitute. Believing Matt to be lonely, Kit offers him her workroom to use as his own apartment and her cook to prepare meals for him, but Matt admits that Kit's attractive presence would prove too great a distraction. Kit proclaims she is attracted to Matt, too, and he agrees both to move in and to take the advertising job. Kit calls Reith's house to leave a message.

ACT II, Scene 1: A few months later, Kit defends before Reith Matt's use of the room in her apartment, believing his art to be original and compelling while her more commercial efforts are second-rate. When Kit doubts if women are capable of works of genius, Reith replies that women's true potentialities have not been realized because they have been forced to live continually in an environment dominated by men's ideals of war and sexuality. Kit attempts to clarify her friendship with Reith, saying she could never marry him because her unconventionality would disappoint the secure and formal life he leads. Reith quickly departs when Matt returns, the latter upset by the gross commercialism of their work in the ad agency, as well as by memories of his mother. Matt responds to Kit's comforting actions, and plans to accept a new ad job with Dick in order to make enough money to marry Kit and start a family. After Kit states a preference for maintaining the freedom they currently enjoy, Matt abruptly exits.

ACT II, Scene 2: Some weeks later, Dick and Do tell a worried Kit that they have finally located Matt and that Reith has placed him in a hospital for rest. They explain how a drunken Matt was found after collapsing in a mission, and they urge Kit to end her relationship with him. Kit, however, remains committed to Matt and vows to marry him and guide him back to health. Dick and Do leave shortly after Reith's arrival. Reith tells Kit he plans to keep Matt sedated until his body recuperates, but he fears congenital drunks such as Matt are doomed to relapse. He, too, urges Kit to abandon Matt before her life is also ruined, and he once again proposes marriage. Kit confirms she would like to have a child, but believes, as does Reith, she should not have one by the genetically plagued Matt. Kit asks to spend one night with Reith with no strings attached, and after he agrees, she goes to him, weeping.

ACT III, Scene 1: The next summer, Kit, now Mrs. Matthew Brooks, has planned a home delivery for her impending childbirth, believing a home to be a far more comforting place than a hospital. Matt brings the ending of his novel to Kit, who cries over its truthfulness and beauty. An ebullient Matt vows never to drink again. Matt speaks of his attraction to family, stemming from childhood nativity stories, although he remarks that Joseph was not really the baby's father. Kit, in sudden pain, calls for the nurse.

ACT III, Scene 2: Early the next morning, Mary arrives to find a brooding Matt, Kit's doctor having been with her all night without delivery. Matt calls for Reith to come help. Mary anxiously brings in a bottle of brandy, but Matt refuses to drink. After Mary speaks of her own stillborn daughter and modern women's propensity to have children at too late an age, Matt succumbs to the brandy before him. Reith arrives and tries to take the glass from Matt. The nurse announces the birth of a baby boy, and Matt angrily wipes away his tears.

ACT III, Scene 3: Some weeks later, Kit and the baby are doing fine. Kit brings Matt letters from Simon and Schuster and *Collier's*, the former wanting to publish his novel and the latter offering a lucrative contract to serialize it. Matt hurriedly leaves to meet with *Collier's* as Reith arrives. Having seen the baby, Reith claims he is the father and threatens to tell Matt. He informs Kit that Matt started drinking again the day of the delivery and will resume again during moments of stress. Kit denies that Reith is the father, and she vows to stand by Matt, who suddenly returns. Having read the letter from *Collier's* in its entirety, Matt is upset that they want many revisions, including the ending. Reith leaves without telling his suspicions to Matt. Kit does not want Matt to change his novel, unconcerned that they may lose a great deal of money. She turns on some music, happy in having Matt, the baby, and their integrity.

Critical Overview--*Three* continues many of Treadwell's usual themes: the interest in the psychology of women, the distinctions between high art and commercialism, the sacrifice that is necessary in love, and the image of Mexico as a place of lost innocence or potential freedom. As Wynn (S186) points out, Treadwell's specific attitudes toward gender are perhaps more pointed here than in other plays. Kit is the epitome of the Treadwell heroine: intelligent, unconventional, capable of an independent, successful life but willing to give up all for sincere love with a man. Reith's explanations for Kit's feelings of women's inferiority most likely reflected Treadwell's own ambivalence at this time, and probably explain why critics such as Wynn conclude that Treadwell believed women were biologically inferior to men.

An earlier version of the play contains a detailed scene in Act Two where Kit explains to Reith her aching need to have a baby to protect her from future loneliness. Reith remains noncommittal over her proposal to have sex.

In Act Three, it is Kit, not Reith, who is tormented by the fact that Matt is not
the baby's father, and Kit expresses a strong desire to have a second baby by
Matt immediately. Gordon, Kit's boyfriend in China, also writes and threatens
suicide after learning of Kit's marriage. Taken together, these details tend to
weaken the overall characterization of Kit, making her less independent.

TO HIM WHO WAITS (c. 1915-18)

   The Characters--MAN: large, heavy, powerful and insistent;
WOMAN: slim, passionate, eerie.

   Plot Summary--The faint music of a violin accompanies an
encounter between a Man and a Woman at a lonely cabin in the mountains.
The Man has made another in a series of trips to the cabin, this time bringing
a ring, cloth for a dress, and food supplies. He passed a lone fox on the trail
up from town, and he tells the Woman she will be unable to live by herself
through the approaching winter. He will lie outside her door until she stops
resisting and receives his advances. The Woman angers the Man by speaking
of her continued companion, a young man who first accompanied her to the
mountains and died months ago. It is his violin she hears. The Man throws
her to the ground, and she escapes into the cabin. The Man beats on the door
until it swings open. He lies down in front of the threshhold to wait her out.
The violin fades and surges, and a lonely animal howls in the distance.
Hesitantly, the Woman goes to the Man and invites him in. The music
abruptly ends, and the sole light in the cabin is blown out as the Man follows
the Woman inside.

   Critical Overview--The work is an unusually lyrical play
from Treadwell's early one-acts. The setting is reminiscent of her earlier
sketch, *Wintering it at Yankee Jim's*, although the tone here is far more somber.
The play, however, depicts a fairly typical theme for Treadwell in her early
plays: the inability of a young woman to follow through on her resistance of
a man's advances. The play seems to reflect Treadwell's intuition that brute
desire will eventually win out over a woman's concerns--the man eventually
proves to be too persistent and too strong. Treadwell makes theatrical use of
light and shadow, as well as musical accompaniment and offstage sound for
dramatic effect. The open violence and brute desire depicted in the work also
separates it from many of Treadwell's other plays. The work is similar in tone
and incident to an early Treadwell scenario for a story titled *Mother Lode*.

TRANCE (copyrighted 1918)

The Characters--MADAME DEVERE: a trance medium; about 50, American, battered and bloodless-looking; CHARLIE: a Cockney loafer, about 45; always a little drunk; JOHN RANDOLPHE: a young American aviator from a good family; in his 20s.

Plot Summary--In a shabby lodging room in London, Madame Devere, a spiritualist, sits alone reading her cards. Her lover of the past year, Charlie, returns from the bar downstairs and bemoans their poor state of affairs. He urges her to resume the hypnotic trances she used to perform before he met her, believing that with a war on people would be eager to pay to talk to their departed loved ones. Madame refuses, saying she merely faked the trances before. Charlie convinces her to trade her last valuable possession, a silver picture frame which has housed a photo of a young boy, in exchange for a bottle of gin to warm them up. As they drink together, Madame tells Charlie of her past life--how she once had everything she could want, but left it for a man. After he deserted her, she could no longer return to her former life, and has since moved from one man to another. A client appears, a young American aviator stationed in France who has spent his leave in London looking for his long-lost mother. His father has only recently told him that his mother is still alive, and he now is trying to find out about her. As the details of the young man's past emerge, Madame recognizes him as her own son, the same son in her prized picture. The young man is revulsed when Madame tries to reveal her true identity to him, and she proceeds to speak of his mother's past as though through a trance. Sensing the young man could not accept her present state of affairs, Madame tells him his mother is dead. The young man is somewhat relieved she is indeed gone and not living in need somewhere. He pays her handsomely and leaves. Charlie returns, not realizing the importance of the encounter, and sees the money on the table as confirmation that trances are what people will pay for in these trying times.

Critical Overview--The play's European setting most likely confirms that Treadwell wrote the one-act shortly after her return to New York after providing journalistic coverage of World War I. One of the surviving manuscripts of the play shows that it was circulated under the pseudonym "John Marn," although there is no evidence that any producer took an interest in it.

Trance captures the shabbiness of Madame and Charlie's life together primarily through poignant pauses and small character details, most notably involving the use of dialect and expositional background. Madame may have served as an initial character study for the principal character of Treadwell's full-length drama of the same period, *Claws*. Both women have suffered the abuses of past relationships, and end up sacrificing their own happiness for that of their children.

WINTERING IT AT YANKEE JIM'S (c. 1906-07)

The Characters--SCHOOLTEACHER: a young woman; YOLLAND: her young male cousin; MARY and RUTH: local women; CLIFFORD and HAROLD ("WINDY"): schoolboys; LOCK SANBORN: a local man; VARIOUS STUDENTS; STAGECOACH DRIVER.

Plot Summary--Although divided into a prologue and three acts, the play is little more than a series of short vignettes depicting the experiences of a young woman schoolteacher at a remote mining town. An introductory scene depicts the schoolteacher and her younger male cousin, Yolland, singing together as they arrive by stagecoach at a barren, snow-covered wasteland. Inside the home of Mary, a local woman, the teacher and Yolland try to suppress their nausea as they eat a meal while being regaled with stories of local calamities, illnesses and death. Later, Yolland and the teacher share a poorly heated hut in the wilderness. The teacher bolts out of bed upon discovering bedbugs, and laments being so isolated from society. In a scene at the schoolroom, the teacher has difficulty controlling the boy pupils, and soon gives them an assignment so she can return to writing the second act of this play. At a final scene at the post office, Yolland, Clifford and Windy chew tobacco and spit. Lock Sanborn, a local, enters and recounts the highlight of his day: discovering legions of ants in an old stump. He warns Windy of the dangers of chewing, and departs after the stagecoach arrives with the mail.

Critical Overview--The play undoubtedly records some of Treadwell's impressions while working as a schoolteacher at Yankee Jim's in Placer County, California. She was joined there during a very snowy winter by her cousin Yolland. Since the play was never typed, and was later kept by Treadwell in a scrapbook rather than with her play manuscripts, it most likely was never intended to be more than a writing exercise or dramatized journal. The scenes are anecdotal and lacking in conflict or clearly defined action.

WOMAN WITH LILIES (copyrighted 1948, 1955; produced 1967)

The Characters--HERCULANO: an old, stupid, often drunk, Mexican servant; LUPE: a handsome, young Indian woman; A LODGER:

a nondescript, middle-aged Mexican; SALVADORA (DORA): the landlady; old, poor, strong, greedy; ANNABEL (ANN): 28, self-assured and ambitious; a successful American fashion artist; RICHARD CRAGG: a gifted American artist; volatile, possessive of a mocking air which hides his despair; CARMEN: a shy, poor, tired, Mexican woman; JUANITO (DON JUAN VILLAVERDE DE MIRAMONTE): a Spaniard, around 30, handsome and corrupt; HARRY BLISS: a small, dapper man, the rich owner of a new nightclub; PEG: a cheap, Irish girl with red hair; A TAXI DRIVER.

      Plot Summary--ACT I: In the courtyard of an old house in Mexico City, Dora, the landlady, recalls a better lifestyle in years past with generals and landowners as her suitors, and her servant Herculano solaces her by playing "La Cucaracha" on the guitar, the only song he knows. Ann, a successful but lonely American career woman, arrives on vacation and rents a room after learning that an American painter is living in the house. Dora hopes Juanito will make money serving as Ann's guide/lover. Richard Cragg enters, anxious for word about the result of a government-sponsored art contest he entered. Lupe, Cragg's young Indian lover, becomes upset over the news of Ann's arrival, fearing Cragg will become interested in the American woman. Dora greets Carmen, a tired Mexican woman with five children and a man who wants to have sex with her three times a day. Dora sells Carmen a sedating drug and tells her to pass the word to her friends that she also sells a drug to help stimulate lovemaking. Lupe is interested in the stimulant, since Cragg spends all his energy on his painting, and Dora gives her a teaspoonful of the drug to try out. Lupe leaves to add it to a bean dish she is cooking. Cragg recognizes Ann as his wife, who divorced him for another man she has since left. He tells Ann how he has been living in the back country of Mexico, in Quezecotacl, up until a few days ago. Ann admits she has pursued Cragg to find out what went wrong in their marriage. Cragg cites as reasons Ann's dislike for sex and, more importantly, her job as an illustrator for the fashion magazine, a job which Cragg felt was a sell-out of her talent. He tells Ann that Lupe is now his girl, and leaves. Dora returns, guessing correctly that Ann wants Cragg and now "he doesn't want to play." Ann returns and decides to hire Juanito as a guide to take her today to Cragg's mountain home in Quezacotacl. She is pleased as Juanito plays her Spanish gypsy music. Harry Bliss, rich owner of a new nightclub, drives up and tells Cragg he heard over the media that he did not win the art competition, but due to his reputation for painting women, he would like to commission a painting for his club. Bliss would like a nude white woman painted against a backdrop of lilies, and Cragg accepts after driving the commission price up to 1000 pesos. As Juanito sings to Ann in her room, Bliss notices how all the women seem to swoon, and he offers Juanito a job try-out at his club. Bliss leaves, telling Cragg he will return tomorrow to review Cragg's initial sketch for the painting. Unhappy with the forced subject of the painting, Cragg curses and throws Lupe's bean dish into the street. Cragg pays Dora rent for three more days and demands that Ann be evicted and her room given to him as a studio. He gives Lupe money, then leaves in search of a model for his painting. Dora orders Herculano to pack up Ann's things, and Lupe leaves to buy a dress and a radio. Herculano, though, having been given money by Cragg to get drunk, merely dumps Ann's things by the door and goes.

ACT II: The next afternoon, Ann's nerves are frayed. She did not sleep last night, worrying about the still-absent Cragg and kept awake by dogs howling in the street, apparently stimulated after eating Lupe's drug-laced dish. Ann knows Bliss will arrive soon to review Cragg's sketch, so she pays Lupe to serve as her model while she makes a sketch. Lupe tells Ann of her simple but romantic life with Cragg. Carmen returns, upset that her man is still sleeping from an overdose of the sedative, but Dora refuses to give her the stimulant to reverse its effect and urges her to accept what the fates give her. Bliss arrives and is pleased by Ann's sketch, thinking it was done by Cragg. He tells Ann that Juanito, a sensation with the ladies at his club, will be on the radio in twenty minutes. Lupe turns down Bliss's offer of a job as a cigarette girl at his club, saying she has a man of her own and that is better than a job. A drunken Cragg returns with a prostitute, Peg. Bliss angrily protests Cragg's intention to use the cheap-looking Peg as the model for the painting, and leaves threatening a lawsuit. When Peg goes in to disrobe for the painting session, Lupe becomes angry that Cragg prefers to paint instead of going to bed with her. Cragg loses his model, however, after Peg learns that he plans to paint her lying on a heap of junk instead of lilies. On the radio, Juanito's rendition of a love song is spoiled when his voice cracks trying to reach a high note. Cragg further angers Lupe by telling her he has spent all of Bliss's advance money, leaving only two third-class boat tickets to Spain. Ann pleads with Cragg to take her, instead of Lupe, with him to Spain, vowing to do things his way this time. Cragg refuses, saying Lupe is dependent on him, and leaves. Ann plans to return immediately to the U.S., but Dora again urges her to spend time with Juanito instead, citing Acapulco as a perfect escape. Ann leaves to find a taxi. Juanito, fired from his job at the club after the radio fiasco, gives a wilted rose to Dora, who tells him of the only man who ever loved her--Herculano, now sleeping off a drunken spree in the corner of the courtyard. Dora urges the despondent Juanito to try again with Ann, who has just returned. They tell her of the beauties of Acapulco, and Dora gives her a coffee mixed with the stimulant. Ann agrees to go to Acapulco with Juanito, and she sends him to wait for her in the taxi. The effect of the drug showing, Ann says she has learned from Cragg how to desire a lover who will place no demands on her. She begins undressing, telling Cragg how she will swim naked in the moonlight in Acapulco, but Cragg grabs her as she swoons. Having grown disgusted with Cragg, Lupe enters and bids him farewell. Ann wants Cragg back and he asks her to pose as the "woman with lilies." Ann reverses her attitude, though, saying she cannot go to Spain with Cragg because of her job. Cragg realizes they would be miserable again together and calls off their reunion. Refusing to be alone anymore, Ann runs down the street after Juanito, who has driven off in the taxi after growing impatient with waiting. Herculano wakes and plays the guitar while Dora sings "La Cucaracha." Cragg, feeling suddenly free, dances alone, stomping and snapping his fingers in a display of male pride.

Critical Overview--*Woman With Lilies* retains the setting and some of the characters and incidents from *The Last Border*. As with *Judgment in the Morning* and *Garry*, Treadwell once again tried to rehash an earlier play. Here, the serious themes of *The Last Border* have been replaced by a greater attention to the comic. Dora, Lupe, Herculano and Juanito all have good comic moments and are far more interesting than the central characters of Ann and Cragg, whose motivations and dialogue remain largely petty, over-written and inconsistent.

The play was produced in 1967 by Peter Marroney, head of the Drama Department at the University of Arizona. Treadwell had approached Marroney about a reading of her play, a suggestion first made by the agent Audrey Wood, who was trying to encourage Treadwell despite her personal dislike for this play. It was Marroney who changed the title to *Now He Doesn't Want to Play*, but Treadwell changed it back after the production and continued marketing the play until June of 1968. No American agent ever showed much interest in the piece, although a Viennese publisher obtained production rights without ever seeing the play realized on stage.

Although Treadwell rewrote the play many times trying to placate agents and directors, relatively little was actually changed in its many versions dating from 1948 to 1967. Several manuscripts, some with the alternate titles *Sauce for the Goose*, *Take My Ear* and *Siempre*, have Ann (or Bonnie Binns in one version) reunited with Cragg (various named Daniel O'Higgins and Bayard Cragg). The plot synopsis provided here is taken from Treadwell's final version of the play, done immediately after its production by Marroney.

YOU CAN'T HAVE EVERYTHING (copyrighted 1925)

The Characters--ZELDA READE: 26, slim, distinguished, somewhat bored; NICHOLAS READE: Zelda's 30-year-old husband; an extremely good-looking advertising director; YOSHI: a Japanese superintendent of the Reade's apartment house; formerly a butler, he now sometimes serves as a caterer to his tenants; LOUISE BLYTHE: a large blonde woman of 35, with a round, childish face; TOM FORREST: a tanned, good-looking, high-spirited man of 28; NEITH DORNE: 30, athletic figure, beautiful red hair, poised but at times indifferent; EVERETT BLYTHE: Louise's heavy, silent, unhappy husband; author of one of the wittiest columns in the New York newspapers; has recently fallen off the wagon.

Plot Summary--ACT I: Nick and Zelda Reade prepare to host an after-theatre party to celebrate the return of their friend Tom Forrest, who has spent the last three years in Honduras. Zelda grows increasingly jealous and angry when she learns Nick has hired Neith Dorne to do artwork for his latest advertising campaign. Once an artist herself, Zelda abandoned painting when she felt she would never be more than second-rate; now she fears her marriage to Tom has made her life stale and second-rate and she begs for the chance to work again. When Nick refuses, she issues an ultimatum about their marriage. The guests arrive: Louise mothers her heavy-set, alcoholic husband, Everett; Tom shows everyone how to make daiquiris and talks of easy divorces in Honduras; and Neith, a free-spirited artist and advocate of free love, captures the attention of all the men. Alone with Louise, Zelda convinces her unhappy friend to join her in a trip to Honduras for a real, or in Lou's case a feigned, divorce. Lou breaks the news to Everett, who cheers, but Nick greets Zelda's news with hostility, believing he is unable to do his work unless he has his wife sitting quietly around him.

ACT II: Six weeks later, much has changed. Everett, who has lost weight and stopped drinking, now lives with Nick, who is grumpy, disheveled and insulting. Neith paints Tom's picture as part of an ad campaign for Nick, and Neith clearly ignores the infatuations of Everett and Tom in favor of caring for Nick. Zelda and Lou return two days before they were expected. Everett is shocked to learn that Lou only pretended to divorce him, and he runs away from her, not wanting to fall back in his old lifestyle. Nick prepares to go to the country with Neith, not wanting to stay in the same house with his divorced wife. Zelda and Nick are reunited, though, after she confesses she is lonely without him.

ACT III: Later that night, Nick is delighted to read a telegram from Zelda informing her that all divorces granted during the recent Honduran revolution were being revoked. Zelda is upset, thinking she had regained her old lover and not wanting to become a mere wife again. A desperate Everett proposes marriage to Neith, who welcomes his attention, but not on an exclusive basis. Abandoned by Nick, Neith agrees to go to the country with Tom, who believes he can win her love despite her protestations. Lou welcomes back a tearful Everett, and begins mothering him again. Nick persuades Zelda, who is packed and ready to leave, that she has indeed won back both her work and her lover.

Critical Overview--The play is similar in style and subject to Treadwell's other New York comedies of manners, *O Nightingale* and *Ladies Leave*. Here, again, the secondary characters seem exceptionally well drawn; Everett and Neith are both more interesting than the temperamental and fickle Zelda and the sombre Nick. Despite a very promising beginning, the action of Act Three tends to fizzle as reconciliations seem both forced and a bit unhappy, especially in the case of Lou and Everett. Treadwell clearly continues her explorations into the nature of gender relationships and self-identity in marriage, and ends as usual with the woman returning to the man. Here, though, Zelda seems to return to Nick from a position of strength, rather than the tired resignation associated with some of Treadwell's other heroines.

PRIMARY BIBLIOGRAPHY

This section lists Treadwell's writings in English in the following order: I. Dramatic Works, II. Fiction, III. Non-Fiction, and IV. Archival Sources (unpublished collected material, including manuscripts of fiction and dramatic works).

I. DRAMATIC PUBLICATIONS
The following is a list of texts in which Treadwell's plays have been either individually published or anthologized.

HOPE FOR A HARVEST

> *Hope for a Harvest*. New York: Samuel French, 1942.
> "Hope for a Harvest" (excerpts). *The Land: a Quarterly Magazine* 2.2 (1942): 97-100.

MACHINAL

> *Machinal*. London: Nick Hern Books, 1993.

Anthologies:
> *American Drama: Colonial to Contemporary*. Eds. Stephen Watt and Gary A. Richardson. Ft. Worth: Harcourt Brace and Co., 1995: 364-402.
> *Plays by American Women: the Early Years*. Ed. Judith E. Barlow. New York: Avon Books, 1981: 243-328; rev. ed. titled *Plays by American Women, 1900-1930*. New York: Applause Theatre Book Publishers, 1985: 171-255.

Twenty-five Best Plays of the Modern American Theatre, Early Series.
Ed. John Gassner. New York: Crown, 1949: 495-529.

II. FICTION
The following is an alphabetical listing of Treadwell's published fiction.
Unpublished fictional works may be found in UALSC (see Section IV of this
Primary Bibliography).

"Bill and a Hatbox" [Pt. I], with William High. *Live Stories* 20.1 (1919): 103-
124.
        Short story of a rich, American munitions manufacturer whose
placid life in Belgium is interrupted by an invasion of German
soldiers. The American finds himself caring for the infant child of
two of his servants, who were shot by the invading Germans. A tale
of unlikely heroism.

"Bill and a Hatbox" [Pt. II], with William High. *Live Stories* 20.2 (1919): 109-
124.
        Conclusion of the short story.

"A Break in the Levee." *Occident Magazine* 50.6 (1906): 233-37.
        Short story of two youths in Stockton, California who
mistakenly shoot a neighbor while trying to protect a river levee from
suspected sabotage by rival Italian farmers.

Lusita. New York: Jonathan Cape & Harrison Smith: 1931.
        With many clear parallels to Treadwell's Mexican encounter
with Pancho Villa, as well as her 1922 Broadway play *Gringo*, this
novel depicts a young male reporter from San Francisco who is sent
to Mexico to cover the apparent abduction of Senorita Luz de Montejo
by the bandit Pancho Zateca. Reviews of *Lusita* may be found in the
Secondary Bibliography under the following catalogue numbers:
R164, R165, R166, R172, R174, and R175.

One Fierce Hour and Sweet. New York: Appleton-Century-Crofts, 1959.
        Novel of a disenfranchised housewife who seeks counsel from
a new neighbor, a retired doctor. Their lengthy conversations function
as both psychoanalytical sessions and moments which build friendship.
Earlier manuscript titles were *The Eye of the Hurricane* and *Deep Well
Center.* Reviews of the published novel may be found in the
Secondary Bibliography under the following catalogue numbers:

R306, R307, R308, R309, R310, R311, R312, R313, R314, R315, and R323.

III. NON-FICTION

The following is an alphabetical listing of Treadwell's published non-fiction. Many of Treadwell's journalistic articles are most easily accessible as clippings, which unless otherwise noted may be found at the University of Arizona Library Special Collections (UALSC). Information on these clippings which is incomplete or unverifiable is bracketed.

A01   Treadwell, Sophie. "A. Lehman Appointed Public Defender of Children by Swann." *New York American* 3 Jan. 1916.
       Interview with Alexander Lehman, a defender in New York's Juvenile Court for the past thirteen years.

A02   ---. "Black Boat, Thirteenth Voyage, 113 Passengers; All Signs Fail." *San Francisco Bulletin* [May 1915].
       The first in a series of "letters" written by Treadwell en route to and within Europe during World War I. This letter is an impressionistic account of the voyage to Europe.

A03   ---. "Boy Starves as Charities Ignore Case." *New York American* [Feb. 1916].
       Profile of twelve-year-old Michael Morales, who has been living alone in a New York apartment since his father was hospitalized a month ago.

A04   ---. "Callan of the 39th." *San Francisco Bulletin* 16 Jan. 1909.
       Admiring profile of E. J. Callan, San Francisco representative to the California legislature.

A05   ---. "Calles Pledges Further Aid to Mexican Labor." *New York Herald Tribune* 23 Nov. 1924.
       Profiles the personality of Mexican President-elect, General Plutarco Elias Calles, and offers predictions about the issues he will pursue in office.

A06   ---. "Carranza's Tragic Flight to Death Described in Full for the First Time." *New York Tribune* 31 May 1920: 1-2.
       Detailed, front-page account of the week-long flight by rail by Don Venustiano Carranza, President of the

Republic of Mexico, on the advent of threatening advances by Mexican revolutionaries. Previous dispatches of the flight appearing in the New York press provided only sketchy outlines of Carranza's final days.

A07   ---. "Carranza's Weird Flight from His Capital." *Literary Digest* 19 June 1920: 51-52, 54-55.
　　　　　Reprints lengthy passages from A06.

A08   ---. "Dead Man's Past Walks at Hearing." [Unsourced clipping, 1914].
　　　　　Second in a series (A15).

A09   ---. "Death Merely Grim Joke to Mexican Bandit." *New York Herald Tribune* 22 Nov. 1924.
　　　　　Continuation of A29.

A10   ---. "Defender in Woman's Night Court Swann Plan." *New York American* [1916].
　　　　　Sympathetic portrait of prostitutes brought forward for conviction in New York's Women's Night Court. The lack of adequate legal counsel and the manner in which the women encounter "The Law," lead Treadwell to comment on a legal system in a manner which prefigues *Machinal*.

A11   ---. "Digging in Mexico for More than Mere Oil." *New York Tribune* 10 July 1921, sec. 5: 12.
　　　　　Profile on the Scotchman William Nevin and his archaeological discovery of artifacts from three different civilizations of Mexico's past. Treadwell ends the article by comparing representations of women from the different eras.

A12   ---. "Fair Grounds Attracts Care-free Crowds." [Unsourced clipping, 5 May 1914.]
　　　　　Humorous report on the gossiping, Sunday visitors to the fair grounds then under construction for the Panama-Pacific International Exposition in San Francisco.

A13   ---. "Fate of Girl Up to Jury." [Unsourced clipping, 1914.]
　　　　　Fourth article in a series (A15).

A14   ---. "Gen. Calles Won Presidency by Force of Arms." *New York Herald Tribune* 17 Nov. 1924: 8.

Details the apathy of the voting populace in Mexico after "long years of disappointment and disillusionment."

A15   ---. "Girl Slayer of Van Baalen Awaits Trial." [Unsourced clipping, 1914.]

First in a series of articles on the San Francisco trial of Leah Alexander for the murder of J. D. Van Baalen, an advertising man and her lover of several years. The article begins with a description which could easily describe the predicament of the Young Woman in Treadwell's later play, *Machinal*: "Next Tuesday morning, before Judge Dunne, a woman--young, handsome and radiant with health--goes on trial for her life. This thing is coming towards her, silent, powerful, inexorable." Treadwell's descriptions of the major players in the trial are filled with insightful details.

A16   ---. "Helen Lackaye Prattles on Cabbages and Kings." [Unsourced clipping, 1908-09.]

Comic profile of a fashion-conscious and pseudo-socialist actress Helen Lackaye.

A17   ---. "Hel=locoed Spelling in New Phone Book Will Set Your Buzzer Goin'." [Unsourced clipping, 1908]

Tongue-in-cheek report on the latest abbreviations used in a telephone directory. Treadwell labelled this her "first story" in her scrapbooks.

A18   ---. "He's All for Clean Stage, He Declares." [Unsourced clipping, 1914.]

Ironic profile of Gilbert & Sullivan star De Wolf Hopper, who despite his abhorrence for the "personal pronoun," egotistically pontificates on his preference for "clean drama" over debased dramas on antisocial subjects.

A19   ---. "The Hopkins Manner." *New York World* 25 Nov. 1928.

Written near the end of the run of *Machinal*, this article attempts to provide first-hand insight into how Arthur Hopkins is regularly able to stage a "miracle." Treadwell refutes the belief that Hopkins merely lets his collaborators alone; rather, he "lets them alone to give him what he wants in their own way." The vision is purely Hopkins's.

A20   ---. "How I Got My Husband and How I Lost Him: the Story of Jean
        Traig." *San Francisco Bulletin* 54 "chapters" beginning 28
        Nov. 1914.
                        Treadwell's first famous serial. First-person narrative
        of the experiences of a twenty-four-year-old woman alone in
        San Francisco. Wynn (S186) notes that the photos published
        of Jean Traig in the serial were actually those of an actress,
        and the "story" is really Treadwell's own, albeit fictionalized.
        It is worth noting that the serial was published at about the
        time McGeehan accepted a job in New York, leaving
        Treadwell in California.

A21   ---. "How the Co-Ed Lives at Berkeley." [Unsourced clipping, 1903-
        06.]
                        Straightforward description of allowances, earnings
        and living conditions of four types of female college students:
        the sorority girl, the boarder, the girl who does housekeeping
        for salary in a boarding house, and the young woman who
        cooks and cleans for a family in exchange for room and
        board. Published under the pseudonym Mary West.

A22   ---. "'I Am Great!' Says Mary of Her Own Self." [Unsourced
        clipping, 1914.]
                        Profile of the singer Mary Garden and her
        opinionated comments about talent, Fate, marriage, and the
        inability of women to succeed in artistic fields other than
        singing and acting.

A23   ---. "I Remembered a Big White House." *New York Herald Tribune*
        14 Dec. 1941.
                        Excellent article full of details about Treadwell's
        California ranch, her childhood memories of it, her work
        restoring it, her failure, and why she wrote *Hope for a
        Harvest* as a metaphor for "Americans, not just about
        farmers." Includes a sketch of Treadwell.

A24   ---. "Is Jack London a Capitalist? No! But is Certainly 'Magnifique,
        By Gosh!'" *San Francisco Bulletin* 28 Feb. 1914.
                        Excellent profile of Jack London from his ranch in
        California. Includes London's opinions on subjects such as
        journalism, prison reform, capital punishment, socialism,
        college experiences, literary critics and marriage. London
        wrote Treadwell a week later expressing his admiration for

her courage in printing his full opinions and inviting her and McGeehan to stay with him at his ranch.

A25   ---. "Kreisler Rehearses with Admiring Symphonists." [Unsourced clipping, Feb. 1914.]
    Profile of violinist Fritz Kreisler.

A26   ---. "Ladies, Son of Nippon is Your Critic." [Unsourced clipping, 1914.]
    Another personality profile in which Treadwell is less than complimentary to the celebrity subject. Here, Treadwell satirizes Tameo Kajiyama, a Japanese ambidextrous calligraphist performing in San Francisco. Treadwell exposes the antiquated views on women's roles lurking in his "double-barrelled brain."

A27   ---. "Lack of Peace in Mexico Laid to 'Oil Question.'" *New York Herald Tribune* 19 Nov. 1924.
    Details the power wielded by oil companies in Tampico, Mexico, and the conflict between interests held by Americans and Mexicans.

A28   ---. "'Land for Indian' is Cry that Stirs Mexico." *New York Herald Tribune* 18 Nov. 1924.
    Explains the impact of Russian socialism on Mexico.

A29   ---. "Mexican Bandit Odd Mixture of Rogue and Hero." *New York Herald Tribune* 21 Nov. 1924.
    Examines how revolutionaries grow from within the Mexican army.

A30   ---. "Mexican People Seen Apathetic to Democracy." *New York Herald Tribune* 4 July 1943.
    As election day approaches in Mexico, Treadwell describes how the nation is still ruled by one party.

A31   ---. "Mexico Backs Labor's Fight for Benefits." *New York Herald Tribune* 20 Nov. 1924.
    Describes the economic conditions and unionization efforts affecting Mexican laborers. Extensively researched.

A32   ---. "Mexico Resents Racial Angle of U. S. Zoot Riots." *New York Herald Tribune* [23 June 1943].
Describes the racial resentment growing in Mexico toward the U.S. after the "zoot-suit war" in Los Angeles. Urges immediate action by "those in high authority in the United States."

A33   ---. "Mexico, International Puzzle, Land of Doubt and Imitation, Begins New Era Under Calles." *New York Herald Tribune* 16 Nov. 1924, sec. 1: 1, 12.
First of nine articles in a series on Mexico. The editorial caption calls Treadwell "one of America's best informed authorities on Mexican affairs." Treadwell states her intention in these articles to "look through the mirage" of Mexico as it has been established by foreign journalists. Here, she recounts the current state of politics and the platform of recently elected President Calles.

A34   ---. "Mexico Moves to Hew Out Her Own Salvation." *New York Herald Tribune* 24 Nov. 1924.
Final article in Treadwell's series on Mexico. Describes deplorable living conditions facing the Indian population in Mexico.

A35   ---. "Mexico's Dislike for Us is Long Standing; a Source of Aggravation is Our Discourtesy." *New York Tribune* 2 Jan. 1921, sec. 7: 7.
Treadwell finds that Mexicans often resent America's "overwhelming worldly success," as well as Americans' "bad manners" and "ill concealed racial disdain" toward Mexicans.

A36   ---. "Miss Illington Thinks So Too." [Unsourced clipping, 1913-14?]
Caustic interview with actress Margaret Illington about the need for minimum wage and an eight-hour work day for women. Treadwell is disgusted that the actress, who is about to perform the role of a working woman onstage, pursues her art without any real knowledge or understanding of the play's subject matter.

A37   ---. "Miss Treadwell Explains Why She Put a $2 Top on Her Play." *New York Herald Tribune* 5 Mar. 1933.
Treadwell explains why she will charge $2 instead of the usual $3 for her new Broadway play, *Lone Valley.*

Treadwell urges reform of business practices on Broadway, finding that current "business customs, conventions and rules" are outdated.

A38   ---. "Miss Treadwell Portrays Herself at 60 in New Play." *New York American* [Apr. 1925].

Treadwell admits that Mme. Istomina in *O Nightingale* is a visualization of herself "as I will be at sixty, just as the part of 'Loney Lee,' played by Miss Martha Brian [sic] Allen, is myself as I was when I was not quite sixteen." Treadwell also relates her summer of study with Boleslavsky, and that the name Vera Istomina was the name of a famous court dancer in Russia before World War I.

A39   ---. "Mrs. Mohr on Trial To-day; Judge Shifted." *New York American*. First in a series of at least sixteen articles, beginning around 10 Jan. 1916.

Details the Providence trial of Elizabeth Blair Mohr as an accessory to the murder of her husband, Dr. C. Franklin Mohr. Mrs. Mohr was accused of hiring three black men, led by her chaffeur George W. Healis, to murder her husband and disfigure for life his housekeeper-lover, Emily Burger. Treadwell's articles, which are not listed separately in this bibliography, continue into the first week of February 1916. Together with her coverage of the Leah Alexander case (A15), these articles show Treadwell a seasoned reporter of sensational murder cases involving women defendants well prior to the Ruth Snyder case.

A40   ---. "News and Views of New Books." *San Francisco Bulletin* 5 June 1909.

Short reviews and notes of eight new books.

A41   ---. "No Clo Clo, No Flo Flo, No Zu Zu. Helas! It Was So Sad, That French Ball." [Unsourced clipping, 1909?]

Satirical description of a disappointing French ball run rough-shod by crude Americans.

A42   ---. "An Outcast at the Christian Door." *San Francisco Bulletin*. Eighteen-part serial beginning 28 Oct. 1914.

A fascinating and compellingly written serial which was prompted by the passing of San Francisco's Redlight Abatement Law, an edict which threatened to displace prostitutes and create more "outcasts" at the doors of Christian charitable organizations. Treadwell's editor, Fremont Older, spurred her into the serial (Wells S107), which forced Treadwell into using her acting talents by going on the streets as a homeless prostitute. The serial sparked a flurry of public commentary, much of which may be found in UALSC. It also included several photos of Treadwell in her disguise. Treadwell found both genuine help and hypocrisy as a result of her investigation. The remaining articles in the serial are not listed separately in this bibliography.

A43   ---. Rev. of *The Goat Song, Hedda Gabler* and *The Great God Brown*. Percy Hammond, "Oddments and Remainders." *New York Tribune* 31 Jan. 1926.
        Treadwell subs for critic Hammond in reviewing three new openings. Her comments on Eugene O'Neill's early success are most interesting; "It is as though, oppressed by the necessity of being great, and thus great, and greater still, he has felt the terrible necessity of bringing into the bright light of the public marketplace . . . all the wares that the back shelves of his mind possess, no matter how commonplace, how uninteresting, how cheap these wares may be." Nevertheless, Treadwell finds O'Neill's new play full of "depth and truth" even if it goes "somewhat to pieces at the end."

A44   ---. "Reviews and Notes of Late Books." [Unsourced clipping, 1913-14.]
        Reviews and overviews of new books.

A45   ---. "Russian Envoy to Mexico Asks a Second Front." *New York Herald Tribune* 27 June 1942.
        At his first press conference in Mexico City, Russian Ambassador to Mexico Constantine A. Oumansky describes war losses, the continued German threat, the need for a second front, and then serves caviar and Russian vodka.

A46   ---. "Screams Story of Wrongs." [Unsourced clipping, 1914.]
        Third in a series (A15).

A47   ---. "Sea Raider Nears; Sailors Make Ready the Life Boats." *San Francisco Bulletin* [May 1915].
        Second in Treadwell's series of "letters" from the

European front (A02). Her ship approaches France.

A48   ---. "She Heard the Call of the Blood of Her Fathers." [Unsourced
         clipping, 1909?]
                Sentimental profile of a young, half-Indian girl
         brought to the U.S. from Mexico four years ago by a wealthy
         Spanish family. The girl, Bertha Rocca, awaits her future in
         a detention home after running away to sleep outdoors,
         supposedly fulfilling the call for nature in her Indian blood.
         Such half-breed waifs "instinctively" displaying their wild
         natures can be found in several of Treadwell's plays.

A49   ---. "Sneers, Poor Food and Hard Beds in Women's City Lodging
         House." [Unsourced clipping, Jan-Feb. 1916.]
                Treadwell again goes undercover, this time to
         investigate conditions in a municipal lodging house for
         destitute women.

A50   ---. "A Tourist Among the Ruins: Lessons of War and Peace in the
         Ghosts of Germany's Shattered Cities." *New York Herald
         Tribune* 11 June 1949.
                After noting Americans' penchant for visiting ruins,
         Treadwell urges her countrymen to visit the "living ruins" of
         post-war Germany: "For they are our ruins. We made them.
         For whatever reason and out of whatever desperate
         necessities, they are our accomplishment." The article proved
         immensely unpopular and generated several irate letters to the
         paper's editor.

A51   ---. "Villa's Voice, the Voice of Mexico, Rings from the Lips of José
         Ruben." [Unsourced clipping, Jan. 1923.]
                Summarizes Pancho Villa's current position as a
         "gentleman farmer" in Mexico, and believes José Ruben in
         Gringo has captured the spirit of such bandits "perfectly."

A52   ---. "A Visit to Villa, a 'Bad Man' Not So Bad." *New York Tribune*
         28 Aug. 1921.
                Detailed profile of Pancho Villa, one which the
         article's editorial caption promises "reveals a Villa hitherto a
         stranger to the American press." Treadwell spent two days
         and nights with Villa on his ranch at Canutillo, and was
         clearly taken with his charisma and gentlemanly hospitality.
         She is also impressed by the order and work ethic fostered by

Villa on the ranch, and she concludes by wishing the
Mexican government would use his talents to head a national
organization of police to make Mexico safe. She leaves the
ranch a clear fan: "I believe in Francisco Villa; in the
sincerity of his feeling for his country and for his people--his
people, the poor, the ignorant, the helpless of Mexico."
Includes two photos of Treadwell, including one of her seated
alongside a rifle-toting Villa.

A53   ---.   "War Tramples Life, But Spirit Triumphs." *San Francisco
               Bulletin* [June? 1915].
                      Another of Treadwell's letters from the war (A02).
               Offers a detailed description of her encounter with a wounded
               Arab soldier in a medical hospital in France.

A54   ---.   "Warlike Paris Hopes and Prays of Peace." *San Francisco
               Bulletin* [June 1915].
                      Another of Treadwell's letters from the war (A02).
               Here, she reports on the new excitement and anxiety in Paris
               since Italy decided "to march." The belief in the city is that
               "the war cannot go on and on much longer." French children
               play at making war and fighting Germans.

A55   ---.   "Weeks of Inquiry Fail to Solve Mystery of Who Killed
               Carranza." *New York Tribune* 9 July 1920: 1, 3-4.
                      This follow-up to Treadwell's initial feature article
               on Carranza's last days (A06) provides more details, and
               raises more questions, about his actual execution.

A56   ---.   "Women in Black." *Harper's Weekly* 31 July 1915: 111-12.
                      Brief profiles of a handful of women in mourning
               Treadwell encountered in France during World War I. She
               contrasts the beauty, charm and grace of the French
               countryside and culture with intricate physical descriptions of
               the effect of grief and loss on the women.

IV. ARCHIVAL SOURCES

Billy Rose Theatre Collection, New York Public Library for the Performing
Arts, Lincoln Center, New York.
       Houses a sizeable collection of material on Treadwell, including
extensive clippings files, playbills, production photographs and limited

correspondence. The scrapbook of Martha-Bryan Allen contains numerous clippings pertaining to the Broadway production of *O Nightingale*, in which she played the leading role. The library also contains typescripts of *Gringo*, *Hope for a Harvest*, *Intimations for Saxophone*, *Ladies Leave*, *The Last Are First*, *Machinal*, *Plumes in the Dust*, and *A String of Pearls*. The library's Theatre on Film and Tape Archive contains a videotape of the 1990 New York Shakespeare Festival revival of *Machinal*.

Library of Congress, Washington, D.C.

The archive houses some thirty-five unpublished, copyrighted manuscripts by Treadwell. The works are listed, along with their registration numbers and copyright dates, in Appendix A of Heck-Rabi's dissertation (S167).

San Francisco Library and Performing Arts Museum, San Francisco.

Maintains a small clippings file related to Treadwell's productions.

University of Arizona Library Special Collections (UALSC), Tucson, Arizona.

Houses the Sophie Treadwell Papers, the largest single collection of material related to the playwright. The Papers may be found under two separate catalogue designations. Under the call number Ms. 124, UALSC houses twenty-seven boxes of the Papers, which were inventoried in 1975. These boxes contain largely professional correspondence, manuscripts of plays, stories, novels, fragments, and scenarios, as well as personal notes kept by Treadwell beginning in college and at various times throughout her later life. The boxes also contain personal interest clippings, Treadwell's lectures for the American Laboratory Theatre, and travel logs. Play manuscripts make up the bulk of these boxes, with several manuscript versions surviving for most plays.

In the fall of 1995, twenty-five more boxes were added to the collection (see "Life and Career" for a discussion on the history of these materials). In order to keep these materials separate from the previous holdings used by scholars, they were assigned a separate call number (Ms. 318). These boxes contain more mansucrits of plays and fiction, extensive personal and professional correspondence, twelve scrapbooks maintained by Treadwell, numerous photographs, and diaries (most of the latter dating from 1942-1970). Some personal artifacts (art objects, passports, etc.) are also in these boxes. A twenty-sixth box is devoted to the William O. McGeehan Papers, which contains a limited amount of correspondence and some fictional and journalistic works.

UALSC maintains typed inventories for the fifty-three boxes which make up the Treadwell collection.

ANNOTATED SECONDARY BIBLIOGRAPHY: REVIEWS

This secondary bibliography lists English-language reviews of significant productions of Treadwell's plays, as well as reviews of her two novels. Much of this material is available only from newspaper clippings, scrapbooks, or microfilm. Many of the clippings in the University of Arizona Library Special Collections (UALSC) are hand dated and sourced by Treadwell. I have indicated in brackets those instances in which information on clippings remains incomplete or unverifiable. Unless otherwise noted, all citations with bracketed information are clippings found at UALSC.

1915-1919

1915

R001   Gleeson, Edgar T. "Actress and Author Share Big Triumph." *San Francisco Bulletin* [1-2 Feb. 1915].
        Reviewing Treadwell's *An Unwritten Chapter*, Gleeson attests to record houses and "genuine enthusiasm" at the Pantages Theater. "Miss Treadwell has brought to the act the same broad sympathy and understanding that characterized her serial in the *Bulletin* on this same subject."

1920-1929

1922

R002   Broun, Heywood. "The New Play." *New York World* 15 Dec. 1922.
        Gringo is probably the most "authentic picture of Mexico" seen on the stage. Nevertheless, Treadwell tried to

tell too much in three acts.

R003   Broun, Heywood. "Seeing Things at Night." *New York World* 24 Dec. 1922.
              Although there is much in *Gringo* that is "excellent" and "exciting," the work contains material "which is of no consequence whether or not it happens to be true."

R004   Corbin, John. "Americans in Mexico." *New York Times* 15 Dec. 1922: 26.
              Corbin is drawn to Edna Hibberd and her characterization of the half-breed Bessie, a character "finely imagined and remorselessly psychologized."

R005   Corbin, John. "The Critic and His Orient." *New York Times* 24 Dec. 1922: 14.
              In his second review of *Gringo*, Corbin again focuses on the character of Bessie, concluding that the play "is a document on the evils of mongrelization." As a play, *Gringo* is "disappointing" melodrama.

R006   Craig, James. "*Gringo*: New Sophie Treadwell Play a Story of Banditry and Tangled Affections in Mexico." *New York Mail* 15 Dec. 1922.
              Craig is disappointed the play did not offer a more nationalistic treatment of Mexican banditry, believing that the action offered "a superlative chance to 'get' a Mexican bandit and thereby make amends for that conspicuous failure in 'getting' [Pancho] Villa." Notes the audience almost stopped the show with applause for Hibberd as Bessie.

R007   Dale, Alan. "*Gringo* Offered at Comedy Theatre." *New York American* 15 Dec. 1922.
              Gringo works too hard to be "colorful." The women characters "were hysterical and possessed of the most loving hearts," while the males were "noisy, demonstrative and melodramatic."

R008   Darnton, Charles. "*Gringo*: Poor White Trash in Mexico." *New York Evening World* 15 Dec. 1922.
              The Mexican characters were treated sympathetically, but the Americans "were a worthless lot."

R009   Field, Louise Maunsell. "Across the Footlights: Comments on the
        Best Plays of the Month." [Unsourced clipping, 1922-23.]
                Faults *Gringo* for having too many plot threads and
        only one character of any sympathy (Stephen Trent).
        Nevertheless, Field anticipates "with much interest"
        Treadwell's next play.

R010   "*Gringo* at the Comedy." *New York Evening Telegram* 15 Dec. 1922.
                This "notable drama" is applauded for its "genuinely
        dramatic story" and especially for its characterization of
        Bessie. The critic takes issue with the ending and Myra's
        choice to stay with "her absolutely worthless mate."

R011   Hammond, Percy. "Lectures and the Drama." *New York Tribune* 24
        Dec. 1922.
                In his second review of *Gringo*, Hammond notes
        Treadwell has revised the play "here and there." He
        especially approves of the new ending, in which Bessie "hits
        the trail" following Tito and carrying his saddlebags.
        Hammond believed the previous ending involving the love
        triangle of Leonard, Myra and Steven Trent "awkward."

R012   Hammond, Percy. "Miss Treadwell's *Gringo* is an Exciting Narrative,
        Employing No Hokum." *New York Tribune* 15 Dec. 1922.
                Gringo is "a graphic, animated story, well told, well
        acted and pretty well scene painted." Calls Treadwell
        "intrepid and original" for employing a central character who
        is unsympathetic.

R013   Marsh, Leo A. "*Gringo* Seen at Comedy Theatre." *New York
        Telegraph* 15 Dec. 1922.
                Believes the play suffers from having two plots, one
        centering on the Americans and the other on the Mexican
        bandits.

R014   "The Only Woman War Correspondent." *New York Tribune* 24 Dec.
        1922.
                Brief notice of *Gringo* as "a story well told in a play
        well acted." Includes a photo of Treadwell.

R015   Playgoer, The. "*Gringo*, Drama of Mexican Life, Comes to the
        Comedy." *New York Evening Sun* 15 Dec. 1922.
                Applauds Treadwell's manipulation of suspense,

finding it "quite impossible . . . to predict what would happen in the last act." The anonymous critic is ultimately disappointed, though, when Myra chooses to stay with her "worthless husband" instead of going off with Trent.

R016   Smith, Alison. "Plays and Players." [*New York Globe* 1922.]
Smith admires the character of Bessie, "the most perfect characterization of a seventeen-year-old girl we have seen for many seasons." She especially appreciates how Treadwell avoids the typical depiction of an ingenue as "delicate and luminous" in favor of one who is "a mixture of rebellion and palpitating hopes."

R017   West, Julia. "*Gringo* Play of Modern Mexico." [Unsourced clipping, 1922.]
West believes Tito to be a thinly veiled depiction of Pancho Villa. She admires Ruben's "ingratiating, sardonic" characterization, McClintic's realistic staging ("including the burro"), and the "splendid affair" found in the last act.

R018   Woollcott, Alexander. "The Incautious Miss Treadwell." *New York Herald* 24 Dec. 1922.
Although Woollcott despairs of "Miss Treadwell ever writing a great popular success," he concludes that *Gringo* was "worth doing."

R019   Woollcott, Alexander. "Miss Treadwell's Play." *New York Herald* 15 Dec. 1922: 14.
Compares *Gringo* to Broadway's ealier play on Mexico, *The Bad Man*, finding Treadwell's play to be "a somewhat richer blend of comedy and melodrama."

1923

R020   Andrews, Kenneth. "Broadway, Our Literary Signpost." *Bookman* 56 (1923): 749-50.
Andrews is disappointed to learn that Mexican bandits are not romantic men having "florid orgies" in "inaccessible hiding places" but rather "pretty dirty people." *Gringo* is "amateurish in construction" and all the characters unsympathetic.

R021   B. "Helen Hayes in Dainty Comedy." *Hartford Daily Times* 13 Nov.
       1923.
              "Loney Lee is a delicate and at times perilously
       fragile comedy, never hilarious, but with touches of delicious
       humor; seldom dramatic, but with moments of near-dramatic
       tensity." Only a small audience saw Helen Hayes's charming
       performance in the large auditorium of Parson's Theatre.

R022   Blitz, Horace. "Helen Hayes in Good Play Here." *Atlantic City
       Gazette-Review* 6 Nov. 1923.
              Finds the "new and delightful role" of Loney to be
       "adapted perfectly" to Hayes's personality.

R023   Ewan, Ruth Osborne. "Loney Lee." *Variety* 8 Nov. 1923: 19.
              Despite calling *Loney Lee* "the female counterpart to
       Merton of the Movies," Ewan dismisses the work as "a mass
       of artificial hokum" unworthy of the talents of Hayes.

R024   *"Gringo."* *Theatre Magazine* Feb. 1923: 19.
              Only José Ruben's performance rises above the
       "theatrical clap-trap" of Treadwell's play. "At no point does
       the piece approach dramatic form much less dramatic power."

R025   Macgowan, Kenneth. "Seen on the Stage: *Gringo."* *Vogue* [Jan.
       1923].
              Calling Treadwell "a writer who has spent too much
       time in Mexico," Macgowan attacks *Gringo* for its unrealistic
       dialogue, its faulty plot construction full of "false leads," and
       its waffling between melodrama and serious psychological
       drama. Director Guthrie McClintic is faulted for a lack of
       ensemble and "inner character" acting.

R026   "Miss Helen Hayes Has Pleasant Play." *Hartford Daily Courant* 13
       Nov. 1923.
              Loney Lee is neither sophisticated enough for New
       Yorkers nor sufficiently naive enough to please the "hokum
       eaters who do abound in the metropolis." The "amusing
       situations" and "shrewd" characterizations are well-acted.

R027   "New Plays Out of Town." *New York Times* 11 Nov. 1923, sec. 8: 2.
              Reprints excerpts from R022.

R028　　Smith, E. F.　"Helen Hayes as Charming as Ever."　[Unsourced clipping, November 1923.]
　　　　　　While built around an "interesting theme," the love affair between Loney and Richard in *Loney Lee* needs more development. The play's second act and Hayes's performance are highlights.

1925

R029　　Abel.　"*O Nightingale*."　*Variety* 22 Apr. 1925.
　　　　　　"It's an ultra 'sweet' show."　While "chatty," the "perfect" casting does much to sustain the action.

R030　　"Author Plays a Part in *O Nightingale*: New Comedy at the Forty-ninth Street Theatre is Entertaining and Well Written."　*New York Times* 16 Apr. 1925, sec. 10: 25.
　　　　　　The story line is rather thin, and often the scenes "run a little down hill at the finish instead of building to their climaxes."　Treadwell as Mme. Istomina is "quite good," but most of the praise goes to Martha-Bryan Allen as Loney.

R031　　Benchley, Robert.　"Drama: Coasting."　*Life* 7 May 1925: 22.
　　　　　　Calls *O Nightingale* a "quite nice" play "performed by nice people."

R032　　Dale, Alan.　"*O Nightingale* is New Offering at the 49th Street."　*New York American* 23 Apr. 1925.
　　　　　　With a subject that demands brevity, Treadwell went to excesses in trying to write a sweet, charming play.　Likens the play to a crocus fighting off winter.

R033　　Davis, Charles Belmont.　"*O Nightingale*, at 49th Street Theater, 'A Genuine Comedy.'"　*New York Herald Tribune* 16 Apr. 1925.
　　　　　　Offers　much　praise　for　*O　Nightingale*--its imaginative story, "true" dialogue and "very natural and . . . human" characters.　The entire cast is "excellent."

R034　　Davis, Charles Belmont.　Rev. of *O Nightingale*.　*Hartford Courant* [Apr. 1925].
　　　　　　Believes the play is due for a long run, especially bcause its humor ranges from the subtle to the broadly farcical and will appeal to any theatregoer.

R035   Davis, Charles Belmont. "The Shop Window." *New York Herald Tribune* 26 Apr. 1925.
         Same review as R034.

R036   Dudley, Bide. "*O Nightingale. New York Evening World* 16 Apr. 1925.
         Although the story "sounds like a lot of tommy-rot," the play "was so delightfully acted and so full of genuine wit" that it will prove an unheralded success. Treadwell's portrayal of Mme Istomina was "excellently presented."

R037   Fife, Peggy. "*O Nightingale* at 49th St. Poor Play with Good Cast." *New York Graphic* 18 Apr. 1925.
         Some good action, but "jerky" and lacking in enough "business" to keep audience interest. "Some clever acting."

R038   Gillette, Don Carle. "*O Nightingale.*" *Billboard* 2 May 1925.
         Incorrectly calls *O Nightingale* a "first play" by Treadwell. Despite its "promising qualities," the play lacks the "kick in the denouement" necessary for success. Constance Eliot [Treadwell] "contributes a natural and clear portrayal."

R039   L., M. "*The Sapphire Ring* Good Drama; *O Nightingale* is Sprightly." *New York Daily News* 16 Apr. 1925: 24.
         A "keenly appreciative audience" welcomed this "highly diverting" comedy. "In these days of the jazz age, we never surmised there was so much innocence in the world, but Martha-Bryan Allen proved it with a fine piece of acting."

R040   Mantle, Burns. "*O, Nightingale* The Broadway." *New York News* 23 Apr. 1925.
         While *O Nightingale* is "a jolly little comedy . . . wittily written and wisely analytical," Mantle "wanted to like it better and couldn't find the excuse." The character of Loney is unrealistically naive.

R041   "New Plays." *Time* 27 Apr. 1925.
         Although not a new story, *O Nightingale* at least has found "new tracks on which to run old wheels."

R042   "*O, Nightingale.*" *Brooklyn Citizen* 17 Apr. 1925.
The play's "Cinderella-like story" is "delightful."
While the story is "rather thin," the performances and
characters are interesting.

R043   "*O Nightingale.*" *Town Topics* 23 Apr. 1925.
Thanks to Allen's performance, the play triumphs.
It is a bit short on story, but is "cleverly put together."

R044   "*O Nightingale.*" *Picture Play Magazine* July 1925: [n.p.].
Despite "excessive lack of sophistication" given to
the character of Loney, "which almost leads you to suspect
that she is not very bright," the play is "full of humor and
poetry" and makes for a "merry and stimulating evening."

R045   "*O Nightingale*--A Play That is Consistently Good.*" *Wall Street News*
18 Apr. 1925.
Calls *O Nightingale* "one of the most refreshing and
most consistently entertaining plays I have seen in many
moons."

R046   "*O Nightingale* at 49th Street Theatre is Pleasing and Witty."
Women's Wear Daily 18 Apr. 1925.
The programme's billing of the play as a "spring
comedy" appropriately reflects the "youthful vivacity of the
principal character." This "extremely well written" comedy
"will undoubtedly become one of the talked of plays of the
season."

R047   "*O Nightingale* at the Forty-ninth.*" *New York Sun* 16 Apr. 1925.
The story is an old one: "It's a yarn Adam must
have told to Eve to keep her home nights." Only Allen as
Loney "approximated what passes for acting on Broadway."

R048   "*O Nightingale* is Charming.*" *Zit's Weekly* 25 Apr. 1925.
Recommends the comedy as a pleasing amusement
highlighted by Allen's performance. Eliot [Treadwell] "could
have been a bit more suave and less noisily temperamental."
The play would make a "good film."

R049   "*O Nightingale* is Refreshing Comedy.*" *Journal of Commerce* 16
Apr. 1925.
Despite a slow first scene, *O Nightingale* "rolls

merrily on to a happy and hilarious finale."

R050   "*O Nightingale* Presented Here." *New York Telegraph* 16 Apr. 1925.
        Allen as Loney "carries the whole performance,"
        while the "adequate" cast is stuck in characters that "have
        nothing very difficult to do."

R051   "*O Nightingale*, Witty and Sparkling Comedy." *New York News-
        Record* 18 Apr. 1925.
                Same as R046.

R052   "*O Nightingale* a Splendid Comedy." *New York Commercial* 18 Apr.
        1925.
                The play is "craftsmanly and of uncommon charm"
        and "soars high among the best of Broadway comedies."

R053   Pollack, Arthur. "Plays and Things: *O Nightingale*." *Brooklyn Daily
        Eagle* 16 Apr. 1925.
                Although the story "has been told in a hundred
        different ways" previously, it remains appealing due to
        Allen's "engaging" performance. Treadwell "did well" with
        Mme. Istomina.

R054   Rev. of *O Nightingale*. *Club Fellow* 22 Apr. 1925.
                Cites Allen's performance as "one of the season's
        most artistic and demure." Treadwell also gave a "perfect
        characterization" as Mme. Istomina.

R055   Rowland, Arthur. "A Spring Comedy." *The Official Metropolitan
        Guide* 10 May 1925: 25.
                Although the premise is "tenuous," *O Nightingale*
        succeeds due to Treadwell's clever dialogue and subtle
        skirting of "the more impossible situations."

R056   S., A. "At the 49th Street Theatre: *O Nightingale*." *New York
        Morning World* 16 Apr. 1925.
                This anonymous critic recalls Treadwell's earlier
        Broadway play, *Gringo*, a play which "was not a conspicuous
        success, probably because a public which loves to sentimalize
        over young girlhood, hates to watch it chase one-eyed Bad
        Men" (Tito).   In *O Nightingale*, Treadwell has
        overcompensated by making her heroine "innocent beyond all
        belief." Despite her shortcomings as a playwright, Treadwell

gives an "excellent performance" in the secondary role of
Mme. Istomina.

R057   Vreeland, Frank. "*O Nightingale*. Sophie Treadwell's Comedy Comes
        to Pass at Last on Broadway." *New York Telegram-Mail* 16
        Apr. 1925.
                O Nightingale is marred slightly by "an occasional
        lapse by Miss Treadwell into the short story technique she
        knows so well," sometimes too casual direction and "first
        night nervousness." The play, though, has potential for
        success.

                                    1927

R058   B., N. J. "Ford's Shows *Wild Honey*, Play of Love." *Baltimore
        American* 18 Oct. 1927.
                "*Wild Honey*'s appeal is only for the very sweet."

R059   "*Bound* Shows Human Nature." *Waterville* [Maine] *Morning Sentinel*
        21 June 1927: 9.
                Review of *Bound* at its "filled to capacity" premiere
        at the Lakewood Theatre. Finds the play "mostly a drab,
        unpleasant story," but applauds Treadwell for not letting her
        subject and characters degenerate into "the sort of 'sex drama'
        that has been nauseating metropolitan audiences several
        seasons back."

R060   D., G. C. "*Wild Honey* Attraction at Ford's Theater." *Baltimore
        Morning Sun* [Oct. 1927].
                Likens the play to old-fashioned melodramas,
        augmented only "by the entire English lexicon of swearing."
        Treadwell's direction was "askew," resulting in the
        supposedly most dramatic moments being met with "highest
        hilarity" by the audience.

R061   Kanour, Gilbert. "Theater Folks Cold to Heroine's Tears." *Baltimore
        Evening Sun* 19 Oct. 1927: 15.
                Review of *Wild Honey*'s tryout in Baltimore. The
        audience "tittered and cackled" at this "innocent" play when
        they were supposed to have been "warm and sympathetic."
        As an experienced playwright, Treadwell "ought to know
        better."

R062   Mullikin, J. C. "Wild, but Not Honey." *Baltimore Daily Post* 18 Oct.
        1927.
                Believes Treadwell tried to rely on the "spectacle of
        a young lady yanking off her dress . . . and a couple of cuss-
        words" to spice up an otherwise old-fashioned melodrama.

R063   Tall. "*Wild Honey.*" *Variety* 26 Oct. 1927.
                Producer "Crosby Gaige must have sunk all of a
        dollar and a half into this production." The single setting
        with few changes of props does little to this "dull and drab
        fable."

R064   "*Wild Honey* New Drama, at Ford's." *Baltimore Evening Sun* 18 Oct.
        1927: 26.
                Mostly recounts plot summary.

R065   "*Wild Honey* Runs Wild at Ford's." *Baltimore News* 18 Oct. 1927.
                This brief review concludes that "*Wild Honey* is
        quite, quite bad."

                                      1928

R066   Anderson, John. "Snyder Case Suggested in a Magnificent Tragedy."
        New York Evening Journal 8 Sept. 1928.
                An ebullient review. *Machinal* "is superb and
        unbearable and harrowing in a way that leaves you bereft of
        any immediate comparison, and leaves you, too, for that
        matter, a limp and tear-stained wreck." Never before in the
        theatre have sound effects been used with such "stunning
        effect." Treadwell's writing possesses a "fine fluency,"
        Arthur Hopkins's direction is "unfailingly effective," and Zita
        Johann's performance is "thrilling" and "heartbreaking."

R067   "At the Theaters." *New Haven Times Register* 3 Sept. 1928.
                Performed before a "large and appreciative audience"
        in New Haven, *Machinal* is a play "sure to create wide-
        spread comment." Robert Edmond Jones and George Schaff
        are praised for their designs.

R068   Atkinson, Brooks. "Against the City Clatter." *New York Times* 16
        Sept. 1928, sec. 3: 4.
                Machinal is "an illuminating, measured drama such

as we are not likely to see again." Atkinson believes other murder plays and news columns have described such a "tawdry yarn" before, but they "have never disclosed it, as *Machinal* does, in terms of an impersonal exposition of character in conflict with environment."

R069   Atkinson, Brooks. "The Play: a Tragedy of Submission." *New York Times* 8 Sept. 1928.
       Machinal cast a "subtly moving spell" on its audience, but Atkinson has a difficult time pinpointing the reasons for the play's power. He finally admits that "the precise quality of *Machinal* escapes definition in this ambiguous review."

R070   Beach, Burton T. "Tolstoy's Stern Note Sounded in Shriek at Chair." *Chicago Post* 14 Sept. 1928.
       Treadwell's story of a "woman's dull, dreary, deadening submissiveness to the monotone" is reminiscent in "motif and key" to Tolstoy's later fiction. Beach believes audiences will leave *Machinal* with "a subtle sense of sorrow" for the central character, as well as a regret that they "did not have an opportunity to kick to death the laughing jackass she married and murdered."

R071   Benchley, Robert C. Rev. of *Machinal*. *Life* 28 Sept. 1928: 17.
       Treadwell has "eliminated most of the trying features" from earlier expressionist plays. The scene between Johann and Clark Gable "was as delicate and lovely an idyl of illicit love as we remember seeing for a long, long time."

R072   Brackett, Charles. "The Theatre: Order, Please." *New Yorker* 15 Sept. 1928: 34.
       Even though Treadwell is able to master the technique of expressionist writing without letting it become a distraction, the character of the Young Woman "is a whining, neurotic girl full of self-pity and repressions," not at all like its real-life model, Ruth Snyder, who possessed "fire, and vigor, and a great lust of life."

R073   "The Broadway Stage." *West Palm Beach Times* 18 Sept. 1928.
       Brief review of *Machinal* along with other recent Broadway openings.

R074   Carb, David. "Seen on the Stage." *Vogue* 27 Oct. 1928: 74-75.
        Provides a lengthy description of Jones's settings, as
        well as the final lighting effect.

R075   Clark, Barrett H. "New Plays on the Broadway Front." *The Drama*
        19 (1928): 45.
        Treadwell simply assumes her audience will find the
        Young Woman deserving of sympathy. Clark, however, feels
        she is "presented as a stupid, sullen, dishonest, uncontrolled
        female." Clark actually "felt sorry" for her husband and
        "would have cheered if he had carried her bodily to the
        window and chucked her out."

R076   Coleman, Robert. "*Machinal* Lacks Greatness, But is Full of Interest."
        New York Mirror [Sept. 1928].
        Credits   Treadwell   and   Hopkins   with   "the
        glorification of a neurotic murderess without becoming
        offensively maudlin." Coleman predicts a "box office smash.
        A real hit. Sexy, sobby and sure fire."

R077   Dash, Thomas R. "Zita Johann Gets Ovation in *Machinal*." *Women's
        Wear Daily* 10 Sept. 1928.
        The play combines a "cogency and palpability of
        theme" with a "technical proficiency" in staging not seen in
        previous expressionist plays.

R078   Davis, Burton. "Divorce, Murder, Suicide?" *New York Sun* 29 Oct.
        1928.
        Discusses *Machinal* as one of four plays in the
        current Broadway season that deals with the problem of
        "What to do with a wife or husband who has become a bore,
        a burden and an annoyance." *Machinal*'s ending in
        electrocution proves that the Young Woman's method "has its
        drawbacks even though it makes magnificent drama when
        sympathetically produced by a genius of stagecraft."

R079   de Rohan, Pierre. "Good Taste and Artistry of Arthur Hopkins Patent
        in Each Scene of *Machinal*." *New York American* 16 Sept.
        1928.
        The play provides "one somber synthesis" of realism
        and expressionism, resulting in a "poignant suffering [which]
        becomes almost unbearable."

R080   de Rohan, Pierre. *"Machinal* Ugly But Great Play." *New York American* 8 Sept. 1928.
         Credits Treadwell for doing for theatre what Theodore Dreiser did for literature: "She has created a complete picture of life's bitterness and essential meanness, painted with the small, oft-repeated strokes of the realist, yet achieving in perspective the sweep and swing of expressionism." Although *Machinal* is "a great play," de Rohan is relatively certain it will not appeal to a large audience: "it was not written for the masses, but about them."

R081   Dick, Leon M. "In New York Town." [Unsourced clipping, 1928.]
         Finds *Machinal* an "adroitly handled" character study that is presented in a "modernistic" style which will "refresh those [spectators] who advance with the theatre."

R082   "The Editor Goes to the Play." *Theatre Magazine* Nov. 1928: 46-7.
         Not since O'Neill's *Strange Interlude* has "the American stage seen so truly a work of dramaturgic art and sincerity as *Machinal*." Treadwell's "forceful, beautiful, thrilling" play has "outstripped" earlier examples of expressionism with its "power and beauty."

R083   Field, Rowland. "Both Sides of the Curtain." [*Brooklyn Daily Times* 1928.]
         Hopkins gives *Machinal* a "tremendously striking production" resulting in one of the more "interesting" plays of the season.

R084   "Flowers for Miss Treadwell." *New York Telegraph* 16 Sept. 1928.
         Praises Treadwell's *Machinal* for depicting "a bedroom scene between a man and a girl married to another without the slightest hint of shame, justification or moral finger-pointing in it."

R085   Gabriel, Gilbert W. "Last Night's First Night: *Machinal,* a Tragedy in Fine Stage Clothing, With Sudden Glory for Zita Johann." *New York Sun* 8 Sept. 1928.
         Although the Snyder-Gray trial has left uncomfortable and "grubby" perceptions in the minds of the public, *Machinal* succeeds in overcoming them, resulting in a play that is "cruelly beautiful and affecting."

R086   Grabe, W. C. "*Machinal* Shubert Play Very Pleasing." *New Haven Journal Courier* 4 Sept. 1928: 3.
> Hopkins, Jones, Schaff, and Johann are highly praised. The play is "tense, interesting" and reminiscent of *An American Tragedy*.

R087   Hammond, Percy. "The Theaters: Bold, but Not Too Bold." *New York Herald Tribune* 16 Sept. 1928, sec. 7: 1.
> Hopkins and Jones match Treadwell's search for theatrical innovation in *Machinal*, the end result of which "is the most honest compromise of adventure with prudence that the recent Drama has known."

R088   Hammond, Percy. "The Theaters: *Machinal*, a Good, Grim and Deftly New-Fangled Story of Why and How a Lady Killed Her Husband." *New York Herald Tribune* 8 Sept. 1928.
> Despite a "delirious" and "frenzied" opening scene, *Machinal* proves "one of the best of the unusual dramas." Johann and George Stillwell are "so excellent that they will never . . . be sufficiently applauded."

R089   Hutchinson, Percy. "As the Theatre Practices the Art of Homicide." *New York Times*, sec. 10: 1.
> Discusses *Machinal* as one of three current Broadway shows using murder as their subject. Dismisses Treadwell's play as too pessimistic and devoid of artistic "beauty."

R090   Ibee. "*Machinal*." *Variety* 19 Sept. 1928.
> Treadwell has removed the "sordidness" from the Snyder trial, and Hopkins's use of lighting in the final scene proved "exceptionally interesting."

R091   Jennings, Mabelle. "Down in Front." [Unsourced clipping, 1928.]
> Hopkins's subtle staging greatly aids Treadwell's *Machinal*, a "monotone" play with readily familiar characters.

R092   Kaufman, S. Jay. "Hopkins does *Machinal* Magnificently." *New York Telegraph* 8 Sept. 1928.
> Kaufman believes the play's title refers to the "dramatic machinations" and scheming "deliberation" of the mind of the central character. Treadwell's story "holds like a vice," even though the opening and courtroom scenes lag.

Hopkins's subtle and truthful direction is so highly praised
that Kaufman urges others directing in New York to go see
the play to "study."

R093   Krutch, Joseph Wood. "Behaviorism and Drama." *The Nation* 26
Sept. 1928: 302.
   Although *Machinal* does not much resemble the
Snyder case, the play does seem to have "that same air of
being at once true and unbelievable" as do many
contemporary crimes reported in the "tabloids." In like
manner, Treadwell too often leaves the facts and motives of
her case unexplained and "indigestible." Hopkins's direction
is highly commended.

R094   Littell, Robert. "Chiefly about *Machinal*." *Theatre Arts* Nov. 1928:
774, 777-80.
   Littell credits Treadwell for not trying to evoke
"sympathy and forgiveness" for the "two monsters" of Snyder
and Gray, but for "the gradual shedding of light in all the
corners of a dark tragedy." He especially praises Treadwell
for her use of suggestiveness and allusion, "giving us
overtones and glimpses and other dimensions which the
ordinary self-contained play is too 'well-made' ever to
tolerate."

R095   Littell, Robert. "The Play: *Machinal*." *New York Evening Post* 8
Sept. 1928.
   The second part of the play reveals Treadwell's
belief that Snyder's execution "shows the vengeance of
society for an act it did not understand well enough to
forgive." The scenes in the honeymoon hotel ("a gem of
quiet horror"), Roe's apartment ("full of melancholy charm")
and the execution (which "leaves you chilled and unstrung")
are singled out as most effective. Hopkins's direction is
superb, and Jones's sets "beyond praise."

R096   Littell, Robert. "Two on the Aisle: a Few Reasons Why *Machinal*
Holds its Head Above the Plays of the New Season." *New
York Evening Post* 15 Sept. 1928.
   Treadwell's use of short scenes and repetition are
particularly innovative, as is her avoidance of the traditional
theatrical articulateness found so often in tragic characters:
"Real feelings, in ordinary people, are bottled up, and trickle

out obscurely, and continue to trickle out, and are never quite unbottled."

R097   Locke, Charles O. "Arthur Hopkins Scores Triumph with Production of *Machinal.*" *Chicago Journal of Commerce* 12 Oct. 1928.
Locke finds it "doubtful if a more significant play than *Machinal* will be seen upon our stage for some time to come." Hopkins grounds the "new dramatic methods" of expressionism with realistic treatment in production details. Locke provides numerous descriptions of staging moments, including the final scene in the dark.

R098   Lockridge, Richard. "*Machinal,* Murder and Motives." *New York Sun* 1 Oct. 1928.
Lockridge takes comfort that Treadwell has offered some explanation for the "monster"-like behavior of Ruth Snyder, but he realizes she has taken great liberties with the facts and "piled on the agony" for her stage heroine. Snyder was not, as is the Young Woman in this play, "hysterical," "sensitive," or "a victim."

R099   "*Machinal.*" *Bulletin of Parents League* Nov. 1928.
Even Johann's suberb performance is not able to rescue the play from the "tawdriness" of its story.

R100   "*Machinal* Proves Absorbing Drama at the Shubert." *New Haven Register* 4 Sept. 1928.
The second half of the play is marred by an overly long courtroom scene. Much detail is given to Jones's "scenic simplification" by using only a cyclorama and one wall.

R101   Mantle, Burns. "*Machinal*--The Perfect Exhibit." *New York Daily News* 8 Sept. 1928.
Mantle remains "puzzled" by his emotional indifference to the play despite his admiration for the "mechanistic perfection" of the whole production.

R102   Mantle, Burns. "The Drama Called *Machinal.*" *New York Sunday News* 16 Sept. 1928: 59.
A week after his initial review of *Machinal,* Mantle is still baffled as to why the production left him emotionally "as cold as a fish." Still, he recognizes it as "the perfect

American tragedy perfectly projected."

R103   Markey, Morris. "Panorama of Plays and Players." *Panorama: New York's Illustrated News Weekly* 1 Oct. 1928.
        Treadwell displayed her heroine's pain, but did not explain it.

R104   McCormick, Elsie. "A Piece of Her Mind." *New York World.* 26 Sept. 1928.
        McCormick laments how "boredom" and "ennui" have become the subjects of modern tragedy and the supposed cause for audience sympathy, especially in regard to women. Nevertheless, McCormick finds much "food for reflection" in *Machinal.*

R105   "Miss Sophie Treadwell." *Town & Country* 15 Oct. 1928.
        Praises *Machinal* for its "terrifying picture of unrecognized murder . . . George H. Jones was a killer." Also provides brief biographical material on Treadwell.

R106   Mulhern, Donald. "The New Play: Hopkins Presents, in Futurist Form, a Parallel to the Snyder Case." *Brooklyn Standard Union* 8 Sept. 1928.
        Compares *Machinal* to *The Hairy Ape*, but concludes that Treadwell's play lacks O'Neill's genius.

R107   Nathan, George Jean. "A Pretentious Zero." *American Mercury* 15 (1928): 376-7.
        In his usual ascerbic tone, Nathan dismisses *Machinal* as pretentious. Hopkins only chose to direct the play so he could show off his stage "hocus-pocus." The play's "hollowness" is plainly evident, and the final lighting effect recalls Belasco's stage wizardry. Such productions ought to bring "opprobrium and tomatoes to the term 'art theatre.'"

R108   "New Plays in Manhattan." *Time* 17 Sept. 1928: 24.
        Machinal sometimes "slips into banality," but nevertheless has "moments which are so true that they are tragic."

R109   "The New York Stage: Expressionism." *Manchester Guardian* 19
        Dec. 1928.
            Machinal is "an uncommonly well-written and
        moving tragedy" influenced by Ernst Toller and Bertolt
        Brecht.

R110   Osborn, E. W. "The New Plays: *Machinal.*" *New York Evening
        World* 8 Sept. 1928.
            Osborn is as baffled by the play's title as by
        Hopkins's decision to stage a play containing "no high nor
        helpful dramatic purpose."

R111   P., H. T. "New Manner, Old Matter, True Tragedy: In *Machinal,* a
        Brave Play Strikes Home for Itself and Breeds an Actress."
        Boston Transcript 29 Sept. 1928: 6.
            This lengthy review contains some of the most
        detailed descriptions of the Broadway staging.

R112   "Plays and Players." *Providence Journal* 16 Sept. 1928.
            Notes the relationship between *Machinal* and the
        Snyder-Gray trial, then excerpts Gilbert Gabriel's review
        (R085).

R113   Pollack, Arthur. "Plays and Things." *Brooklyn Daily Eagle* 30 Sept.
        1928.
            Praises Treadwell's blending of expressionism with
        realism, as well as her portrayal of the Babbitt-like husband
        without "sticking loud labels on him."

R114   Pollack, Arthur. "The Theaters." *Brooklyn Daily Eagle* 8 Sept. 1928.
            Machinal is "fine and gentle and delicate," and is
        strongly preferred over earlier ventures in expressionism. The
        final "actorless scene is one of the most impressive things the
        theatre has offered," and Johann's performance is "something
        very close to perfection."

R115   Rev. of *Machinal. F.P.A. World* 15 Sept. 1928.
            Machinal is "a fine tragick play" if a bit "verbose."

R116   Rev. of *Machinal. Brooklyn Times* 16 Sept. 1928.
            Machinal's success is due in part to Johann and the
        overall production, but "mainly because it is such a thorough
        piece of dramatic craftsmanship."

R117   Rev. of *Machinal. Town & Country* 1 Oct. 1928.
        Praises the first half of the play, but beginning with
        the courtroom scene it "drops to the plane of not too skillful
        melodrama."

R118   Ruhl, Arthur. "Off-Stage and On." *New York Herald Tribune* 20
        Sept. 1928.
        One of the few critics to assert that *Machinal* bears
        the stamp of a "feminine" writing style, one that contains "a
        kind of desperate intensity, at once wistful, defiant, and
        fiercely in earnest."

R119   Ruhl, Arthur. "Second Nights." *New York Herald Tribune*, sec. 7:
        [n.p.].
        Ruhl provides excellent descriptions of staging
        details in *Machinal*. He marvels at the emotional effect of
        the drawing-room scene between Johann and Stillwell, even
        though "Almost nothing is said."

R120   "Ruth Snyder Motif Features *Machinal*, New Broadway Hit." *New
        York Herald* [Paris] 3 Oct. 1928.
        "According to those who were present," the final
        scene in the play was "a faithful reproduction of the death of
        Mrs. Snyder."

R121   Sayler, Oliver M. Rev. of *Machinal. Footlight and Lamplight: a
        Weekly Review of Plays, Books and Periodicals Broadcast
        from Gimbel Brothers, New York* 17 Sept. 1928.
        Credits the play as "one of the first . . . by an
        American dramatist successfully to merge and fuse
        expressionist form and expressionist content." It surpasses
        O'Neill's *The Emperor Jones* and *Strange Interlude* in its
        depiction of the subconscious.

R122   Seldes, Gilbert. "The Theatre." *The Dial* 85 (1928): 445-6.
        Machinal is "riddled with faults," including a
        combination of styles, an inconsistent realization of the
        central character and an overly "repulsive" portrayal of the
        Husband.

R123   Smith, Alison. "The New Play: Mills of the Gods." *New York World*
        10 Sept. 1928: 13.
        Not since Georg Kaiser's *From Morn to Midnight*

has expressionism as a theatrical style "been so completely realized." Although *Machinal*'s theme is "honest and moving," Treadwell has weighted her story too heavily in favor of the Young Woman, depicting the males in the play as "monsters of brutality and treachery."

R124   Terrett, Courtenay. "*Machinal* Slated to be 'Important' Season Play, but Doomed to Oblivion." *New York Evening Telegram* 8 Sept. 1928.

Although *Machinal* is a "shrewdly and often beautifully written" play, Terrett feels it is doomed to be remembered solely as "the play about Ruth Snyder." Terrett is convinced Treadwell wrote the work to capitalize on public interest in the executed murderess.

R125   V., W. "*Machinal*." *Drama Calendar* 25 Sept. 1928.

The play is "simple and universal," the cast "perfect," the settings "inspired," and the direction "masterly." *Machinal* "will long set a standard by which plays of this type will be judged."

R126   Watts, Richard, Jr. "Applying the Pulmotor to Modernist Drama." *New York Herald Tribune* 23 Sept. 1928.

Machinal supplies a much-needed "pulmotor" to the developing expressionist dramas, and Treadwell's choice of this style matches her theme perfectly. Watts also claims, via a report from Whitney Bolton, that the Young Woman's comic explanation in court as to why she did not divorce her husband was taken directly from Snyder's trial testimony.

R127   Winchell, Walter. "*Machinal* at the Plymouth." *New York Graphic* [8 Sept. 1928].

Winchell, who covered the Ruth Snyder murder trial, believes the play recalls Snyder's "unhappy life," especially in the courtroom scene, "where much of the testimony was taken verbatim from the trial." It is one of "the few intelligent presentations to be seen."

R128   Winchell, Walter. "Your Broadway and Mine." *New York Graphic* [20 Sept. 1928].

Winchell refutes Alison Smith's claim that *Machinal* was not based on Snyder. "Golly, even Miss Johann's attire during the courtroom scene was almost identical to that worn by Mrs. Snyder at the time. The same black hat pattern, the same black ensemble, too." Winchell goes on to claim that the Young Woman's "cries of despair in the cell scene were copied almost word for word from those uttered in the execution chamber" by Snyder.

R129   Winslow, Thyra Samter. "Playthings." *New York Jewish Tribune* 21 Sept. 1928.
        Although *Machinal* is "a bit too harrowing if you're nervous," altogether it is "a thrilling and touching play."

R130   Young, Stark. "Joy on the Mountains." *New Republic* 31 Oct. 1928: 299-300.
        Young believes there is "a kind of bravery . . . in the nakedness of [Treadwell's] themes" that is exhibited in scenes such as those between the Young Woman and her husband. The scene in Roe's apartment contains "an underlying tone of a certain bare sorrow and fatal desire." The play begins to break down for Young with the introduction of too much realism in the courtroom scene.

1929

R131   Barnes, Howard. "*Ladies Leave* Proves Amusing Satire on Morals." *New York Tribune* 2 Oct. 1929.
        Mildly favorable review of this "pleasantly amusing if not very compelling satire on contemporary morals."

R132   Bellamy, Francis R. Rev. of *Ladies Leave*. *Outlook* 16 Oct. 1929: 272.
        Decries the morals of Zizi in *Ladies Leave*.

R133   Cushman, Howard. "*Ladies Leave* a Bright Unassuming Comedy by a Miss Sophie Treadwell." [Unsourced clipping, New York Public Library for the Performing Arts] 3 Oct. 1929.
        Although "no theatrical milestone," Cushman finds the play "funny as hell."

R134   Dudley, Bide. "*Ladies Leave*." *New York Evening World* 2 Oct. 1929.
        Dudley cannot figure out what the play is about. The play was received "calmly and quietly" by the audience.

R135   F., C. F. *"Ladies Leave*, a New Sophie Treadwell Play at the Charles
        Hopkins." *Brooklyn Times* 2 Oct. 1929.
                Compared to *Machinal, Ladies Leave* is "a total
        collapse." Finds the story "lacking" in climaxes, the ending
        unclear, and the "leading characters, especially Zizi, coldly
        indifferent to the properties of life."

R136   Krasna, Norman. "Another New Play." *New York Graphic* [Oct.
        1929].
                The Treadwell who "screamed out the wretchedness
        of the machine-age in tragic symbols and vulgar finger-
        pointing [in *Machinal*] has changed [in *Ladies Leave*] into a
        nice, motherly woman who uses a soft and insinuating
        crooning."

R137   *"Ladies Leave."* *Theatre Magazine* Dec. 1929: 68.
                Treadwell's play lacks "sprightliness" and "becomes
        eventually boring."

R138   *"Ladies Leave*, a Play of Polite Theatre." *New York Times* 2 Oct.
        1929: 28.
                This anonymous critic is disappointed that Treadwell
        cannot sustain the gaity of high comedy.

R139   *"Ladies Leave*, at the Hopkins, Is Modern Problem Comedy." *New
        York American* 3 Oct. 1929.
                Treadwell's simple comedy depicts the "eternal
        triangle" problem, but fails to resolve it: it "simply rotates on
        and on and never comes to end."

R140   *"Ladies Leave*: Sophie Treadwell's New Play Again Tells of
        Discontented Women." *Brooklyn Eagle* [2 Oct. 1929].
                Finds the subject matter of "a discontented wife" and
        her ensuing affair to be "a theme that is no longer new."

R141   Longacre, Betty. *"Ladies Leave."* *New York Standard Union* 2 Oct.
        1929.
                Longacre is one of the few New York critics to
        boldly praise *Ladies Leave*, calling it "the most sophisticated
        play of the season." The production is "perfectly cast."

R142   "Miss Treadwell Has a Smart Comedy in *Ladies Leave*." *New York News* [3 Oct. 1929].
The strong cast produces much fun, and Robert Edmond Jones's sets are praised.

R143   P., E. "Smart Comedy." *Brooklyn Citizen* 2 Oct. 1929.
Complimentary review of this "smart comedy," especially the first two acts.

R144   Rathbun, Stephen. "*Ladies Leave* Opens: Comedy by Sophie Treadwell at the Charles Hopkins." *New York Sun* 2 Oct. 1929.
Rathbun likes the last act, but not the first two. Says Zizi is "interested only in men. She lives in a man-centered world." Thus, she is not really a feminist and that is why *Ladies Leave* "is an unimportant play." Cites over-acting throughout the cast.

R145   Riley, Wilfred J. "*Ladies Leave*." *Billboard* 12 Oct. 1929.
This "flimsy, over bearing effort" takes a good idea and ruins it with "inept" execution. Most of the company is guilty of over-acting. Jones's sets are "as usual excellent."

R146   Smith, Alison. "In the Order of Their Appearance: More about the Ladies." [*New York World*] 6 Oct. 1929.
The opening of *Ladies Leave* missed "by only a few weeks the exact date of the arrival of *Machinal* last season." This new play is an "after-thought on the same theme."

R147   Smith, Alison. "Other New Play." *New York World* 2 Oct. 1929.
Smith dismisses *Ladies Leave* as "a flippant cartoon . . . a sort of comic strip of a marital triangle." Unfavorably compares the situation of the play to that of Ibsen's *A Doll's House*.

R148   Spewack, Samuel. "*Ladies Leave* Opens in Hopkins Theatre." *New York Telegram* 2 Oct. 1929.
Treadwell's new play is " a frothy little piece" not up to the "magnificent *Machinal* of last season." Notes the overacting of Henry Hull.

R149   U., W. A. *"Ladies Leave* at Hopkins with Henry Hull." *New York Journal* 2 Oct. 1929.
       Ladies Leave has "but little form and no substance."

R150   Waldorf, Wilella. *"Ladies Leave."* [Unsourced clipping, Oct. 1929.]
       Waldorf notes the audience's clear disapointment in comparing this play with *Machinal*. "So insipid and trifling is the conversation that it is necessary for the people of the play to work themselves into a temper and rush frantically about the stage in order to challenge any sort of attention."

R151   Warren, George C. "Daring Play Produced in Berkeley." [Unsourced clipping, 1929.]
       Review of the Playhouse Association of Berkeley's production of *Machinal*, a play that "comes close to the line of greatness . . . with a fatality like that of the Greek tragedies." This production seems to have followed the lead of last year's Broadway production in terms of simplified staging.

1930-1939

1931

R152   B., B. "Gloomy American Drama of Murder by a Business Girl." *London Daily Mirror* 16 July 1931.
       Although the play garnished praise in America, *The Life Machine*'s appeal in England "is likely to be restricted to those with whom depression is a hobby." The play is "morbid and gloomy."

R153   Baughan, E. A. "Ruth Snyder Case in a Play." *London News Chronicle* 16 July 1931.
       The Life Machine's central character "is so essentially without character or brain that her agonies never become tragedy." The play is "unpleasant, morbid and pretentious."

R154   Brown, Ivor. *"The Life Machine."* *London Observer* 19 July 1931.
       "The play is too sordid to be wholly tragic, the woebegone lady is too small and tiresome to be a heroine commanding all our sympathy."

R155   D., W. A.   "*Life Machine* at Garrick: Satire and Grand Guignol."
London Daily Telegraph 4 Aug. 1931.
Treadwell throws too much sympathy to the Young
Woman. "The husband has damp hands. It is enough. He
must die." Disapproves of the attempt to lure audiences by
billing the play on posters "for adults only."

R156   D., W. A.   "A Play of Mixed Styles--Expressionism and Grand
Guignol." *London Daily Telegraph* 16 July 1931.
The Life Machine is "an astounding mixture" of
expressionist satire and Grand Guignol realism. The play's
theme is "not artistically conceived" and the work "falls to
the ground with a resounding thump."

R157   "Execution in a Play--Grim Sounds Heard 'Off." *London Daily Mail*
16 July 1931.
The Life Machine proves "one of the very few
interesting plays of the summer season." Two "remarkable"
scenes are singled out: the honeymoon scene ("which is
frank enough to border on the unpleasant") and the final
scene ("when the audience actually hear the sound of the
execution off the stage"). David Horne's portrayal of the
husband is "almost embarrassing in its truth to a certain
type."

R158   G., M.   "A Play About a Girl in Torment." *London Evening News* 16
July 1931.
This critic is one of the few in London to praise *The
Life Machine*'s use of expressionistic techniques, believing
"there is something Greek about its mixture of abstraction
and humanity."

R159   H., H.   "*The Life Machine*." *London Observer* 9 Aug. 1931.
Mary Grew's performance as the Young Woman
"clearly gives melodrama the appearance of tragedy."

R160   L., S. R.   "Revolting Scenes in *The Life Machine*." *The Morning Post*
[London] 16 July 1931.
Treadwell's play is "a horrible thing," justifiably
banned by the censor. Some scenes are "revolting": the
honeymoon scene is "brutal in its intimacies"; the hospital
scene "a spectacle of torture"; the trial "a familiar thrill."

R161   *"The Life Machine."* *London Times* 16 July 1931.
          By the play's end, the Young Woman is little more
        than "a wounded animal blindly struggling to tear itself out
        of a trap," while the audience has "lost track of her motives."

R162   *"The Life Machine."* *London Sunday Times* 9 Aug. 1931.
          The play is "intellectually dishonest" in its
        insinuation that "all young women employed in offices are
        miserable." The husband "is really not a bad sort," and his
        coarseness is excusable, being married to "a hyper-sensitive,
        neurotic *pretentieuse*." Treadwell seems to have intended her
        heroine as a "Hedda Gabler of the masses."

R163   *"The Life Machine* at the Garrick." *London Times* 5 Aug. 1931.
          Mary Grew's performance rises above both the play
        itself and the cheap advertisements promoting its graphic
        nature.

R164   Lowrey, Flora. "Love Plus Banditry in Mexican Locale Make Lively
        Novel." [Unsourced clipping, 1931.]
          Cites Treadwell as an authority on Mexico before
        concluding that her story in *Lusita* "is a corking good one."

R165   *"Lusita."* *Birmingham News* 1 Nov. 1931.
          "It is a novel of rapid action and subtle analysis of
        character."

R166   "Mexican Adventure." *New York Times Book Review* 1 Nov. 1931: 7.
          Admires Treadwell's "credible" story and "delightful
        touches of humor" in *Lusita*. The villain is sympathetic and
        the hero "charming, likable and unheroic."

R167   "The Playhouses." *The Illustrated London News* 15 Aug. 1931.
          Despite "a general slackening of interest" during the
        numerous blackouts between scenes, *The Life Machine* at
        least "holds the attention to some extent." The Husband's
        numerous repetitions amount to a form of burlesque which
        seems out of place.

R168   "Plays & Pictures." *New Statesman and Nation* 25 July 1931: 110.
          The Young Woman's actions in *The Life Machine*
        are "childish in their spontaneity."

R169   "Realism Carried Too Far in an Excellent Drama." *London Daily Sketch* 16 July 1931.
    "Many girls marry fat men for their money and yet manage to be reasonably happy." The "realism" of many of the scenes in *The Life Machine* transcends good taste.

R170   Rev. of *The Life Machine*. *The Stage* [London] 23 July 1931.
    Most of the scenes are "studies in nastiness of some sort or another." Apparently a license will be granted for public performance of the play if certain dialogue is cut.

R171   Rev. of *The Life Machine*. *London News* 15 Aug. 1931: 272.
    Review of *The Life Machine*.

R172   S., B. "Rapid Action Romance." [Unsourced clipping from Chicago newspaper] 2 Nov. 1931.
    Brief review of *Lusita*, "a romance full of rapid action and true to the life and color of the Mexican country."

R173   Shackleton, Edith.   "Speak-Easy Scene on the Stage--Grim Expressionistic Play from America." *London Evening Standard* 16 July 1931.
    The heavy-handedness of *The Life Machine*'s expressionistic devices "seem to anticipate stupidity or callousness in the audience." Despite its "crudities," though, the play "is sometimes moving."

R174   Shaw, Robert. "Sophie Treadwell's *Lusita* Banishes Life's Humdrum." [Unsourced clipping from San Francisco bay area newspaper, 1931.]
    Praises the compelling story, calling Treadwell "a writer who does not know how to be dull."

1932

R175   "Bad Man." *New York Herald Tribune Books* 3 Jan. 1932, sec. 11: 13.
    Brief review of *Lusita*. "The plot is so closely knit that one forgets it is far from plausible."

R176   Beckwith, Ethel. "*The Island*, New Treadwell Play Receives Tryout."
        [Unsourced clipping] 12 Aug. 1932.
                Brief review of Treadwell's "not-so-hot" new play,
        The Island. Beckwith is appalled that the three women
        characters "literally beg their respective boyfriends, 'Please
        take me.'"

R177   Garland, Robert. "Cast and Miscast." *New York World-Telegram* 1
        July 1932.
                Unusual, highly personalized review of the *Lone
        Valley* tryout in Nyack, New York. Garland notes how
        Treadwell, a "charming lady with God's great gift of poise,"
        watched the performance of her play "Calm eyed, collected
        . . . as though she had not met the work before." He
        discusses the play, along with *Machinal*, with a local
        bartender named Tim after the show.

R178   "*Lone Valley* Draws Praise from Audience." *Nyack Daily News* 30
        June 1932.
                Praiseworthy review of *Lone Valley*'s tryout.
        Provides a detailed description of the events following the
        final curtain: the "prolonged applause" and shouts of
        "Author, author!"; Treadwell's confusion over the shouts,
        thinking them intended for the cast; the "more insistent"
        shouts, and Treadwell's final realization of whom the
        audience wanted. "Only a few saw her throw her white lace
        scarf around her shoulders and slip out the door of the box to
        the street and around to the front of the theatre." Concludes
        that "the best-known newspaper wom[a]n in the United
        States" is shy. Predicts a successful Broadway run.

R179   Perkins, Albert R. "*Lone Valley* Has Best Cast of Any Production So
        Far." *Rockland County Evening Journal* 30 June 1932.
                Although predictable, Treadwell's play is "effective"
        and moving. The production garnishes praise for its realistic
        detail, right down to the performance of a talking parrot.

R180   "Play Has Premier in Newtown Hall." *New York Post* 12 Aug. 1932.
                Review of *The Island*, a play full of "thrilling
        climaxes," in Newtown, Connecticut. Provides professional
        credits for the cast, who are scheduled to stay with the show
        when it moves to New York in the fall. Mentions celebrities
        in attendance.

1933

R181   Atkinson, Brooks. "The Play: Desire in *Lone Valley*." *New York Times* 11 Mar. 1933: 18.
          Atkinson finds the play derivative, "out of the theatre's old clothes closet." He wonders why Treadwell, who displayed great "mental agility" in *Machinal*, could not recognize this play's shortcomings.

R182   Gabriel, Gilbert. "*Lone Valley*: Sophie Treadwell Produces Her Own Play in the Plymouth." *New York American* 11 Mar. 1933, final ed., sec. 1:11.
          The play's talkiness and over-earnestness contributes to a "dead level of unexcitement."

R183   Hammond, Percy. "The Theaters." *New York Herald Tribune* 11 Mar. 1933.
          Hammond believes *Lone Valley* is based on factual circumstances known to Treadwell and hence she erroneously thought it stageworthy. Calls Treadwell "one of the loveliest ladies this side of heaven," but concludes that her casting this time was "inadequate."

R184   Lockridge, Richard. "The New Play: *Lone Valley*, a Play of Youth's Awakening." [*New York Sun* Mar. 1933].
          The play is sincere but lacking in dramatic complications. Dislikes the forced happy ending.

R185   "*Lone Valley*." [Unsourced clipping, 1933.]
          The play is "a shapeless, drab affair" with "no sense of the commercial theatre." All of the characters are underdeveloped.

R186   "*Lone Valley*." *The Stage* Apr. 1933.
          Finds it a "pity that so much honest craftsmanship" in writing and producing was wasted on such a "mediocre" play.

R187   "*Lone Valley* on a Morning After." [Unsourced clipping, 1932].
          The play turns out to be "a boo-boo and a bore."

R188   *"Machinal." Variety* [June 1933].
            Reviewing *Machinal* in Moscow, this reviewer notes
        that director Alexander Tairov "has done his best, Soviet
        fashion, to turn the characters into symbols." George H.
        Jones becomes "Capitalism incarnate." Nevertheless, the
        critic predicts it will not meet with approval by Soviet
        officials. The Young Woman does not embody the spirit of
        the proletariat and the play lacks an appropriate "Marxian
        moral." The staging is "one of the finest" Moscow has seen
        in years, and Alice Koonen "brilliantly performed" Helen.

R189   Mantle, Burns. *"Lone Valley* an Author's Orphan." *New York Daily
        News* 11 Mar. 1933.
            Calls *Lone Valley* another of Broadway's "orphans,"
        plays loved desperately by their "parents" but unwanted by
        everyone else. It is not much more than "a sad little drama."

R190   "A Playgoer's After Thoughts: *Lone Valley." The Stage* 10 (1933): 8.
            Treadwell's writing and direction reflects "honest
        craftsmanship," but the plot is too familiar.

R191   Pollack, Arthur. "The Theaters." *Brooklyn Daily Eagle* 11 Mar.
        1933.
            Despite the familiarity of the plot, Treadwell has
        staged her own drama "rather well."

R192   R., G. *"Lone Valley* Put on View." *New York World Telegram* 11
        Mar. 1933.
            Although the play "is an earnest little effort, it is,
        bluntly, as arid as the drought-stricken *Lone Valley* where it
        all takes place."

R193   Rev. of *Lone Valley. New York Herald Tribune* 19 Mar. 1933.
            Cites many positive merits, including a "refreshing
        truthfulness," but also numerous faults ("bits of cloudy
        symbolism and overstressed sentiment").

R194   Sobel, Bernard. *"Lone Valley* is Presented at Plymouth." [*New York
        Mirror* Mar. 1933.]
            Believes the play to be a re-hash of O'Neill's *Anna
        Christie* and argues that Treadwell has stretched "coincidence
        to the breaking point."

R195   Waldorf, Wilella. "*Lone Valley* Arrives: Sophie Treadwell Presents a New Play From Her Own Pen at the Plymouth Theatre." *New York Evening Post* 11 Mar. 1933.

The play "is not brilliant enough either in the writing or playing to make up for the dreary familiarity of its plot."

R196   Watts, Richard, Jr. "Moscow Sees *Machinal* and Approves of It." *New York Herald Tribune* 18 June 1933: 2.

Watts provides a number of specific descriptions of Tairov's staging before concluding that the Russian production "is more effective visually, [but] probably lacks something of the sympathy that Mr. Hopkins put into his version." Still, Watts finds *Machinal* "a fine, moving and beautiful play, one of the most distinguished works of the modern theatre."

1934

R197   Leyda, Jay. "News from Moscow." *Theatre Arts Monthly* Apr. 1934: 282.

Leyda provides a brief comparison of Tairov and Reuben Simonov's productions of *Machinal* in Russia, the former preferred due to its less naturalistic approach and "striking scenic effects."

1936

R198   Allen, Kelcey. "*Plumes in the Dust*." *Women's Wear Daily*, 9 Nov. 1936, sec. 1:16.

The play's episodic structure made the story "jerky and left much to the imagination." Henry Hull's performance as Poe is the finest of his career.

R199   Anderson, John. "*Plumes in the Dust* at 46th St. Theatre." *New York Evening Journal* [7-10 Nov. 1936].

Treadwell's dialogue sounds "pompous" and does not adequately recreate the historical period. Depicting a person of genius convincingly on stage is difficult, and Treadwell's effort is "sheer theatrical hankey-pankey."

R200   Atkinson, Brooks. "On the Life of Poe." *New York Times 15 Nov. 1936*, sec. 11: 1.

Atkinson believes it is "impossible to write of Poe on the stage without turning him into an actor." Hull "swashbuckled" through his scenes. The lack of "social warmth" in Poe's own writings makes dramatizing his life a difficult task.

R201   Atkinson, Brooks. "*Plumes in the Dust*, in Which Henry Hull Acts the Part of Edgar Allan Poe." *New York Times* 7 Nov. 1936, sec. 11: 14.

Too many speeches are given to Poe in defense of his behavior and attitudes. The theatrical part of Poe's life is unworthy of dramatic portrayal.

R202   Bell, Nelson B. "Henry Hull is Given Ovation in New Drama." *Washington Post* 27 Oct. 1936: 13.

Bell stresses the play's "insistent note of defeatism . . . that is continuously and thoroughly depressing." Hull's performance is highly praised.

R203   Benchley, Robert. "One of Those Weeks." *New Yorker* 14 Nov. 1936: 38.

Benchley was predisposed in favor of the production until the last act, which included " a little too much tedium," especially during Poe's prolonged death scene.

R204   Bolton, Whitney. "The Stage Today: *Plumes in the Dust* a Stalwart Play Though Sophie Treadwell Has a Task." *New York Morning Telegraph* [Nov. 1936].

Treadwell's "uneven" play is saved by Hopkins's "astute, sympathetic direction" and Hull's "rich" performance.

R205   Bowen, Stirling. "Poe Has Anti-Climax." *Wall Street Journal* 7 Nov. 1936.

Treadwell reveals that Poe's seeming arrogance and occasional bad taste were actually expressions of "a fierce hatred of the shams with which in his art he was in desperate competition." Hull's performance is "confident, spirited."

R206   Brown, John Mason. "Henry Hull Appears in *Plumes in the Dust*." [*New York Evening Post* 7 Nov. 1936.]

Brown finds the play's title an apt description for the

sufferings "Poor Poe" had to endure in Treadwell's drama.
The play is the sort of sprawling epic "which all of us used
to write when we were thirteen."

R207   Coleman, Robert. "*Plumes in the Dust* a Pageant of Edgar Allan
       Poe." *New York Daily Mirror* 7 Nov. 1936.
              The play's episodic nature makes it appear more like
       a pageant than a play.

R208   "Come and Gone: *Plumes in the Dust*." *Stage* 14 (1936): 10.
              Treadwell and Hull "deserve credit . . . for the try,"
       but the "real Edgar Allen [sic] Poe eluded them both."

R209   Craig. "Plays Out of Town." *Variety* 28 Oct. 1936: 58.
              Treadwell lets "one of the greatest, most-poignant,
       most-discussed tragedies of modern times . . . slip through
       [her] fingers as sensational melodrama." She has "neglected
       to give her portrait a frame."

R210   Drake, Herbert. "*Plumes in the Dust*." *Cue: the Weekly Magazine of
       Metropolitan Entertainment* [Nov. 1936].
              Plumes is "a magnificent playwrighting feat."

R211   Field, Rowland. "The New Play: *Plumes in the Dust* Stars Henry Hull
       in the Role of Edgar Allan Poe Under the Auspices of Arthur
       Hopkins." [Unsourced clipping,] 7 Nov. 1936.
              Hull's performance is the finest of his career, and the
       production "provides a fascinating entertainment."

R212   Gabriel, Gilbert W. "*Plumes in the Dust*: Mr. Hopkins Presents Us a
       Play About Mr. Poe." *New York American* 7 Nov. 1936,
       final ed., sec. 1:7.
              Notwithstanding the "elaborate production" involving
       a half-dozen sets, large cast and historical costumes, "lacking
       much conflict, it can never be much of a play."

R213   Gabriel, Gilbert W. "Poets in Plays: From Poe to Byron." *New York
       American* 15 Nov. 1936.
              Only "one play out of ten" about poets manages to
       present an "actively heroic" central character. Treadwell's
       effort, while "scrupulously honest" and "authentic," fails to
       make Poe's "torturesome, grubby, grievous life over into stuff
       of an attractive stage."

R214   Gilbert, Douglas. "Tragic Story of Edgar Allan Poe is Retold in *Plumes in the Dust*." *New York World-Telegram* 7 Nov. 1936: 8A.
Treadwell's attempt to glorify Poe is undermined by scenes and dialogue that confirm him as "a self-pitying weakwill." The death scene is "embarrassing."

R215   "Henry Hull's New Role." *New York Times* 26 Oct. 1936: 21.
Notes that *Plume*'s world premiere in Princeton "brought a round of applause [at the end] which lasted for more than fifteen minutes, during which time Mr. Hull and other members of the cast took a dozen curtain calls."

R216   Hynes, Betty. "*Plumes in the Dust* Opened Last Night at the National." *Washington Herald* 27 Oct. 1936.
Treadwell has chosen espisodes from Poe's life which "move with leaden feet across the stage, losing themselves in the slough of hopeless sentimentality."

R217   Ibee. "Plays on Broadway: *Plumes in the Dust*." *Variety* 11 Nov. 1936: 54.
Plumes is "fine writing and the season may not disclose a more meritorious display of authorship." Hopkins's direction is his best effort in years.

R218   Kelley, Andrew R. "Play on Poe Opens." *Washington Times* 27 Oct. 1936.
Unlike other Washington critics of *Plumes*, Kelley finds Treadwell "a friendly biographer" of Poe who "softens" the details of his addiction to alcohol. He is extremely complimentary of Hull's performance.

R219   Kirkley, Donald. "*Plumes in Dust* at Ford's Theater." [Unsourced clipping, 1936.]
Review of the Baltimore tryout of *Plumes*, which was given a strong ovation by the audience. The play's achievement is in providing audiences with a "complete picture of [Poe] as he must have seemed to his contemporaries."

R220   Lockridge, Richard. "The Stage in Review: Borrowed Plumage." [*New York Sun*] 7 Nov. 1936.
Applauds Treadwell's compassionate depiction of

Poe, but wishes Hopkins had forced her to "prune her scenes and lines to the dramatic bone."

R221   Mantle, Burns. Rev. of *Plumes in the Dust. New York Daily News* 7 Nov. 1936.
           Laments that "even in death" Poe cannot escape injustice in Treadwell's "depressing story without redeeming contrasts." What is lacking is a "sustained emotional attack" unifying the "detached scenes."

R222   Mantle, Burns. "Plumes in the Theatre: The Biography of Edgar Allan Poe." *New York Sunday News* 15 Nov. 1936.
           Recalls the play's turbulent history with John Barrymore and concludes that if the actor had produced it in the early 1920s "near the peak of his stage career . . . I believe it would have achieved a popular success." Mantle laments the play's impending closure as "an inevitable failure."

R223   Melcher, E. de S. "Play About Poe's Life is Sad and Intelligent." *Washington Evening Star* 27 Oct. 1936: B16.
           Melcher offers exceptional praise for Hull's performance, but laments that the play moves too slowly in the beginning and end.

R224   "New Plays in Manhattan." *Time* 16 Nov. 1936: 89.
           Plumes seems mostly "concerned with an unpleasant man surrounded by unpleasant people, presented with all the dramatic impact of a glass of sour milk."

R225   "*Plumes in the Dust.*" [Unsourced clipping, San Francisco Performing Arts Library & Museum, Oct. 1936.]
           Review of the Washington tryout. The action is "slow, episodic and gloomy," but Hull's performance is a personal success.

R226   "Stage: Tobacco Road's First Jeeter Lester Has a Field Day." *Newsweek* 14 Nov. 1936: 58--59.
           Plumes lacks dramatization and Hull lacks variety. Includes statements by Hull about his research for the role.

R227   Thorp, Willard. "Hull's Acting. Sure and Often Inspired . . . "
         [Unsourced clipping, Oct. 1936.]
                  Review of the *Plumes* tryout in Princeton. Although
         Treadwell's depiction of Poe "is the sober truth about him,"
         Thorp overheard audience members wishing the play offered
         an added theme or explanation for Poe's behavior.

R228   Vernon, Grenville. "The Play & the Screen." *Commonweal* 20 Nov.
         1936: 104.
                  Credits the work of Hull, Hopkins and designer
         Thompson. Treadwell's script, though, somehow "misses
         fire."

R229   Watts, Richard, Jr. "The Theaters." *New York Herald Tribune* 7 Nov.
         1936: 10.
                  "With her usual sympathetic understanding,"
         Treadwell "persuades you that her central figure actually is a
         great literary artist, with a burning, inexhaustible passion for
         artistic creation." Poe, perhaps, is a poor subject for drama,
         due to the "monotonous grayness of his doom."

R230   Watts, Richard, Jr. "The Theaters." *New York Herald Tribune* 15
         Nov. 1936, sec. 7: 1.
                  Wishes Treadwell had placed the causes for Poe's
         demise within the man himself, rather than blaming Fate.

R231   Wyatt, Euphemia Van Rensselaer. "The Drama." *Catholic World* 144
         (1936): 336-7
                  Review of *Plumes in the Dust*.

R232   Young, Stark. "Hamlets." *New Republic* 25 Nov. 1936: 116.
                  Faults Treadwell for not adequately developing a
         point of view about her subject and for writing scenes that
         "often lacked development in details."

                              1940-1949

                                 1941

R233   Allen, Kelcey. "*Hope for a Harvest*." *Women's Wear Daily* 27 Nov.
         1941.
                  Harvest "just misses being a good play." The last

act is action-filled, the first two "entirely too dull and wordy."

R234   Anderson, John. "*Hope for a Harvest* Presented by Guild." *New York Journal American* 27 Nov. 1941.
        Dismisses *Harvest* as "a tedious symposium littered with words and almost empty of drama."

R235   Anderson, John. "The Drama." *New York Journal American* 7 Dec. 1941.
        Anderson doubts that Treadwell is as optimistic herself about the cure for America's problems as are her characters. The ending is filled with "artificial rainbows."

R236   Atkinson, Brooks. "Back to the Soil." *New York Times* 7 Dec. 1941, sec. 10: 5.
        The play seems to deserve admiration, but upon reflection its conclusion is overly simplistic.

R237   Atkinson, Brooks. "The Play in Review: *Hope for a Harvest*." *New York Times* 27 Nov. 1941.
        Treadwell's "daring theme" is worthy of "a better exposition than she has given it." Fredric March's performance is "the best acting he has contributed to the Broadway stage."

R238   Bell, Nelson B. "The Marches Triumph in Guild Play." *Washington Post* 22 Apr. 1941.
        Review of the Washington tryout of *Harvest*. The play "possesses those warm qualities of human understanding, sympathy and mutual helpfulness that make it a particularly inspiring document at just this juncture in dislocated national and international affairs." Its subject is reminiscent of *The Grapes of Wrath*, but is devoid of Steinbeck's "ugliness."

R239   Bessie, Alvah. "Poor Harvest." *New Masses* 9 Dec. 1941: 26.
        Despite good intentions, the play degenerates into "treacly comedy and material for inconsequential celluloid." The play might have been less "naive" if Treadwell had spent more time examining the "causes for the tragedy she portrays."

R240   Bone. "Plays Out of Town: *Hope for a Harvest*." *Variety* 9 Apr. 1941.
        The tryout performance in New Haven "has struck a chord here that should eventually find a response throughout the land."

R241   "Brilliant Cast Presents Moving Play at Shubert." [Unsourced clipping] 5 Apr. 1941.
        The writing and acting are in "perfect" sympathy in this "intensely moving drama."

R242   Brown, John Mason. "*Hope for a Harvest* Deals with Farmer's Deterioration." *New York World-Telegram* 27 Nov. 1941.
        The play's theme is "valid enough," but seems "slightly remote to those of us in New York." Treadwell's subject is "true, timely and tragic," but she "writes about it with the earnestness of an editorial writer turning out his first editorial."

R243   Burr, Eugene. "New Plays on Broadway: *Hope for a Harvest*." *Billboard* 6 Dec. 1941: 15.
        The immediacy of Treadwell's message to American audiences makes for "splendid stuff" onstage.

R244   Carmody, Jay. "The Marches Bring a Play of Merit to the National." *Washington Evening Star* 22 Apr. 1941: B20.
        Praiseworthy review of *Harvest* in Washington. Treadwell's play fits the "mood" of the time, and is "simple, sincere, honest and human in the light of this dark day."

R245   Clark, Norman. Rev. of *Hope for a Harvest*. *Baltimore News-Post* [May 1941].
        Reviewing the Baltimore tryout, Clark finds *Harvest* "a thoughtful and most interesting drama, done in that superb style for which the Guild has long been famous." Hopes Treadwell will do some editing on the first act.

R246   Cohen, Harold V. "Fredric Marches Bring Sophie Treadwell's New Guild Play to the Nixon." *Pittsburgh Post Gazette* 29 Apr. 1941: 27.
        Review of *Harvest* in Pittsburgh. While *Harvest* is not as good a play as *Machinal* ("few dramas will ever be"), the combination of Treadwell's writing and the presence of

the Marches may bring success.

R247   Coleman, Robert. *"Hope for a Harvest* Pedestrian Play." [*New York Daily Mirror* 27-28 Nov. 1941].
        Harvest is "often dull and seldom arresting."

R248   Craig, Don. *"Hope for a Harvest*: March and Eldridge Score in Theater Guild Story of California Farmers." *Washington Daily News* 22 Apr. 1941.
        This "satisfying" new play succeeds in its realistic dialogue and characterizations.

R249   Doyle, Peggy. "Marches' New Play, *Hope for a Harvest*, Happily Received at Colonial." *Boston Evening American* 8 Apr. 1941.
        Reviewing the tryout in Boston, Doyle finds *Harvest* "not as light-hearted as it seems, nor yet as important as was somehow anticipated."

R250   Eager, Helen. *"Hope for a Harvest* Brings the Marches to Colonial." *Boston Traveler* 8 Apr. 1941.
        This "frequently absorbing" play is "honest, sympathetic and eloquent." The play is marred by a "let-down" in the second act.

R251   Ferris, John. "Post-War Farm Play Brings Stage Team Back to Broadway." *Toledo Blade* 1 Dec. 1941.
        Ferris's syndicated review states that Treadwell's treatment of her theme in *Harvest* "bears a little too heavily on the optimistic side."

R252   Freedley, George. *"Hope for a Harvest* First Truly Adult Play of Present Broadway Season." *New York Morning Telegraph* 28 Nov. 1941.
        Treadwell has "at last fulfilled the brilliant promise which she gave in *Machinal* many years ago." The ending, however, is contrived.

R253   Gibbs, Wolcott. "Ants and Grasshoppers." *New Yorker* 6 Dec. 1941: 46.
        Treadwell's conclusion in *Harvest* is little more than "pretty rudimentary economics" and the play itself "fairly dull and unlikely."

R254   Harrison, Bernie. *"Hope for a Harvest* Proves Inspiring Play."
        Washington Times-Herald [21-22 Apr. 1941].
                The play's "stirring" patriotism produces a work that
        is "beautiful and inspiring." The husband-wife team of
        Fredric March and Florence Eldridge performs excellently.
        Harrison notes Katherine Hepburn's presence amongst the
        opening night crowd at the Washington tryout.

R255   Holtzmann, H. M. and J. A. Kneubuhl. "Curtain Call." *Yale Daily
        News* [5-6 Apr. 1941].
                Review of the New Haven tryout of *Harvest.* The
        play lacks conflict, bungles the plot and subplot, and utilizes
        "awkward characterizations." Unfavorably compares the play
        to Sidney Howard's play of the Napa Valley, *They Knew
        What They Wanted.*

R256   *"Hope for a Harvest* Has Premiere." *New York World-Telegram* 5
        Apr. 1941.
                Brief notice of the capacity audience's response to
        Harvest in New Haven. The cast drew nine curtain calls.

R257   *"Hope for a Harvest* Seen: Treadwell Play, with March & Eldridge,
        Opens in New Haven." *New York Times* 5 Apr. 1941.
                Review from an AP wire release which also appears
        in other New York newspapers on this date. Notes the hearty
        reception to the play in New Haven.

R258   Hughes, Elinor. *"Hope for a Harvest* Opens 2-Week Boston Stay at
        Colonial." *Boston Herald* 8 Apr. 1941:12.
                Reviewing *Harvest* in Boston, Hughes finds
        Treadwell's latest effort to be "an honest, earnest and pretty
        talky play."

R259   Hutchens, John K. "Return of the Native." *Boston Transcript* 8 Apr.
        1941.
                Review of the Boston tryout of *Harvest.* The play
        is "interesting as an idea, feeble as a story."

R260   Ibee. *"Hope for a Harvest." Variety* 3 Dec. 1941.
                The play's "comedy touches" in the third act may
        redeem the "very talky and rather dull" early scenes.

R261   Johnson, F. R. "Last Night's Play: *Hope for a Harvest* Compelling."
        New Haven Journal-Courier 5 Apr. 1941.
                The drama's "crisp up-to-dateness marks it for a play
        not to be overlooked," and the production's "top-notch stars"
        helped produce the "intense enthusiasm" at the New Haven
        opening last night.

R262   Jordan, Elizabeth. "Theatre." *America* 13 Dec. 1941: 274.
                This "interesting, amusing and dramatic" play should
        benefit from a long run.

R263   Kanour, Gilbert. "For Theater Goers." *Baltimore Evening Sun* 6 May
        1941.
                The production "stacks up well" with the best the
        Guild has offered, and the "prolonged" applause and "many
        curtain calls" at the Baltimore tryout seemed well deserved.

R264   Keen, J. H. "*Hope for a Harvest.*" *Philadelphia Daily News* 11 Nov.
        1941.
                Keen found the play a bit too didactic, "a sort of
        living editorial." While thought-provoking, it is not always
        good drama.

R265   Kirkley, Donald. "*Hope for a Harvest.*" *Baltimore Sun* 6 May 1941.
                Treadwell's theme is an important one, and it is
        presented in a form which avoids preachiness.   March
        superbly makes Elliott's defeatism unsympathetic.

R266   Kronenberger, Louis. "Hope Talks Itself Out of a Harvest." *New York
        Newspaper "PM"* 27 Nov. 1941.
                If the play were written by a young dramatist, it
        might show "a certain promise," but coming from the author
        of *Machinal*, written over a dozen years earlier, it is nothing
        less than a "deep disappointment."

R267   Krug, Karl. "New March-Eldridge Comedy Opens in Nixon Theatre:
        Superb Cast Backs Star in Guild Play." *Pittsburgh Sun
        Telegraph* 29 Apr. 1941: 20.
                Harvest is "a generally charming, leisurely and frail
        play, adroitly performed" by a fine cast.

R268   Krutch, Joseph Wood. "Gas Station and Juke Box." *The Nation* 13
        Dec. 1941: 621-2.
                Although Treadwell's plays have always been
        received by critics with a "certain seriousness," Krutch says
        none "aroused much genuine enthusiasm." The "verdict" is
        the same with *Harvest*.

R269   Leyendecker, Frank S. Rev. of *Hope for a Harvest*. *About Town*
        [Dec. 1941-Jan. 1942].
                Harvest is a "thoughtful" play enhanced by "decisive
        performances" by the Marches.

R270   Lockridge, Richard. "*Hope for a Harvest*, by Sophie Treadwell,
        Opens at the Guild Theatre." *New York Sun* 27 Nov. 1941.
                The numerous plot incidents "rather too patly . . .
        prove the author's point."

R271   Mantle, Burns. "Early American Virtues the Plea of *Hope for a
        Harvest*." *New York Daily News* 27 Nov. 1941.
                Like the Marches, *Harvest* is "wholesome, human,
        honest and socially conscious." The early scenes contain "a
        good deal of discussion and precious little action."

R272   Mantle, Burns. "Most of this Season's Plays with Morals Attached
        Have Had Tough Going." *New York Sunday News* 7 Dec.
        1941.
                Reviews *Harvest* in the context with several other
        recent shows on Broadway with serious themes. Although
        "wordy," it proves "a rewarding evening in the theatre."

R273   Martin, Linton. "*Hope for a Harvest* Opens on Walnut Stage."
        Philadelphia Inquirer 11 Nov. 1941: 24.
                Reviewing the Philadelphia tryout, Martin finds the
        play a bit "long on atmosphere and short on action," although
        he credits Treadwell with having something "pertinent" to
        say.

R274   McCloud, Don. "Broadway Echoes." [Unsourced clipping, New York
        Public Library for the Performing Arts, 1941.]
                Harvest is a "fascinating study" of the present
        generation of Americans, most of whom are "looking for
        something for nothing." The Guild's production is "splendid"
        and the casting "perfect."

R275   Monahan, Kaspar. *"Hope for a Harvest* Challenges America."
        Pittsburgh Press [28 Apr. 1941].
            This timely play is "simple and direct." Monahan
        wishes Treadwell could have displayed her central theme a
        little earlier in the first act.

R276   Murdock, Henry T. "March & Wife Costarred in Walnut Play."
        Philadelphia Evening Public Ledger [11-12 Nov. 1941].
            "It is the first play of the new season to lay claim to
        stature and yet one of its chiefest charms is that there is
        nothing pretentious about it." March is "perfect."

R277   Murdock, Henry T. "Farm Drama: *Hope for a Harvest* Good Bucolic
        Script--Says Expert." *Philadelphia Evening Public Ledger* 15
        Nov. 1941.
            Murdock especially admires the play's "authenticity"
        of detail and language. Includes an interview with the
        Marches.

R278   "New Play in Manhattan." *Time* 8 Dec. 1941: 39.
            Harvest contains "sound points," but its "pulpit
        manner is a bore and its Santa Claus ending a betrayal."

R279   Norton, Elliot. "Author of *Hope for a Harvest* Has Courage: Second
        Thoughts of a First-Nighter." [*Boston Post*] 13 Apr. 1941.
            The play is static at times, narrative, melodramatic
        and glib in its ending. But it is ultimately "arresting,
        provocative and stimulating."

R280   Norton, Elliot. "Stirring Play at Colonial." [*Boston Post*] 1 Apr. 1941.
            Review of *Harvest* in Boston. Norton fears
        Treadwell will be called "a reactionary and an enemy of
        progress," but many will find this "beautiful" play to be
        "profoundly stimulating."

R281   O'Hara, John. "Stage Wait." *Newsweek* 8 Dec. 1941: 68.
            Short review of *Harvest*, which largely failed to hold
        his attention despite his admiration for the Marches.

R282   Parry, Florence Fisher. "I Dare Say: Being an Appreciation of the
        Earnest Devotees of Theater." [*Pittsburgh Press*, 1941.]
            Reviewing *Harvest* in Pittsburgh, Parry is impressed
        by the production values the Theatre Guild brings to this

"slight" play.

R283   Peet, Creighton. "News of Broadway." *Los Angeles News* 2 Dec. 1941.

        Harvest is "thoughtful, provocative, and full of the warmth and glow of life." Unfortunately, though, the play "wanders about a good deal and lacks any forceful dramatic incident."

R284   Pollack, Arthur. "*Hope for a Harvest* Gets the Farmer Back to Earth." *Brooklyn Daily Eagle* 27 Nov. 1941: 5.

        The play is not "deep," but its "sincerity is obvious."

R285   Pollack, Arthur. "Sophie Treadwell's *Hope for a Harvest*." *Brooklyn Daily Eagle* 30 Nov. 1941.

        Harvest oversimplifies the plight of today's farmers with its "thin" plot.

R286   Russell, Fred. H. "Fredric March Play at Klein Proves to be Excellent Theater." *Bridgeport Sunday Post* 9 Nov. 1941: B10.

        Review of *Harvest* in Bridgeport, Connecticut. Russell finds it "a grand play," citing the excellent performances by the Marches.

R287   Schloss, Edwin H. "*Hope for a Harvest* at Walnut." *Philadelphia Record* [Nov. 1941].

        Review of *Harvest* in Philadelphia. Although the play at times resembles a "dramatization of a U.S. Department of Agriculture report on crop rotation and soil conditions," Schloss admires the production's "human values" and "obvious sincerity."

R288   Sensenderfer, Robert. "The Living Theater." *Philadelphia Evening Bulletin* [Nov. 1941].

        Review of *Harvest* in Philadelphia, praising it as "a warm, pulsing . . . fascinating" play with "vibrant" performances, especially by March and Alan Reed.

R289   Sloper, L. A. "*Hope for a Harvest* Features Mr. and Mrs. Fredric March." *Christian Science Monitor* 11 Apr. 1941: 16.

        In the Boston tryout, Sloper finds the dramatic "machinery" in *Harvest* a bit too visible, especially in the contrived entrances and exits, the "sudden" and "facile" conclusion, and the unsympathetic character of Elliott.

R290   "The Stage: Colonial Theatre--*Hope for a Harvest.*" *Boston Daily Globe* 8 Apr. 1941.
Review of *Harvest* in Boston. Although Treadwell uses her characters too much as mouthpieces for her own views, "by Jove, she's right, absolutely right" in her message.

R291   Waldorf, Wilella. "*Hope for a Harvest* New Comedy at the Guild Theatre." *New York Post* 27 Nov. 1941.
The plot is conventional, and the subplot involving Tonie's pregnancy "tiresome."

R292   Waldorf, Wilella. "The Guild's *Hope for a Harvest* Speaks Out on a Timely Subject." *New York Post* 19 Dec. 1941.
Waldorf revisits *Harvest* after the attack on Pearl Harbor and recent journalistic calls for Americans to regain their drive and ingenuity if they plan to win the war. Waldorf now finds *Harvest* one of the "more interesting and timely" plays currently on Broadway. Treadwell's theme compensates for the deficiencies of the script.

R293   Warner, Ralph. "*Hope for a Harvest.*" *Daily Worker* 29 Nov. 1941: 7.
Although *Harvest* is "unquestionably the most interesting play produced this season," Treadwell has misrepresented the causes of the American farmers' misfortunes and oversimplified their remedy. "Hard work is simply not enough" to solve the problems of unemployment and a lack of adequate markets for farm produce.

R294   Watts, Richard, Jr. "The Theaters: California." *New York Herald Tribune* 27 Nov. 1941.
Watts is sympathetic to Treadwell's cause, but says that the play uses "unpersuasive and undramatic" devices.

R295   Watts, Richard, Jr. "The Theater: When Critics Differ." *New York Herald Tribune* 7 Dec. 1941.
Watts tries to explain why *Harvest* was so admired by out-of-town critics yet dismissed by New York reviewers. The play is "mild and rather monotonous in its storytelling," a fact the New York critics foregrounded, while out-of-towners focused on the play's theme. Watts wishes Treadwell

had been able to achieve more lasting success in the theatre, for her plays always contain "an original approach, sensitivity, an idealistic viewpoint, thoughtfulness, sincerity and an independence of mind and emotion."

R296   Young, Stark. "Stage Traffic." *New Republic* 13 Dec. 1941: 762.
        Harvest contains "worthwhile" themes, but is "overexplicit, pedestrian and dull."

1942

R297   Gilder, Rosamund. "Broadway in Review." *Theatre Arts* 26 (1942): 5, 12-13.
        Harvest is a play "for those who see the theatre in other terms than fireworks, who can contemplate character, milieu and event and follow an idea with as much enthusiasm as they give to the disentangling of a murder clue."

R298   Mantle, Burns. "Choice was Limited and Selection Tough, But There Were Some Good Shows." *New York Sunday News* 14 June 1942.
        A re-cap of the critical response to *Harvest*.

R299   Wyatt, Euphremia Van Rensselaer. "The Drama.". *Catholic World* 154 (1942): 472-3.
        Harvest is an overwritten but "sound-hearted American play" buoyed by excellent performances. "The final curtain particularly is a good ten minutes overdue."

1948

R300   "Comedy Plays to Packed and Pleased House." [*Newtown Bee* Aug.-Sept. 1948.]
        Praiseworthy review of *Highway* by the Town Players, a little theatre in Newtown, Connecticut. *Highway* "most expertly" reveals the "symptoms of unrest, unhappiness, loneliness and despair, without providing us with a convincing cure." Director Treadwell coached her amateur actors into "real personalities" which garnished more enthusiasm from the audience than Treadwell's play. Ann Raynolds as Zepha leads the cast. Harrie Wood's stage set

"is perfect in every detail."

1950-1959

1953

R301   Chan. "Television Followup Comment." *Variety* 18 Nov. 1953.
Review of Norman Lessing's adaptation of *Hope for a Harvest*, televised on the U.S. Steel Hour, ABC-TV. As produced by the Theatre Guild, *Harvest*'s story proves "mature," "provocative" and "dramatic." The one-hour adaptation reduces some of the play's situations into a manner which is too "pat." The direction and cast are "excellent."

R302   Crosby, John. "Radio and Television: the U. S. Steel Hour." [Unsourced clipping, 1953.]
The teleplay of *Harvest* was a "well meaning enterprise," says Crosby, "but frankly it bored the dickens out of me."

1954

R303   Gould, Jack. "Television Reviews: Joan Lorring in *Machinal--The Rise of Carthage--Author* Returns." [Unsourced clipping, Jan. 1954.]
Review of last week's telecast of *Machinal*, a work whose theme "has gained pertinency with the passing of the years. . . . The very intimacy of the home screen heightened the sense of heart-rending yet inevitable disaster."

1958

R304   Powr. Rev. of *Machinal*. *Variety* 14 Apr. 1958.
Review of *Machinal* at the Hollywood Center Theatre. This brief review states that "although some of the techniques used in *Machinal* is [sic] now dated, the theme itself is as pertinent as it ever was." This "experimental" production by Quadrivium Productions is "interesting, if not very lively."

R305   Stinson, Charles. "*Machinal* Given Striking Production." *Los Angeles Times* 12 Apr. 1958, sec. 3: 3.
        This revival by the newly formed Quadrivium Productions is "theatrically sharp and emotionally satisfying." Modernizations to the play--such as television and the mambo--"were effected cleverly and discreetly." Incorrectly states that the play was based on the "Winnie Ruth Judd" case of the 1920s.

1959

R306   B., S. "On a Sea of Woman Chatter." *Bridgeport Post* 15 Nov. 1959.
        One Fierce Hour and Sweet is a novel as "oddly put-together" as ever was. As a man, this reviewer finds the novel's progress "from nowhere to nowhere on a sea of woman-talk" to be a "chastening experience."

R307   Crowther, Florence. "Sinners of Exurbia." *New York Times* 12 Dec. 1959.
        Although at times "engrossing as gossip," Treadwell's novel would have fared "a great deal better as a daytime drama on television."

R308   Manney, Florence. "Lady Doctor Aids Matron." *Ft. Wayne News Sentinel* 19 Dec. 1959.
        One Fierce Hour and Sweet is an "interest-holding" novel with a convincing character, the retired doctor Mary Morrow.

R309   Melvin, Wally. "Surburbia Story Fails to Hold Interest." *Pensacola News-Journal* 8 Nov. 1959.
        Treadwell gives a "brave stab at a realistic resolution," but this novel is little more than "weak closet drama at best."

R310   "New Fiction." *Savannah Press* 6 Dec. 1959.
        One Fierce Hour and Sweet "has all the fascination of a psychoalalysist's [sic] case book."

R311   O'Leary, Theodore M. "Understanding the Basis of Compassion." *Kansas City Star* 7 Nov. 1959.
        While not "escape reading," Treadwell's novel does

"enlarge the reader's understanding of the sort of suffering
that the person undergoing it usually tries to conceal."

R312   Rev. of *One Fierce Hour and Sweet*. [*Independent-Press-Telegram
        Southland Magazine*, 1959.]
                Treadwell's novel "is not unlike listening in on a
        psychiatrist and his patient."

R313   Rev. of *One Fierce Hour and Sweet*. [*Washington News*] 7 Nov.
        1959.
                This extremely brief review finds Treadwell's novel
        "a dull explanation of how one of those violently
        discontented surburban matrons came to realize that her legal
        partner was fit to live with."

R314   Ross, Mary. "A Housewife's Discontents." *New York Herald Tribune*
        13 Dec. 1959.
                The novel will appeal to those interested in "what an
        actual psychiatrist once described as 'the nervous housewife.'"

R315   Scratch, Patty.   "*One Fierce Hour* Tells Plight of Housewife."
        [Unsourced clipping] 4 Dec. 1959.
                Treadwell's novel is "timely," "thoughtful," and
        "convincing."

                                1960-1969

                                   1960

R316   Aston, Frank. "*Machinal* at the Gate." *New York World Telegram
        and Sun* 8 Apr. 1960.
                This revival of *Machinal* is "grimly entertaining,
        neatly and compellingly executed."

R317   Atkinson, Brooks.   "East Side Drama: Two New Productions on
        Second Avenue." *New York Times* 17 Apr. 1960, sec. 2: 1.
                Atkinson likes director Gene Frankel's stylized
        staging of *Machinal* as a "bitter ballet." Calls the production
        "one of off Broadway's most vivid."

R318   Atkinson, Brooks. "Theatre: *Machinal* Revived at Gate." *New York Times* 8 Apr. 1960: 27.
Director Frankel's production is "resourcefully designed and thoroughly disciplined in movement, spectacle and characterization."

R319   Brustein, Robert. "A Director's Theatre." *New Republic* 25 Apr. 1960: 21.
In a column primarily on American directors, Brustein chooses to "dispense briefly" with the *Machinal* revival by dismissing it as "one of those banal tabloid stories." The staging, though, is as "well orchestrated as a symphony and as imaginatively designed as a ballet."

R320   Burm. "Off-Broadway Reviews: *Machinal.*" *Variety* 20 Apr. 1960.
Machinal is still capable of producing "a lot of impact." Frankel's stylized staging employs masked scene shifters who "snake in and out" of the action to choreography by Sophie Maslow. The concept proves "sufficiently arresting" to overcome its "sometimes pretentious posturing."

R321   Crist, Judith. "*Machinal* Revival Staged by Gene Frankel at Gate." *New York Herald Tribune* 8 Apr. 1960.
This revival is more a "dance drama set to dialogue" than a play. The production, though, is "impressive and engrossing," and all the performances "perfection."

R322   Field, Rowland. "Dated Revival: *Machinal* is Worthy Fable of Memorable Murder." [Unsourced clipping from Newark newspaper, Apr. 1960.]
Although *Machinal*'s subject is dated and its "rather cryptic devices and symbolism" pretentious, it "retains a liberal measure of fascination." The text has been "slightly revised" for this production.

R323   Gregor, Ann. "A Woman's Role." *Newark News* 3 Jan. 1960.
Treadwell's *One Fierce Hour and Sweet* is a "fine vehicle" through which she expresses her views on women's roles in modern American society.

R324   Hayes, Richard. "The Stage: Expressionism as Style." *Commonweal* 17 June 1960: 306.
Although Hayes finds *Machinal* lacking in

complexity or originality of ideas, he admires Treadwell's mastery of the expressionist form.

R325   Hewes, Henry. "Broadway Postscript." *Saturday Review* 30 Apr. 1960: 27.
        Short review which finds *Machinal*'s expressionism a form of dated didacticism.

R326   Lewis, Theophilus. "Theatre." *America* 30 Apr. 1960: 203-4.
        Lewis likes *Machinal*'s expressionist style but is intolerant of its central character, "from the start a reluctant and fretful wife."

R327   Malcolm, Donald. "Off Broadway: the Romance of Helen Jones." *New Yorker* 16 Apr. 1960.
        Malcolm believes the play "looks very much like a soap opera" and dismisses it in several barbed quotes, especially some concerning Treadwell's apparent misanthropy.

R328   McClain, John. "Glowing Praise for *Machinal*." *New York Journal American* 8 Apr. 1960.
        The play seems "untarnished by the years," and many individuals receive praise: Frankel for his direction, Ballou's unit set, and the principal cast members, especially Dolores Sutton, who is "outstanding."

R329   "Theatre." *Cue* 16 Apr. 1960.
        This anonymous critic liked the staging in the revival of *Machinal*, but hated the play. "The sauces are piquant, but the meat's so-so."

R330   Watts, Richard, Jr. "Good Revival of a Drama of 1928." *New York Post* 8 Apr. 1960.
        Machinal proves just as effective "without the advantage of topical allusion" provided by the Snyder-Gray case. The production's "stylized moments," while "slightly pretentious," have the advantage of creating sympathy for the heroine "by showing her moving to her doom in a kind of confused trance that blinded and bewildered her."

1967

R331   Keating, Michelene. *"He Doesn't Want to Play* Ought Not To."
        Tucson Daily Citizen 26 July 1967: 19.
                 Harsh review of Treadwell's final play, produced at
        the University of Arizona. "If ever a play had a crying need
        not to be played, this one is it." The plot is "threadbare" and
        the characters stereotypes. Above all, Treadwell's style,
        especially when compared to contemporary playwrights like
        Harold Pinter and Edward Albee, "seems quaintly dated."

R332   Sears, Barbara. "Top Effort Fails to Brighten Play." *Arizona Daily
        Star* [Tucson] 23 July 1967.
                 Although Sears applauds the choice of a new,
        "unproven" play for university students and Tucson
        audiences, ultimately she finds Treadwell's plot "hackneyed"
        and her characters stereotypical.

1970-1989

1973

R333   "Women's Lib, 1928." [Unsourced clipping, Sept. 1973.]
                 Recaps the history of Treadwell and *Machinal*, and
        gives brief summaries of the critical responses to the play in
        recent productions in Warsaw and Moscow.

1983

R334   Weiner, Bernard. "S. F. Repertory Resurrects a Melodrama from the
        '20s." *San Francisco Chronicle* 7 May 1983: 36.
                 Weiner finds that *Machinal* "still resonates today--
        and not only for women." Michelle Truffaut directs the
        production "fluidly."

1984

R335   Arnold, Stephanie. Rev. of *Machinal*. *Theatre Journal* 36 (1984):
        108-10.
                 Arnold offers vivid descriptions of the "striking

theatrical cubism" found in the designs and acting in the San Francisco Repertory's revival of *Machinal*. Arnold details how the double-casting further illuminates the play's themes and how director Truffaut's revised ending achieves a powerful moment for the Young Woman, a character written too much as a victim. Includes a production photo.

1988

R336   Smith, Sid. "Lifeline Theatre Dusts Off Heirloom." *Chicago Tribune* 19 Feb. 1988, sec. 2: 2.
    "For every obvious gesture or social lecture, Treadwell injects a poetic or revealing note." *Machinal* is "no masterpiece" but is "still a treasure."

R337   Weiss, Hedy. "Lifeline's Curious *Machinal* Explores Passion and Despair." *Chicago Sun-Times* 20 Feb. 1988.
    At the "tiny space" used by Chicago's Lifeline Theatre, *Machinal* proves "a rather curious play that is a strange blend of film noir despair, tawdry scandal-sheet documentary, poetic romance and feminist tract."

1990-1994

1990

R338   Barnes, Clive. "Perfect Period Piece." *New York Post* 16 Oct. 1990. In *New York Theatre Critics' Reviews*, 1990: 173-74.
    Machinal is "a find, a virtually lost, or at best mislaid, American classic." The staging in the New York Shakespeare Festival revival is "superb." Jodie Markell as the Young Woman is "tremulously appealing" and the rest of the cast offers a "beautifully" created ensemble. *Machinal* is "a wonderful play so perfectly of its time that it transcends any such boundaries."

R339   Beaufort, John. "Atmospheric Revival of Murder Drama Captures '20s Mood." *Christian Science Monitor* 31 Oct. 1990. In *New York Theatre Critics' Reviews* 1990: 172.
    Beaufort believes modern audiences will find the "dramatic substance" of *Machinal* on the "slight side."

R340   Brustein, Robert. "She-Plays, American Style." *New Republic* 17
        Dec. 1990: 27-28.
                Brustein compares the play to Rice's *The Adding
        Machine*, as well as other works inspired by the Snyder-Gray
        case, including James M. Cain's *The Postman Always Rings
        Twice*. Mostly, Treadwell's play is "declarative, predictable,
        simplistic."

R341   Kirkpatrick, Melanie. "Domestic Tragedy." *Wall Street Journal* 26
        Oct. 1990. In *New York Theatre Critics' Reviews*, 1990: 172.
                Michael Grief's "rapid-fire" direction makes
        Machinal "riveting" and "surprisingly effective." Jodie
        Markell's half-screaming delivery of the Young Woman's
        monologues clearly suggests that character's "capacity for
        murder."

R342   Kissel, Howard. "She's a Victim, So's Audience." *New York Daily
        News* 16 Oct. 1990. In *New York Theatre Critics' Reviews*,
        1990: 173.
                The Young Woman is presented as too much a
        victim, and though the dialogue has occasional "bite" it fails
        when it "aspires to something loftier."

R343   Oliver, Edith. "The Theatre: Noises On." *New Yorker* 29 Oct. 1990:
        114.
                The script of *Machinal* is "earnest and humorless and
        deeply condescending toward working people and toward its
        heroine as victim."

R344   Rich, Frank. "A Nightmarish Vision of Urban America as Assembly
        Line." *New York Times* 16 Oct. 1990. In *New York Theatre
        Critics' Reviews*, 1990: 171.
                Grief's "imaginative, unpatronizing" direction and
        Treadwell's script produce "a startling collision of past and
        present." The play is "far more contemporary" than other
        social protest plays of the '20s and '30s.

R345   Simon, John. "Mechanical." *New York* 29 Oct. 1990: 96.
                As a play, *Machinal* is "indigestible." It lacks the
        "poetry" of similar expressionist plays, and Treadwell has
        "loaded the dice" in favor of her heroine. Includes a
        production photo.

R346   Watt, Doug. "*Machinal*: Joltingly Executed Drama." *New York Daily News* 19 Oct. 1990. In *New York Theatre Critics' Reviews*, 1990: 173.
Machinal is "superbly directed, designed, lighted and performed."

R347   Weales, Gerald. "Young Woman in a Web." *Commonweal* 23 Nov. 1990: 698-99.
Treadwell relies on "cliche and repetition" in creating a heroine who is "too squashed a cabbage to be the central figure in a play." Jodie Markell, at least, brings wit and assertiveness to the character.

R348   Winer, Linda. "Sophie Treadwell's Everywoman Revival." *New York Newsday* 16 Oct. 1990. In *New York Theatre Critics' Reviews*, 1990: 170.
This revival "makes one wonder where Treadwell has been all our theatrical lives." Grief has staged the play "with a punchy, staccato black-and-white savvy that hooks right into Treadwell's pulp, unsentimental documentary style."

1991

R349   Smith, Sid. "Rediscovered *Machinal*." *Chicago Tribune* 21 July 1991, sec. 5: 5.
The revival by A Fly's Eye Production in Chicago lacks a "stylistic imprint and interpretive coloring" in this "threadbare, rough" staging.

1992

R350   Bradley, Jeff. "*Machinal* Still Jolting." *Denver Post* 1 Apr. 1992: 3F.
As produced by CityStage Ensemble in Denver, this "post-modern" staging of *Machinal* includes live musical accompaniment, "giant" TV monitors, and gender-blind casting. While the production "may not succeed on every level," especially in the casting of an "alluring" woman as Roe and in Helen's unexplained character transformation, "going along for the ride is exhilarating."

R351   Dolan, Jill. Rev. of *Machinal*. *Theatre Journal* 44 (1992): 96-97.
Insightful review of the 1990 revival from a materialist feminist point of view. Dolan discusses Treadwell's depiction of "heterosexual romance [as] simply another discursive strategy engaged to constrain women." She applauds the multi-racial production for also considering issues of race and ethnicity, but notes that the acting choices range from an appropriate form of broad two-dimensionality in the hospital scene to an overly romanticized portrayal of the Young Woman as victim. "The Public's production clarifies the prescience, poignancy, and relevance of Treadwell's play."

1993

R352   Abarbanel, Jonathan. "The Eclipse Co.'s Star is Rising." *Backstage* 10 Dec. 1993: 17.
Praiseworthy review of the newly founded Eclipse Theatre Company and its production of *Machinal*. Staged with "precision and clear understanding" by director Susan Leigh.

R353   Billington, Michael. Rev. of *Machinal*. *Manchester Guardian* 18 Oct. 1993. In *Theatre Record* [London], 1993: 1184-85.
Treadwell's "startling" play is "Pinteresque" in its economy and suggestion. The staging approach by director Stephen Daldry and designer Ian MacNeil, however, "seems out of scale with the tone and texture of the writing."

R354   Billington, Michael. "Theatre." *Country Life* [London] 28 Oct. 1993.

Machinal is a "stark, short, embittered, proto-feminist play" that is crushed by a monumental design scheme. The "Pinteresque economy" of the dialogue is "startling." Includes a photo from the hospital scene.

R355   Cohn, Ruby. "At *Machinal*." *Plays International* Dec. 1993: 17.
"The whole production is unforgettable." Includes a photo of the play's opening scene.

R356   Coveney, Michael. "Fiona, dea ex *Machinal.*" *London Observer* 24
        Oct. 1993: 10.
                Machinal is "an overwhelming experience, a
        fantastic discovery." Coveney's review is filled with
        numerous descriptions of setting and action. The execution
        scene echoes the actual, "illicit" photograph of Ruth Snyder's
        execution. Fiona Shaw's "Irish mania . . . translates the
        misery of disappointment [of the Young Woman] into the
        tragic ecstasy of despair."

R357   de Jongh, Nicholas. Rev. of *Machinal. London Evening Standard* 18
        Oct. 1993. In *Theatre Record* [London], 1993: 1187.
                de Jongh says the Royal National Theatre's revival
        of *Machinal* proves to be "one of the most devastating
        theatrical experiences of my life." Treadwell is "a lost
        heroine of modern American theatre."

R358   Doughty, Louise. "Pillage Idiot." *Mail on Sunday* [London] 23 Oct.
        1993.
                Although *Machinal's* politics seem a bit "simplistic"
        today, Doughty found the execution scene a "shocking
        denouement." The curtain call afterward should be dropped:
        "I was too stunned to applaud." Includes a production photo.

R359   Edwardes, Jane. Rev. of *Machinal. Time Out* 20 Oct. 1993. In
        Theatre Record [London], 1993: 1187.
                Daldry's staging at times distorts the sense of the
        play. "The lingering impression is of the horrors of capital
        punishment rather than male oppression."

R360   Gross, John. Rev. of *Machinal. London Sunday Telegraph* 24 Oct.
        1993. In *Theatre Record* [London], 1993: 1187-88.
                Gross is disturbed that Helen shows no feelings of
        guilt over the murder, and nothing more than "a perfunctory
        twinge when she thinks about its consequences for her child."

R361   Hagerty, Bill. "*Machinal* the Marvellous." *Today* [London] 18 Oct.
        1993.
                The production of this "long neglected play" is
        "magnificent. I want to see it again."

R362 Hassell, Graham. Rev. of *Machinal*. *What's On* 27 Oct. 1993. In *Theatre Record* [London], 1993: 1186.

Daldy's staging is dazzling, but overwhelming for such a "threadbare" play: "It's hard to dispel the feeling that he's using a sledgehammer to crack a nut." Shaw's performance, then, is all the more remarkable for conveying the "still centre" of the play amidst the staging.

R363 Hepple, Peter. "Ghosts in the *Machinal*." *The Stage and Television Today* [London] 28 Oct. 1993: 14.

Director Stephen Daldry's production of *Machinal* "is one of the most spectacular pieces of staging ever seen at the National." Hepple wonders, though, if Treadwell's "curiously uninvolving," episodic script is "worth" the massive staging it receives. Includes two production photos.

R364 Howes, Cathy. "Mscellany Onstage: *Machinal*." *Ms. London* 1 Nov. 1993.

Although "not entertainment per se," *Machinal* is a "memorable production nonetheless." Includes a photo.

R365 Lahr, John. "The Virgin and the Dynamo." *New Yorker* 22 Nov. 1993: 112-16.

Lahr's detailed review of the Royal National Theatre's revival of *Machinal* is interspersed with excerpts from his interview with Shaw. Lahr believes Treadwell was "ahead of her time" in her dramatic debate "about family, male authority, and women's rights." However, he concludes that this important play is not really a "good" one due to its inability to provide "substantial character development" for its central character. "Even Fiona Shaw . . . admitted that 'the play is legless,' and said, 'It's like fighting with one hand behind your back.'"

R366 Leon, Ruth. Rev. of *Machinal*. *London Sunday Express* 24 Oct. 1993. In *Theatre Record* [London], 1993: 1195.

In staging *Machinal*, "Stephen Daldry has once again chosen a flawed and old-fashioned play for the kind of make-over teenage girls pray for from fashion editors."

R367 Morley, Sheridan. Rev. of *Machinal*. *London Spectator* 23 Oct. 1993. In *Theatre Record* [London], 1993: 1188.

Treadwell's play is "scarcely a play at all but a series

of short-sharp-shock scenes" pulled from headlines of American newspapers.

R368   Nathan, David. Rev. of *Machinal*. *London Jewish Chronicle* 22 Oct. 1993. In *Theatre Record* [London], 1993: 1188.
          Daldry's staging is "stunning."

R369   Nightingale, Benedict. "Broken Up by the Machinery." *London Times* 19 Oct. 1993: 32.
          Shaw's performance is at times "almost too painful too watch." Undoubtedly, many today will still identify with the play's depiction of society's attacks on a woman's "emotional privacy."

R370   Nordern, Barbara. "Death in Metroland." *The Times Literary Supplement* 22 Oct. 1993: 20.
          The role of Helen seems "made for" Fiona Shaw. "The graphic quaking of [Shaw's] body as it is seared by the electric current, while a rainbow spectrum colours the smoke that rises from it, is extremely harrowing."

R371   O'Mahoney, John. "'Til Death Do They Partake In." *Irish Post* 6 Nov. 1993.
          This review of *Machinal* also profiles two of the Irish actors in the cast, Fiona Shaw and Ciaran Hinds. The Royal National Theatre production "is a masterful achievement," although Shaw admits to wondering at times if the play might "have been better served with some silence rather than this noise" from the setting and sound design. Shaw also speaks of the play's "excessive relentlessness. It really is on the wrong side of good taste which is the way a lot of life actually is. Treadwell could have put in a nice witty scene here and there. But she just doesn't bother." Includes a production photo of Shaw and Hinds.

R372   Paton, Maureen. Rev. of *Machinal*. *London Daily Express* 16 Oct. 1993. In *Theatre Record* [London], 1993: 1183.
          The play "is simple-minded 'wimmin's' propaganda of the most mechanical kind." The central character is "a doddering ninny . . . clearly on the verge of a nervous breakdown."

R373   Peter, John. Rev. of *Machinal*. *London Sunday Times* 24 Oct. 1993.
        In *Theatre Record* [London], 1993: 1186-87.
                Daldy and MacNeil are praised for resurrecting this
        play of "deep feeling and cool objectivity." John Woodvine
        gives a "masterly"performance as George H. Jones.

R374   Price, Victor. "London Theatre: *Machinal*." *The Scotsman* [Edin-
        burgh] 8 Nov. 1993.
                Admires Shaw's performance as Helen, as well as
        Daldry's conceptual staging.

R375   Raymond, Gerard. "London Reviews: *Machinal*." *TheaterWeek* 22
        Nov. 1993: 38.
                Noting the tendency in contemporary theatre to
        "stage straight plays like over-blown musicals from the '80s,"
        Raymond wishes director Daldry had allowed *Machinal* to
        "breathe" without being "smothered" by all the visual and
        aural distractions onstage. Shaw's "heart-wrenching
        performance blazes miraculously through the clatter."

R376   Rutherford, Malcolm. "*Machinal*." *London Financial Times* 18 Oct.
        1993: 13.
                The electrocution scene is particularly "moving," but
        there is "no excuse" for the Young Woman killing her
        husband, who is "not *that* bad." Includes a production photo.

R377   Shaw, Roy. "Theatre." *The Tablet* [London] 20 Nov. 1993.
                Machinal is an "unforgettably powerful piece, which
        is highly relevant to the way we live now. Shaw, Daldry and
        MacNeil receive high praise.

R378   Sierz, Aleks. Rev. of *Machinal*. *London Tribune* 29 Oct. 1993. In
        Theatre Record [London], 1993: 1188.
                This "superficial" play "fails to challenge the
        stereotype of woman as a neurotic victim unable to live
        independently." The sets steal the show.

R379   Spencer, Charles. "A Howl of Rage." *London Daily Telegraph* 18
        Oct. 1993: 17.
                Stephen Warbeck's dissonant musical score is
        "extraordinary," and Shaw is "terrific." The end result is "far
        from depressing"; the play leaves you "strangely exhilarated."

R380 Tanitch, Robert. *"Machinal."* *Plays & Players* Nov. 1993: 5.
Tanitch recounts the history of the original London production, and draws parallels between *Machinal* and O'Neill, Rice, Odon von Horvath, Mamet, and Gertrude Stein. Includes a photo of the honeymoon scene.

R381 Taylor, Paul. Rev. of *Machinal*. *London Independent* 18 Oct. 1993. In *Theatre Record* [London], 1993: 1185-86.
This production of *Machinal* is "embroiled in an exhilarating irony," for the play's "damning" indictment of mechanization is tempered by the "uplifting *celebration* of the vast mechanical resources of the Lyttleton." The husband in the play may be "crassly materialist," but he is not "unkindly." The staging is the real "masterpiece."

R382 Tinker, Jack. Rev. of *Machinal*. *London Daily Mail* 16 Oct. 1993. In *Theatre Record* [London], 1993: 1184.
Treadwell's dramatic technique and Daldry and MacNeil's "bravura wizardry" produce a show that "simply takes the breath away."

R383 Trewin, Wendy. "New Plays: *Machinal*." *The Lady* [London] 16-22 Nov. 1993: 26.
Treadwell's play gives a "consistently one-sided view of modern life in which the women suffer and there are few decent men." Includes a photo of Shaw in the hospital scene.

R384 Wardle, Irving. Rev. of *Machinal*. *London Independent on Sunday* 17 Oct. 1993. In *Theatre Record* [London], 1993: 1186.
As Helen's husband, John Woodvine "emerges as a kindly chap who takes his wife's frigid tantrums in his stride." Daldry tries to overcome the play's weaknesses by enlisting a "large cast and vast scenic resources."

R385 Woddis, Carole. "Bitter Indictment." *The Herald* [Glasgow] 30 Oct. 1993.
Daldry's "audacious" staging of *Machinal* is "thrilling--though oddly unmoving."

R386 Wolf, Matt. *"Machinal."* *Variety* 6 Dec. 1993: 34.
Daldry and MacNeil's "ferocious expressionism risks constituting its own cliché." While the New York Shakespeare Festival revival of *Machinal* "heightened"

Treadwell's vision, Daldry's approach "pummels away at it in a display of physical coups that make *Starlight Express* look modest." Only Fiona Shaw is true to the play.

1994

R387   Goggins, William O. *"Machinal. "* *San Francisco Weekly* 8 June 1994.
        Review of the revival by the Actors Theatre of San Francisco. The 1928 drama appears "both time-bound and timeless" in this production.

R388   Green, Judith. "The Odd Human in an Assembly-Line World." *San Jose Mercury News* 29 June 1994.
        Incorrectly cites the Actors Theatre of San Francisco's production of *Machinal* as the play's west coast premiere. Despite compelling designs and performances by the supporting actors, "it's uninteresting to watch [Nadja] Kennedy [as the Young Woman] play 100 minutes of non-stop victimization."

R389   Harvey, Dennis. "Play Ball." *San Francisco Bay Guardian* 8 June 1994.
        "*Machinal* intrigues as both antiquated staged experiment and still-provocative protest." Harvey compares the play to literary works such as Kate Chopin's *The Awakening* and Charlotte Perkins Gilman's *The Yellow Wallpaper*, where "female 'hysteria' is understood to be rebellion's only possible outlet."

ANNOTATED SECONDARY BIBLIOGRAPHY: BOOKS, ARTICLES, SECTIONS

This secondary bibliography lists English-language critical commentary on Treadwell's writings, as well as significant biographical material pertaining to her career as a dramatist and actress. Brief articles on stage productions, such as advance notices or profiles, photos and sketches of actors, have been omitted. Also omitted are most articles dealing with Treadwell's journalistic writings, unless they have a direct relationship to her work for the theatre. As with the secondary bibliography of reviews, notation is provided in brackets when a citation remains incomplete or unverifiable. Unless otherwise noted, all citations with bracketed information are taken from clippings at the University of Arizona Library Special Collections.

1904-1909

1904

S001   Birdsall, Osra. "In Lighter Vein at the University." *Overland Monthly* 44.3 (1904): 207-12.
        This overview of recent theatrical performances at the University of California at Berkeley includes a photo of Treadwell as Matilda in the farce *Of Royal Blood*. Birdsall credits Treadwell's performance for that play's success: "There are few actresses on the professional stage who could get more fun out of the part."

S002   "1906 Presents Real Farce at Junior Day Celebration." [Unsourced clipping, 1904.]
        Complimentary review of Treadwell's performance in the university production of a farce called *Just About Now*.

S003   "Strange Happenings at Sophomore Party." [Unsourced clipping, 1904.]
       Treadwell is cited as chairman of the sophomore women's entertainment committee and as being among "the most clever of the juvenile actresses."

S004   "University Students Plunge into Theatricals." [*San Francisco Bulletin*, clipping, 1904.]
       Brief article on the "talented students" involved in university dramatics at Berkeley. Includes a photo of Treadwell in the farce, *Of Royal Blood.*

1905

S005   "Co-Eds in Vaudeville Stunts Burlesque Their Professors: All Males Barred from Laughable Performance." [Unsourced clipping, 1905.]
       Review of a vaudeville show which included a comic sketch, *Tom, Dick and Harriet*, with songs by Treadwell. Includes a photo of Treadwell and Isabel McReynolds, who wrote the sketch.

1906

S006   "Cast is Chosen for Dramatic Clubs' Play." [Unsourced clipping, 1906.]
       Treadwell is cast as "Constantine Gage" in a comedy by Henry Arthur Jones titled *The Manoeuvers of Jane.*

S007   "Changes Made in Extravaganza Cast." [Unsourced clipping, 1906.]
       Treadwell will perform the role of "Maybelle" at the university commencement extravaganza.

1907

S008   Stevens, Otheman. "Fitch Play Lacks Both Wit and Plot." *Los Angeles Examiner* 10 Dec. 1907: 6.
       Brief report the day after Willia Williams's [Treadwell's] "eminently successful" vaudeville debut. "She established herself at once with her audience, and was

recalled until her repertoire was exhausted. Her songs with their dainty acting and illustrative music, are a novel and refreshing form of vaudeville."

S009   Stevens, Otheman. "Pretty San Francisco Girl Will Seek Fame on Stage." *Los Angeles Examiner* 10 Dec. 1907.
        Announces the debut of Willia Williams [Treadwell] in a variety act at Fischer's Theatre. Includes a full-length photo of Treadwell in her variety act costume.

1909

S010   "Drops Pen for Footlights: Miss Sophie Treadwell, Newspaper Writer, Goes on Stage." *Oakland Enquirer* [1909, clipping, San Francisco Performing Arts Library and Museum].
        Announces Treadwell's participation with an Oakland stock company, Ye Liberty Playhouse.

1910-1919

1912

S011   Anthony, Walter. Rev. of *The Toad*. *San Francisco Call* [3-5 July 1912].
        In this review of a drama of ancient Egypt, Anthony singles out performances by Treadwell (as Queen of Acortis) and Helen Cooke (as Seeres of Amon) as exemplary, especially in the scene where they fight over a hunchbacked dwarf (the "toad" of the title).

S012   "Forest Theatre Glows in Mystic Beauty; Carmel's Big Night Thrills Aesthetes." *San Francisco Examiner* 4 July 1912.
        Cites the environment of open air, forest and sea at Carmel-by-the-Sea as creating a Greek-like atmosphere for drama. The principal actors in *The Toad*, including Treadwell, "were often applauded."

S013   "Literary Colonists Give Realistic Touch to Dramatic Tangle of Love in Queen Ismae's Court--Difficult Roles Interpreted with True Art." [Unsourced clipping, July 1912.]
        Treadwell "struck every note in her points of

intensity with the sure pitch of genuinely dramatic mind."

1915

S014   "Jean Traig Wins Way to the Stage: Will Appear at Pantages in One-Act Play Written for Her by Sophie Treadwell." [Unsourced clipping, Jan. 1915.]

As a result of Treadwell's serial in the *Bulletin*, "How I Got My Husband and How I Lost Him," Jean Traig "is probably the most discussed young woman in San Francisco today." Treadwell's one-act, *An Unwritten Chapter*, is based on a "hitherto unpublished incident in the life of this girl" as told to Treadwell.

S015   "Jean Traig Appears at Pantages Sunday." [Unsourced clipping] 30 Jan. 1915.

Treadwell's serial, with its accompanying 50+ photos, have made Jean Traig "the center of interest and curiosity here." Traig makes her theatrical debut in Treadwell's play.

1917

S016   San Francisco Bulletin. *The Bulletin Book: a Compilation of Noteworthy Articles by Staff Members of the San Francisco Bulletin and Others Which Have Appeared in This Paper in the Last Few Years.* San Francisco: n. pub., 1917: 49-55.

Reprints excerpts from Treadwell's serial, "An Outcast at the Christian Door."

1920-1929

1922

S017   "Author of *Gringo* an Actress and Writer Too." *New York Herald* 16 Dec. 1922.

Brief biographical profile of Treadwell. States that Modjeska encouraged Treadwell not to pursue acting after she received a letter from one of her former pupils, a young woman who was "starving to death in New York" because "no manager would engage her because of her lack of beauty."

S018   "Concerning Miss Sophie Treadwell." *New York Tribune* 16 Dec. 1922.
        Recounts a story that Treadwell would repeat often-- that Modjeska urged her not to change one of her early playscripts to suit the tastes of a theatrical producer. Treadwell misleads her interviewer by stating that she began playwriting while studying with Modjeska and that Treadwell "did the actual writing" of Madame's memoirs.

S019   Rice, Willis B. "Pro-*Gringo*." Letter to the Dramatic Editor. *New York Times* 24 Oct. 1922, sec. 7: 1.
        Rice takes issue with John Corbin's review of *Gringo*, believing that those who have lived in Mexico will admire Treadwell's portrayal of that country.

S020   Smith, Alison. "Plays and Players. *New York Globe* 4 Aug. 1922.
        Smith is the first to identify Treadwell as the author of Guthrie McClintic's second major directing task--*Gringo*.

1923

S021   Hammond, Percy. "Oddments and Remainders." *New York Tribune* 7 Feb. 1923: 8.
        Reports on Treadwell's participation in a summer retreat of theatre study with Richard Boleslavsky.

S022   "Helen Hayes in *Loney Lee*, a Hugh [sic] Success at Apollo." [Unsourced clipping, 6 Nov. 1923.]
        Provides some statistical background behind the plot situation in *Loney Lee*. Citing the Bureau of Statistics in New York City, the article claims that between 10,000-15,000 girls came to the city in 1922 from small towns across America in order to go on the stage. Of that number, no more than 75 are now on the stage, fewer than 200 ever "got a chance to show what they could do," and no more than 25% returned home. Treadwell's play describes what happens to "one of these girls."

S023   "Helen Hayes in *Loney Lee*, at the Apollo this Week." *Atlantic City Evening Union* 6 Nov. 1923.

        Loney Lee was hastily contracted to producer George C. Tyler only after Israel Zangwill was unable to complete his play, *We Moderns*, due to heavy lecture engagements.

S024   Mantle, Burns, ed. *The Best Plays of 1922-23*. Boston: Small, Maynard & Co, 1923: 12, 500.

        Gringo is "a colorful Mexican drama" which was "well written" by Treadwell. A cast list and plot synopsis are also provided.

1924

S025   "Accuses Barrymore of Stealing *Poe* Play." *New York Evening Bulletin* 16 Oct. 1924.

        Description of Treadwell's initiation of court action against John Barrymore for plagiarism of her play on Edgar Allan Poe. Treadwell is suing for payment or the return of her original manuscript. This account states that Treadwell wrote the play with McGeehan.

S026   Acton, Harry. "Over the Gangplank with Harry Acton." *New York Telegraph* 6 Nov. 1924.

        Extremely condescending dismissal of Treadwell's charges against Barrymore.

S027   "Barrymore Abandoned *Poe* Paly [sic] After Hearing." *New Orleans Item* 17 Oct. 1924.

        Summary of Barrymore's manager, Arthur Hopkins's, statement in defense of his client.

S028   "Barrymore Sued by Miss Treadwell for Mss. of Her Play." *New York Telegraph* 16 Oct. 1924.

        This brief account reports that Barrymore had written to Treadwell in September to notify her he could not use her Poe play because his wife had written one "much like it."

S029   "Barrymore Sued for Poe Play: Sophie Treadwell Alleges That Wife's Production is a Copy." *New York Evening World* 16 Oct. 1924.

        Standard wire service account of the lawsuit includes

photos of Barrymore's wife, Michael Strange, and Treadwell.

S030   "Barrymore to Scan *Parsifal* as Spoken Part." *New York Herald &*
Tribune 6 Nov. 1924.
On his way out of the country, Barrymore calls
Treadwell's plagiarism accusations "ridiculous."

S031   Brastow, Virginia. "Movie Stars Set New York Fashions." *San*
Francisco Argonaut 1 Nov. 1924.
This society column intersperses details about the
legal "situation" between Barrymore and Treadwell with
descriptions of the playwright as a lady of fashion and wife
of McGeehan.

S032   "Denies Libel in *Poe* Suit." *New York Post* 28 Oct. 1924.
Very short overview of Michael Strange's countersuit
against Treadwell for libel and damages due to stoppage of
her play production. Treadwell welcomes the chance to
mediate the dispute in court.

S033   "Devoted." *Pittsburgh Post* 3 Nov. 1924.
Photo of Barrymore on ship's deck before sailing to
join his wife, who is upset over the lawsuit.

S034   "Gives Barrymore Side of Poe Play Dispute: Miss Treadwell Not
Harmed, View of Hopkins, Theatrical Manager--Actor
Fishing." *New York Times* 17 Oct. 1924: 18.
The sub-heading pretty much tells it all: Arthur
Hopkins defends Barrymore while the actor is fishing in
Florida. Hopkins gives his version of the chronology of the
events leading up to the suit.

S035   Hammond, Percy. "Oddments and Remainders." *New York Herald &*
Tribune 2 Nov. 1924.
Stating he is friends of both Barrymore and
Treadwell, Hammond claims not take sides. His sympathies
seem clearly with Barrymore, though.

S036   "Hopkins, Producer, Defends Barrymore in Treadwell Suit." *New*
York Tribune-Herald 17 Oct. 1924.
Quotes at length from Hopkins's prepared statement
about Treadwell's court action against Barrymore.

S037   "John Barrymore Seeks New Play." *Detroit Free Press* 6 Nov. 1924.
Barrymore announces plans to act in the Poe drama after the "alleged plagiarism case" has been resolved, a comment in contradiction to Hopkins's statement of 17 October, in which he states all plans for production are cancelled.

S038   "John Barrymore Sued for Play." *New York Sun* 16 Oct. 1924.
Provides detailed descriptions of Treadwell's interaction with Barrymore and the reasons for her suit.

S039   "Mrs. Barrymore Sues." *Cincinnati Billboard* 8 Nov. 1924.
States that Barrymore encouraged Strange to offer counter-suit against Treadwell "because of the insinuation that he was a party to the alleged piracy."

S040   "Mrs. Barrymore Sues Author, Charging Libel." *Springfield* [Mass.] *Evening Union* 28 Oct. 1924.
Treadwell welcomes Strange's countersuit, saying she hoped the matter would be tried in court "for the sake of all playwrights and authors."

S041   "Mrs. Barrymore Sues Playwright for $200,000." *New York Herald & Tribune* 28 Oct. 1924.
Condensed copy of S040.

S042   "Mrs. John Barrymore Sues Sophie Treadwell for Libel." [Unsourced clipping] 28 Oct. 1924.
Treadwell "laughed heartily" when informed of the news of Strange's countersuit and said: "If she had an original play why didn't she have it produced? She the wife of the leading actor in the country and then to say I prevented her from having her play produced!   It's ridiculous."

S043   "Mrs. John Barrymore Sues Sophie Treadwell Over Play." *New York Journal* 28 Oct. 1924.
A summary of Strange's countersuit.   States that Treadwell's original manuscript was returned to her on Monday.

S044   "Obtains Writ for Play Held by Poe." *New York Daily Mirror* 16 Oct.
        1924.
                    Brief report on Treadwell's suit.

S045   "Plays and Plagiarism." *New York Evening Sun* 1 Nov. 1924.
                    Indirectly dismisses the validity of Treadwell's suit
        by examining it alongside ten other unsuccessful accusations
        of plagiarism in the theatre.

S046   "Playwright Sued by Mrs. Barrymore." *New York Times* 28 Oct. 1924:
        18.
                    A statement issued from Arthur Hopkins's office
        regarding the Strange countersuit attempts to undermine
        Treadwell's credibility by attacking her motives for bringing
        legal action: "she ha[s] set out upon a course of self-
        advertising, reckless of the consequences of her false
        accusation."

S047   "Playwright Sues John Barrymore." *New York American* 16 Oct.
        1924.
                    Brief account of Treadwell's accusations.

S048   "Sophie Treadwell Replevins Play She Says John Barrymore Retains."
        New York Morning World 16 Oct. 1924.
                    The accusations against Barrymore are accompanied
        by a photo of Treadwell.

S049   "Sues Barrymore to Get Back Her Play About Poe." *McKeesport*
        [Penn.] *News* 22 Oct. 1924.
                    This nice photo of Treadwell includes a captioned
        summary of her lawsuit and activities as a member of the
        Lucy Stone League.

S050   "Sues John Barrymore to Recover Poe Play: Woman Says His Wife
        Used Her Manuscript." *New York Times* 16 Oct. 1924: 1.
                    News of Treadwell's suit against Barrymore made
        page one of the *Times*.

S051   "Sues to Recover Play from John Barrymore." *Cincinnati Billboard*
        25 Oct. 1924.
                    Standard account of the first week of events
        surrounding the plagiarism lawsuit.

S052   "Suit Over Play Hits Barrymore." *New York News* 16 Oct. 1924.
        One paragraph announcement of Treadwell's suit.

S053   "Woman Sues Barrymore as Play 'Pirate.'" *New York Tribune-Herald*
        16 Oct. 1924.
        Lengthy account of Treadwell's dispute with
        Barrymore. Treadwell's description of her confrontational
        meeting with Barrymore matches the typed transcript of this
        meeting found in Heck-Rabi (S167) and UALSC.

S054   "Woman Writer Sues Barrymore for Play." *New York Evening Post*
        16 Oct. 1924.
        This brief account of Treadwell's legal action
        includes direct quotes from the complaint filed in the New
        York Supreme Court.

S055   Woollcott, Alexander. "Plays and Players in These Parts." *New York
        Evening Sun* [Oct.-Nov. 1924].
        A big admirer of Barrymore's, Woollcott makes
        casual mention of the "Treadwell-Strange litigation."

S056   "Writer Sues Barrymore." *New York Evening Journal* 16 Oct. 1924.
        Standard account of Treadwell's court action.

                                    1925

S057   "Americans Take Satire with Good Nature." *New York Sun* [Apr.-May
        1925].
        Quotes Treadwell at length regarding her use of the
        French Marquis in *O NIghtingale* to represent the European
        point of view toward American men.

S058   "Author to Act." *New York Graphic* 14 Apr. 1925.
        Treadwell will perform in *O Nightingale* rather than
        postpone its opening due to the departure at the "eleventh
        hour" by a "temperamental player."

S059   Baker, Colgate. "Sophie Treadwell and *O Nightingale* Regular K. O."
        New York Review 9 May 1925.
        Lengthy profile of Treadwell which focuses on her
        attitudes toward playwriting and producing. Corroborates
        much of the information in a profile published two weeks

previously (S069). An old friend of Treadwell's from California, Baker wonders why Treadwell has not pursued her acting career, and cannot imagine why George C. Tyler and other producers would have let a play like *O Nightingale* slip through their fingers. Baker recounts Modjeska's influence on Treadwell, and incorrectly says she studied theatre with Stanislavsky, not Boleslavsky. He refers to McGeehan as Treadwell's "Friend-Husband."

S060   "Cast and Forecast." *New York World* 28 Apr. 1925.
            It appears Treadwell's play on Edgar Allan Poe will be the first of several in circulation to be produced. The article fails to mention who will produce the play.

S061   "Clever Playwrights Who Are Also Their Own Playwrights." *Vanity Fair* July 1925: 48.
            The caption under a severe-looking photo of Treadwell reads: "When not busy exploring Mexico, writing plays, marrying W. O. McGeehan, or suing Mrs. John Barrymore, Miss Treadwell is not above playing roles in her own dramas."

S062   "In Her Own Comedy." *New York Review* [Apr. 1925].
            Identifies Treadwell as the actress Constance Eliot in *O Nightingale*.

S063   Mantle, Burns, ed. *The Best Plays of 1924-25*. Boston: Small, Maynard & Co., 1925: 578.
            Provides a plot synopsis and cast list for *O Nightingale*.

S064   "Miss Treadwell to Make Further Productions." *New York Telegram* 28 Apr. 1925.
            Coinciding with *O Nightingale*'s transfer from the 49th Street Theatre to the Astor Theatre, Treadwell announces plans for a series of future productions, including her play on Poe.

S065   "*O Nightingale* Characterizations." *Wall Street News* 24 Apr. 1925.
            Treadwell claims the character of Gormont in *O Nightingale* is not based on any particular theatre producer, despite rumors to the contrary.

S066   "Play-Things." *New York Telegram* 10 Apr. 1925.
Treadwell, "being naturally a bold, intrepid person," will open *O Nightingale* without the benefit of a tryout or even "an invitation dress rehearsal."

S067   "7 or 11 Out." *Variety* 6 May 1925: 23.
Wonders why the transfer of *O Nightingale* to the Astor Theatre is warranted, since its sales at the 49th Street Theatre have been modest.

S068   "A Sob Sister Becomes a Broadway Producer." [Unsourced clipping, Apr.-May 1925.]
Recounts Treadwell's previous experiences with New York theatre, including the Barrymore lawsuit and Tyler's abrupt dismissal of *O Nightingale*. Calls her "Broadway's bravest woman."

S069   Stone, Percy N. "Many-Sided Sophie Treadwell Places Playwright Side First." *New York Herald Tribune* 26 Apr. 1925, sec. 6: 14.
Excellent profile on Treadwell's views on theatre, as well as insights into her personality. With *O Nightingale* she is Broadway's only "playwright-producer-director-actress." Treadwell has abandoned a career as an actress to dedicate her time to writing: "the typewriter," she says, "has played the obbligato to my life."

S070   "Theatre Notes." *New York News* 26 Apr. 1925.
Treadwell plans to produce her Poe play next fall.

S071   "To Do Feminist Play." *New York Telegram* 7 May 1925.
Treadwell states there has been "so much interest" by feminists in her "comedy," *Rights*, that she has "advanced [it] on her list of plays for early production." Like her plans for the Poe play, this production never got off the ground.

S072   [Untitled clipping.] *New York Post* 23 Apr. 1925.
Treadwell denies rumors that the character of Gormont in *O Nightingale* was based on a well-known theatre manager. Treadwell's "solemn" denials that the rumors lack truth, though, "indicates subtly that it isn't so."

S073   "Who's Who in the Theatre." *New York Times* 26 Apr. 1925, sec. 8:
        2.
                One of the best early sources of biographical
        information on Treadwell. She reports that *Rights* grew out
        of her involvement with the Lucy Stone League, and that she
        was the "first accredited woman war corespondent for
        American newspapers during the World War, with a portfolio
        in the War Office."

1926

S074   Older, Fremont. *My Own Story.* New York: Macmillan, 1926: 277.
                Passing mention of Treadwell as one of Older's
        "little group" from the *San Francisco Bulletin* who took an
        interest in an abandoned wife of an ex-convict who tried to
        run away from her life as a high-class prostitute by going on
        the stage. Older was Treadwell's editor on the *Bulletin.*

1927

S075   "Lakewood Audiences to See First Production Treadwell Drama."
        [Unsourced clipping, June 1927.]
                Notes with anticipation the pre-Broadway production
        of Treadwell's *Better to Marry* at the Lakewood Theatre in
        Skowhegan, Maine. Provides some otherwise undocumented
        information about Treadwell's work as a journalist during
        World War I.

1928

S076   Anderson, John. "Footnotes on Spotlights." *New York Evening
        Journal* [1928].
                Cites Arthur Hopkins's unusual but oddly appropriate
        action of placing an ad in yesterday's *Journal* praising his
        own production: "*Machinal* is brilliantly written, thrillingly
        acted. It will arouse you."

S077   "Cast and Forecast." *New York World* 8 Aug. 1928.
                Brief reports on rumors that Hopkins is rehearsing a
        new play, *Machinale.* "Some say Mr. Hopkins is the author."

S078   "Editorial." *Drama Calendar* [Sept.-Oct. 1928].
            This letter to the drama editor praises *Machinal*, a
production through which New York theatre "has reached its
zenith."

S079   "Hopkins' *Machinal* Mirrors Snyder Case." *Variety* 5 Sept. 1928.
            Two days before *Machinal*'s opening, *Variety* reports
that the play is a dramatization of the Ruth Snyder-Judd Gray
murder case. Hopkins has "forbidden" the cast to talk of the
play's theme to the press. Treadwell "unofficially" covered
the trial, and Hopkins "is said to have also had a hand in on
the script."

S080   "Immorality of Actors." *New York Times* 16 Sept. 1928.
            This editorial praises *Machinal* as being "so
detached, impersonal and abstract that it seems timeless. In
a hundred years it should still be vital and vivid."

S081   Littell, Robert. "Front and Inside Pages." *Theatre Arts Monthly* Oct.
1928: 704.
            Littlell's article on the current Broadway season
includes two sketches by Robert Edmond Jones for *Machinal*:
the courtroom and the prison cell.

S082   "The Talk of the Town." *New Yorker* 29 Sept. 1928: 15.
            This brief column humorously records the many
questions heard in the theatre during a performance of
Machinal.

S083   [Untitled clipping.] *New York World* 9 Aug. 1928.
            Hopkins responds to yesterday's report on *Machinal*
by confirming that Treadwell is the author of the play. He
has been secretive because "certain revolutionary methods of
staging" are still being worked out by Jones, and George
Schaff is designing special lighting equipment for the
production.

S084   [Untitled clipping.] *New York World* 23 Sept. 1928.
            Notes the difficulty a fellow critic had in identifying
which actors played which parts in *Machinal*, due to
Treadwell's archetypal naming scheme. The reviewer praised
Hal K. Dawson when he should have honored Clark Gable.

S085   [Untitled clipping.] *The Spur* Oct. 1928.
        Believes Treadwell's many exploits, have "helped her
        cultivate a broad and searching mind."

1929

S086   "Five Playwrights Who Will Contribute to the Coming Season."
        Theatre Magazine Sept. 1929: 20.
        Vandamm photo of Treadwell with caption
        announcing her upcoming production of *Ladies Leave*.

S087   Mantle, Burns, ed. *The Best Plays of 1928-29*. New York: Dodd,
        Mead, 1929: 225-51, 350, 369.
        Machinal is listed as one of Mantle's ten best plays
        of the 1928-29 season. This volume provides a plot
        summary, dialogue excerpts, a production photo, and a brief
        overview of the play's reception. A biographical note on
        Treadwell and a cast list are also included.

S088   "The Play That is Talked About--*Machinal*: a Play in Two Parts and
        Ten Scenes." *Theatre Magazine* Jan. 1929: 32-34, 58, 62.
        Provides a plot summary with dialogue excerpts,
        along with three photos from the Broadway production.

1930-1939

1930

S089   Mannes, Marya. "Robert Edmond Jones: a Scene Designer Who Has
        Achieved Distinction in Many Styles and Moods." *Theatre
        Guild Magazine* Nov. 1930: 14-19, 62-63.
        Speaks of the air of "aristocracy" evident in all
        Jones's designs, even for those plays that seem rough or
        earthbound, such as *Machinal*.

1931

S090   Mantle, Burns, ed. *The Best Plays of 1929-30*. New York: Dodd,
        Mead, 1931: 410.
        Provides a cast list for *Ladies Leave*, along with a

very brief plot summary.

S091   McGeehan, W. O. *Trouble in the Balkans*. New York: Dial Press, 1931.

Tongue-in-cheek account of McGeehan eating and drinking his way through Europe in the spring of 1931 with Treadwell and a Bavarian guide named Otto. McGeehan never fully identifies Treadwell by name, referring satirically to her instead as "the lady who is driving me." The book provides a colorful companion to Treadwell's unpublished and more factual "Log of a Chrysler," located in the archive at UALSC. McGeehan's chapters were originally published as essays in his "Down the Line" column for the *New York Tribune*.

1933

S092   "Authoress of *Lone Valley* Interviewed." *New York American* [Undated clipping, Mar. 1933].

This anonymous interviewer knew of Treadwell's journalistic exploits and expected, when meeting her for the first time, to find a "robustious person who wears chaps to breakfast, uses a six-shooter-barrel to stir her coffee and leads a Gila Monster through Central Park on a leash." What the interviewer found instead was a "completely feminine person, scared to death of interviewers and shrinking painfully from publicity's glare." Treadwell commends Arthur Hopkins as the "kindest man in the world," and the interviewer concludes that Treadwell herself is the "ideal of the gentle and gracious."

S093   "Comment on Theatrical Activities Along Broadway and Here in Brooklyn." *Brooklyn Daily Eagle* 5 Mar. 1933: E2.

This announcement of *Lone Valley*'s opening is accompanied by a sketch of Treadwell in profile.

S094   "From the Russian Theatres." *Theatre Arts Monthly* Dec. 1933: 941-44.

Includes photos from Tairov's production of *Machinal*.

S095   Rubinstein, Raphael. "A Word from the Soviet Theater On Its
        Production of *Machinal*." *New York Herald Tribune* 28 May
        1933.
                Rubinstein, the "literary advisor" for Moscow's
        Kamerny Theatre, reports on Tairov's production of *Machinal*
        in an attempt to refute claims by Western journalists that the
        Soviet stage only produces propaganda. In quoting Tairov at
        length, however, the article reveals the director's views on the
        play's indictment of capitalism, and discusses how his staging
        reinforced his interpretation.

S096   "Sophie Treadwell Given Play Royalties in Moscow: Soviet Sets
        Precedent Through Recognizing *Machinal*." *New York
        Herald* [Paris] 24 Aug. 1933.
                Treadwell has won in her efforts to secure
        production royalties from the Soviet Union. A run of "a year
        or more" is predicted for *Machinal* at the Kamerny.

S097   "Soviet Royalty On Play Won by U.S. Dramatist." *New York Herald
        Tribune* 28 Aug. 1933.
                Reports on Treadwell's royalty payment from the
        Soviets. A "number" of provincial Russian theatres are
        planning production of *Machinal*. Includes a photo of
        Treadwell.

S098   "They Stand Out from the Crowd." *Literary Digest* 23 Sept. 1933: 9.
                Brief announcement that Treadwell has become the
        first American playwright to obtain royalties from Soviet
        Russia. Includes a photo of Treadwell.

S099   [Untitled caricature.] *New York Times* 5 Mar. 1933, sec. 9: 2.
                Caricature of Treadwell.

                                    1934

S100   Hopkins, Arthur. "Ten of My Favorite Plays." *New York Sun* 26
        Mar. 1934.
                Machinal makes Hopkins's top ten list.

S101   Mantle, Burns, ed. *The Best Plays of 1932-33*. New York: Dodd,
        Mead, 1934: 475.
                Lists cast and summarizes plot of *Lone Valley*.

1935

S102   Markov. P. A. *The Soviet Theatre*. The New Soviet Library, 3. New
        York: G. P. Putnam's Sons, 1935: 104-05.
                Discusses Tairov's production of *Machinal*, in which
        the director "makes a general expression of soulless,
        mechanical life in America."

S103   "Sophie Treadwell's *Lusita*." *New York Herald Tribune* 6 Jan. 1935.
                Report that Treadwell, while revising *Promised Land*
        for producer Thomas Mitchell, has completed a stage
        adaptation of her novel, *Lusita*. Producer Alexander McKaig
        "has acquired the show and plans to exhibit it next month."
        There is no record in Treadwell's papers that such a
        production took place, nor has any manuscript of this
        adaptation survived.

1936

S104   "Famed Bay Author Waits Premiere of Her New Play." [Unsourced
        clipping, 1936.]
                Feature article on Treadwell and *Plumes in the Dust*.
        Summarizes some biographical details of Treadwell's
        background in California, and states that *Machinal* "was
        produced in every capital in Europe."

S105   Houghton, Norris. *Moscow Rehearsals*. New York: Harcourt, Brace
        & Co., 1936.
                Houghton provides descriptions of the two Moscow
        productions of *Machinal*, one by Tairov and the other by
        Simonov. He greatly admires Vadim Ryndin's settings and
        projections for the former, but he is more "deeply moved"
        over the plight of the Young Woman in the latter.

S106   Ross, Ishbel. *Ladies of the Press*. New York: Harper & Brothers,
        1936.
                Excellent early source of biographical information on
        Treadwell. Provides details of Treadwell's work on the *San
        Francisco Bulletin* and *New York American*, as well as her

marriage to McGeehan.

S107   Wells, Evelyn. *Fremont Older*. New York: D. Appleton-Century, 1936.

This biography of Treadwell's editor at the *Bulletin* includes a description of the events leading up to Treadwell's assignment on the serial, "An Outcast on the Christian Door." Wells remembers Treadwell as "a dark, slender, sensitive young woman with hair-trigger perceptions." Wells also states that Herbert Bashford, book editor of the *Bulletin*, turned the "Outcast" serial into a play "which reaped him a small fortune." Wells may be confusing this play with Treadwell's *An Unwritten Chapter*, as I have found no evidence of such a play by Bashford.

1937

S108   Hopkins, Arthur. *To a Lonely Boy*. New York: Book League of America, 1937: 243-47.

Hopkins's impressionistic autobiography includes Treadwell among a list of journalists who also made good playwrights, and discusses *Machinal* and the artists associated with its initial production.

S109   Mantle, Burns, ed. *The Best Plays of 1936-37*. New York: Dodd, Mead, 1937: 8, 428-29.

Reprints the cast list for *Plumes in the Dust* and summarizes its plot.

S110   Mersand, Joseph. *When Ladies Write Plays*. New York: Modern Chapbooks, 1937: 13.

This slim volume, often derided as a work of condescending chauvisinism, refers to *Machinal* as "one of the most lucid of all expressionistic plays."

1938

S111   Flexner, Eleanor. *American Playwrights: 1918-1938--The Theatre Retreats from Reality*. New York: Simon & Schuster, 1938: 283.

This excellent study of early twentieth-century

American drama lists *Machinal* as one of the notable plays of this era written by playwrights not regarded as our nation's leading dramatists.

S112   Mantle, Burns. *Contemporary American Playwrights*. New York: Dodd, Mead, 1938.
Includes a brief paragraph on Treadwell.

1939

S113   Cornell, Katharine. *I Wanted to be an Actress*. New York: Random House, 1939: 57.
Mentions *Gringo* as one of husband Guthrie McClintic's "two failures in quick succession" at a time when the couple was experiencing financial hardship.

1940-1949

1941

S114   "Creator of *Machinal* Returns to Broadway with Guild Play." *New York Herald Tribune* 23 Nov. 1941.
This profile provides numerous details about Treadwell's life and personality, including her recent purchase of a home in Newtown, Connecticut. The author, however, confuses Modjeska with Adah Isaacs Menken.

S115   "*Hope for a Harvest*." [Unsourced clipping, 1941.]
Notes Treadwell's use of her experiences on the family ranch in Stockton as source material for her new play, *Hope for a Harvest*. The ranch also served as subject matter for a 1914 story by McGeehan for the *Saturday Evening Post*.

S116   Jones, Robert Edmond. *The Dramatic Imagination*. New York: Theatre Arts Books, 1941: 132.
Mentions [*For*] *Saxophone* as one of the few exceptions to a tendency toward literalness and prosaicness in contemporary plays.

S117   "Pancho Villa Source of Material for Play: War-Time Interview with
        Bandit Helps in Writing Color Stories." [*New York Morning
        Telegraph*, 3 Dec. 1941.]
                Anecdotal article on Treadwell's Villa interview and
        latest play, *Hope for a Harvest*. "Her detailed account of
        Carranza's fatal flight from the capital city to Vera Cruz is
        now a newspaper classic."

S118   Parker, R. A. "In the Drama Mailbag." Letter to Drama Editor. *New
        York Times* 14 Dec. 1941.
                Rebuffs the dismissal of *Harvest* by the New York
        critics. Believes Treadwell the first American playwright "to
        dramatize The Machine as the villain of the human tragedy
        as it is being enacted by society today." The article was
        perhaps written by Treadwell's close friend, editor Robert
        Allerton Parker.

S119   Powers-Waters, Alma. *John Barrymore: the Legend and the Man.*
        New York: Julian Messner, 1941: 200-01.
                Discusses the Treadwell-Barrymore dispute in the
        context of the actor's troubled marriage to Michael Strange.

S120   "Theatre Guild Plays Up Out-of-Town Reviews on *Harvest* After N.Y.
        Nix." *Variety* 3 Dec. 1941.
                Reports on Lawrence Langner's "radical idea" of
        taking out large ads for *Harvest* which excerpted out-of-town
        rather than New York critics.

                                    1942

S121   Mantle, Burns, ed. *The Best Plays of 1941-42.* New York: Dodd,
        Mead, 1942: 7, 349-84, 390, 417.
                Provides a detailed plot summary and dialogue
        excerpts from *Harvest*, as well as a biographical note on
        Treadwell and a cast list.

                                    1943

S122   Malvern, Gladys. *Curtain Going Up! The Story of Katharine Cornell.*
        New York: Julian Messner, 1943: 126.
                Mentions *Gringo* as one of two productions which

lost the money Guthrie McClintic had just made from his Broadway directing debut with *Dover Road*.

S123   Martin, Boyd. *Modern American Drama and Stage*. London: Pilot Press, 1943: 62, 94.

Cites Treadwell as one example of "a generous amount of writing talent that knows its way around a theatre."

1949

S124   Gassner, John. Introduction to *Machinal*. *Twenty-five Best Plays of the Modern American Theatre, Early Series*. Ed. John Gassner. New York: Crown, 1949: 494.

Citing *Machinal* as "One of the most unusual plays of the twenties," Gassner says the play appeared onstage "almost as if it had been deliberately produced to sum up trends in the theatre of that period." Treadwell's "unique" form of expressionsim, transformed the "commonplaces of adultery and murder" into a "story representative of many lives." The play contained a "very high degree of artistry that not everybody was able to recognize" when first produced. Gassner's introductory essay to the anthology mentions *Machinal* as a "theatrical *tour de force*" amongst plays depicting the plights of working class characters (xxxvi).

S125   Morehouse, Ward. *Matinee Tomorrow: Fifty Years of Our Theater*. New York: Whittlesey House, 1949: 275.

"Fredric March and Florence Eldridge found that they could do little with Sophie Treadwell's *Hope for a Harvest*."

1950-1959

1951

S126   Langner, Lawrence. *The Magic Curtain*. New York: E. P. Dutton, 1951: 335, 478.

Refers to Treadwell as one of his and his wife Theresa Helburn's "closest friends." Also recounts how his placing ads for *Harvest* quoting non-New York critics backfired: "Even those New Yorkers who had bought tickets seemed to want their money back!"

1953

S127   Stock, Morgan Evan. "The Carmel Theatre from 1910-1935." M.A. thesis, Stanford U, 1953.
        History of the Carmel theatre where Treadwell appeared in *The Toad.*

1954

S128   Hunt, Lawrence E. "Historic Treadwell Estate Sold to G. L. Capps." [Unsourced clipping, 1954?]
        Announces the sale of Treadwell's ranch in Stockton.

1955

S129   Black, Eugene Robert. "Robert Edmond Jones: Poetic Artist of the New Stagecraft." Diss. U Wisconsin, 1955: 181-275.
        Discusses the designs for *Machinal* in light of Jones's continued development as a designer. Excerpts critical reviews pertaining to the script and Jones's designs.

S130   "E. L. T. Production Canceled." [Unsourced clipping, 1955.]
        Brief announcement that the previously announced production of *Machinal* by the Equity Library Theatre has been cancelled.   Rights were not cleared pending a prospective musical treatment of the play, which is being adapted by Abby Mann.

S131   McClintic, Guthrie. *Me and Kit.* Boston: Little, Brown & Co., 1955: 327.
        McClintic erroneously recalls directing *Gringo* in 1927.

S132   Sievers, W. David. *Freud on Broadway: a History of Psychoanalysis and the American Drama.* New York: Hermitage House, 1955.
        This influential study includes discussions of

Machinal in several different chapters. Sievers discusses the play in terms of Freudian analysis, and mentions that it "contributed greatly to the gradual removal of the taboo on such themes as homosexuality." Treadwell's other plays were not departures from realism, and *Ladies Leave* was "a somewhat inept drawing room satire on psychoanalytic faddists."

1957

S133   Ferguson, Phyllis Marschall. "Women Dramatists in the American Theatre, 1901-1940." Diss. U Pittsburgh, 1957.
Sketchy and uneven discussion of Treadwell within the larger context of American women playwrights.

S134   Gorchakov, Nikolai A. *The Theater in Soviet Russia*. Trans. Edgar Lehrman. New York: Columbia UP, 1957: 350.
Dense discussion of Tairov's interpretation of *Machinal*, which was attacked for "dragging in hypocritical bourgeois liberalism" to the Soviet stage.

1958

S135   Pendleton, Ralph, ed. *The Theatre of Robert Edmond Jones*. Middletown [Conn.]: Wesleyan UP, 1958: 68-69, 165, 167.
Includes Jones's sketch for the courtroom scene in *Machinal*.

1960-1969

1960

S136   Blum, David, ed. *Theatre World: Season 1959-1960*. Philadelphia: Chilton, 1960: 161.
Reprints the cast list and three production photos from the Gate Theatre revival of *Machinal*.

S137   Calta, Louis. "*Machinal* Opens at Gate March 9." *New York Times* 10 Feb. 1960: 42.
In this interview, Treadwell admits to being "awfully

bitter" over the critical response to *Hope for a Harvest*. She calls *Machinal* her "favorite play," but disputes that it is in any way "allegorical."

S138   Dusenbury, Winifred L.   *The Theme of Loneliness in Modern American Drama*. Gainesville: U Florida P, 1960: 113.
        Cites *Machinal* as one of several post-World War I plays to deal with the "debilitating effects upon human character of the crushing forces of the capitalistic economic system."

S139   Little, Stuart W.   "1928 Drama, *Machinal*, In Revival." *New York Herald Tribune* 7 Apr. 1960.
        Describes how *Machinal* was "redesigned, re-rehearsed, re-scored and choreographed" after Gene Frankel replaced Louis MacMillan as director for the Gate Theatre revival.

S140   Little, Stuart W.   "Vernon Rice Awards Given Playwrights First Time." *New York Herald Tribune* 10 May 1960.
        The Gate Theatre's revival of *Machinal* receives a Vernon Rice Award for best "all-around" off-Broadway production this season. Dolores Sutton is cited for honorable mention for her performance.

S141   "*Machinal*, 4 Playwrights Get Rice Awards." *New York Times* 10 May 1960: 45.
        Announces the awards for *Machinal*.

S142   Morgenstern, Joe.   "*Machinal* Evades Success." *New York Herald Tribune* 8 May 1960.
        Morgenstern laments that the *Machinal* revival lacks good box office sales despite favorable reviews. In excerpts from interviews, director Frankel explains his staging concept for the production and Dolores Sutton tells how she visited Treadwell in Connecticut and gained her approval for the revival. This latter account contradicts an earlier report (S137) that Treadwell gave producer Richard Karp permission to revive the play, pending their agreement in finding a suitable actress. In yet another account of the production's genesis, a press release by Karp dated 5 February 1960 states that Treadwell had withheld rights to the play for the past ten years, waiting for the right combination of producer and

actress.   After seeing Sutton on television one night, Treadwell supposedly "called the studio and offered her the role on the spot" (UALSC).

S143   "New Writers Take Four Rice Awards." *Village Voice* 11 May 1960.
Announces the awards for *Machinal.*

S144   "Plea for *Machinal.*" *New York Times* 28 Apr. 1960.
Actors in the Gate Theatre revival staged a demonstration in Shubert Alley on behalf of their production, which may close unless ticket sales pick up.

1961

S145   Hansen, Delmar J. "The Directing Theory and Practice of Arthur Hopkins." Diss. U Iowa, 1961.
Includes discussion of how the productions of *Machinal* and *Plumes in the Dust* relate to Hopkins's directing philosophy and working methodology.

S146   Swanberg, W. A. *Citizen Hearst.* New York: Charles Scribner's Sons, 1961: 292-93.
Brief mention of William Randolph Hearst's admiration for Treadwell's journalistic work for the *San Francisco Bulletin*, which resulted in his hiring of her for the *New York American.*   Treadwell calls Hearst "the most generous of employers."

1964

S147   Tillinghast, John Keith. "Guthrie McClintic, Director." Diss. Indiana U, 1964.
Passing mention of *Gringo.*

S148   Valgemae, Mardi. "Expressionism in American Drama." Diss. U California at Los Angeles, 1964.
Dissertation which formed a later published study (S162).

1965

S149   Edwards, Christine. *The Stanislavsky Heritage.* New York: New
        York UP, 1965: 239-40.
             Confirms Treadwell's attendance at Boleslavsky's
        public lectures at the Princess Theatre in 1923.

1967

S150   Benton, Pat Moran. "Premiere of a Play: a Lot of Hard Work."
        Arizona Daily Star [Tucson] 20 July 1967: C1.
             This preview of *Now He Doesn't Want to Play* is
        accompanied by several photos of the cast, director Peter
        Marroney and Treadwell in rehearsal.

S151   Gassner, John.   "Realism in the Modern American Theatre."
        American Theatre. Stratford-upon-Avon Studies, 10. Eds.
        John Russell Brown and Bernard Harris. London: Edward
        Arnold, 1967: 27.
             Cites *Machinal* as one of several American dramas
        whose "documentary character" would have proved
        "tiresomely obvious" without some "theatrical distancing of
        the material by formal and stylistic means."

S152   Pavillard, Dan. "A New Treadwell." *Tucson Daily Citizen* 24 June
        1967.
             Brief profile of Treadwell's theatrical and journalistic
        careers. Includes a photo of Treadwell in her 80s.

1969

S153   Nadel, Norman. *A Pictorial History of the Theatre Guild.* Introd.
        Brooks Atkinson. New York: Crown, 1969: 173-74.
             Summarizes the critical response to *Harvest* found in
        S126. Includes production photos.

S154   Tairov, Alexander. *Notes of a Director.* Trans. and Introd. William
        Kuhlke. Coral Gables [Fla.]: U Miami P, 1969: 36.
             Passing mention of *Machinal* as one of the plays he
        produced from Western Europe and America.

1970-1979

1970

S155   Obituary. *New York Times* 14 Mar. 1970.
Treadwell's obituary mentions her major plays and journalistic achievements, a novel, husband McGeehan, and an adopted son who survives. Incorrectly cites her age as 79.

S156   Obituary. *Variety* 18 Mar. 1970.
Almost identical to S155.

S157   "Sophie Treadwell Dies; Noted as Playwright." *Arizona Daily Star* [Tucson] 24 Feb. 1970: A2.
Obituary notice. The only source to identify Treadwell as a play doctor for "many playwrights." Mentions she was engaged in writing a play at the time of her death.

S158   "Sophie Treadwell Dies; Playwright, Newspaperwoman." *Tucson Daily Citizen* 23 Feb. 1970: 4.
Obituary notice. Remembrances were suggested to the University of Arizona Drama Department.

1971

S159   Halverson, Bruce Rogness. "Arthur Hopkins: a Theatrical Biography." Diss. U Washington, 1971.
Quotes from Treadwell's article on Hopkins (A19), but otherwise provides few details on Hopkins's working process on *Machinal* or on *Plumes in the Dust*.

S160   Oblak, John B. *Bringing Broadway to Maine.* Terre Haute [Ind.]: Moore-Langen, 1971: 78, 155.
In this history of the Lakewood Theatre, Oblak describes Treadwell's presence at the opening performance of her play, *Bound.* [A photo of Treadwell with Lakewood Theatre personnel is housed in the New York Public Library for the Performing Arts.] Oblak incorrectly states Crosby Gaige produced the show on Broadway the following year, and he misspells the last name of actor Harold Vermilyea.

1972

S161   Matlaw, Myron. "Sophie Treadwell." *Modern World Drama: an Encyclopedia*. New York: Dutton, 1972: 771-72.
Brief but well-written encyclopedic entry on Treadwell.

S162   Valgemae, Mardi. *Accelerated Grimace: Expressionism in the American Drama of the 1920s*. Carbondale: Southern Illinois UP, 1972.
Examines *Machinal* in light of the entire body of American expressionistic drama of the 1920s and ranks it in the top dozen in terms of being "aesthetically satisfying." Valgemae also provides a paragraph description of *For Saxophone*. See S148.

1973

S163   Brockett, Oscar G. and Robert Findlay. *Century of Innovation*. Englewood Cliffs: Prentice-Hall, 1973: 527.
The authors improperly lump Treadwell in with a listing of "left-wing" dramatists of the 1920s and 30s who "for the most part were dismissed as mere propagandists and were encouraged only by workers' theatre groups."

S164   Salem, James M., ed. *A Guide to Critical Reviews: Pt. I: American Drama, 1909-1969*. Metuchen [N.J.]: Scarecrow, 1973: 538-40.
Bibliography of major reviews for Treadwell's Broadway productions.

1974

S165   Shafer, Yvonne B. "The Liberated Woman in American Plays of the Past." *Players* 49.3-4 (1974): 95-100.
Brief discussion of *Machinal* as one of several American plays of the early twentieth century to advocate the education and liberation of women.

1975

S166   Churchill, Allen. *The Theatrical Twenties.* New York: McGraw-Hill, 1975: 280-81.
        This amply illustrated documentary of Broadway in the 1920s includes a brief mention of *Machinal.* Includes a photo of the speakeasy scene.

1976

S167   Heck-Rabi, Louise Evelyn. "Sophie Treadwell: Subjects and Structures in 20th Century American Drama." Diss. Wayne State U, 1976.
        The first dissertation completed on Treadwell's career. Heck-Rabi provides a general discussion of the evolution of Treadwell's career, as well as critical assessments of her plays. She concludes that Treadwell's greatest weaknesses as a playwright were the inability to create sympathetic protagonists and a certain journalistic objectivity in her writing. Useful appendices include a register of copyrights of Treadwell's works and Treadwell's typed transcript of her meeting with John Barrymore over the Poe play dispute.

S168   Himmelstein, Morgan Y. *Drama Was a Weapon.* New Brunswick: Rutgers UP, 1976: 151-52.
        Dismisses *Hope for a Harvest,* saying neither Treadwell nor the Theatre Guild "had treated the exploited proletariat with sufficient solemnity."

S169   Tornabene, Lyn. *Long Live the King: a Biography of Clark Gable.* New York: G. P. Putnam's Sons, 1976: 107-09, 113, 150.
        Discusses Gable's performance in *Machinal,* and includes reminiscences by fellow cast members Zita Johann and Hal K. Dawson.

1977

S170   Kobler, John. *Damned in Paradise: the Life of John Barrymore.* New York: Atheneum, 1977: 159.
        Kobler's discussion of the Treadwell-Barrymore

plagiarism dispute is filled with inaccuracies about Treadwell's residence at the time, Barrymore's reaction to her script, and the timing regarding Barrymore's return of Treadwell's manuscript. [Kobler is the author of an interesting 1938 study, *The Trial of Ruth Snyder and Judd Gray*.]

S171   Marshall, Herbert A. *A Pictorial History of the Russian Theatre*. Introd. Harold Clurman. New York: Crown, 1977: 119.

A brief discussion of Tairov's interpretation of *Machinal* is accompanied by three production photos.

S172   Torda, Thomas Joseph. "Alexander Tairov and the Scenic Artists of the Moscow Kamerny Theater 1914-1935." Diss. U Denver, 1977: 593-607.

The most extensive account in English of the staging, critical response and "historical significance" of Tairov's production of *Machinal*. Includes photocopied reproductions of numerous production photos. Torda also provides a translated excerpt of an article by Treadwell in a Russian newspaper extolling her admiration for the production.

1978

S173   Mosel, Tad and Gertrude Macy. *Leading Lady: the World and Theatre of Katharine Cornell*. Boston: Atlantic Monthly Press, 1978: 166-67.

Having produced *Gringo* from his own bank account, Guthrie McClintic kept the show running longer than warranted by actual ticket sales.

1980-1989

1980

S174   Bronner, Edwin J. *The Encyclopedia of the American Theatre: 1900-1975*. San Diego and New York: A. S. Barnes, 1980.

Provides brief production details and memorable phrases from critical reviews pertaining to Treadwell's plays.

S175   Gianakos, Larry James. *Television Drama Series Programming: a Comprehensive Chronicle, 1947-1959.* Metuchen [N.J.]: Scarecrow, 1980: 380.
Lists airing dates and principal cast members for *Harvest* and *Highway.*

S176   *New York Theatre: Vandamm Collection.*   Cambridge [Cambridgeshire]: Chadwyck-Henley, 1980.
This microfiche collection of theatrical photographs from the Vandamm studio includes production and/or publicity shots from *Machinal, Plumes in the Dust* and *Hope for a Harvest.* The original photos are in the New York Public Library for the Performing Arts.

1981

S177   Barlow, Judith E. "Introduction." *Plays by American Women: the Early Years.* New York: Avon Books, 1981: ix-xxxii.
Briefly recounts Treadwell's work as a journalist and playwright, and compares *Machinal* to both the Ruth Snyder case and fellow playwrights Susan Glaspell and Zona Gale.

S178   Chinoy, Helen Krich. "Art Versus Business: the Role of Women in American Theatre." *Women in American Theatre.* Eds. Helen Krich Chinoy and Linda Walsh Jenkins. New York: Crown, 1981: 7.
Cites *Machinal* as thrusting "a powerful image of women's anguish and revolt at audiences."

S179   Heck-Rabi, Louise. "Sophie Treadwell: Agent for Change." *Women in American Theatre.* Eds. Helen Krich Chinoy and Linda Walsh Jenkins. New York: Crown, 1981: 157-62.
In an excerpt from her dissertation (S167), Heck-Rabi believes that in *For Saxophone* Treadwell "accurately predicted the ubiquitous popularity of music in all stage and cinema work."

S180   Mordden, Ethan. *The American Theatre.* New York: Oxford UP, 1981: 80, 255.
Compares *Machinal* to *The Adding Machine.* Mordden dismisses the 1960 revival of the play as part of Off-Broadway's "movement for the revelation of not merely

new but 'difficult' authors."

S181   Olauson, Judith. *The American Woman Playwright: a View of Criticism and Characterization.* Troy [N.Y.]: Whitson Publishing, 1981: 50.
        Provides an overview of *Hope for a Harvest*, "the only sustaining play to be written by a woman" in 1941.

1982

S182   Coven, Brenda. *American Women Dramatists of the Twentieth Century: a Bibliography.* Metuchen [N.J.]: Scarecrow: 1982: 205-06.
        Brief bibliographic entry of Treadwell's plays and select reviews of productions.

S183   Greenfield, Thomas Allen. *Work and the Work Ethic in American Drama 1920-1979.* Columbia: U Missouri P, 1982: 60-61.
        Briefly discusses *Machinal* and *Harvest* in relation to other American labor dramas of the 1920s and `30s. *Machinal* is derivative of *The Adding Machine*, while *Harvest* is "a racist rallying cry to WASPs who have been demoralized by the intrusion and success of hard-working immigrants." The play's central character, Elliott Martin, is a figure-head for the "orthodox liberal position" which decries racism, while Treadwell's main purpose was to urge "her white audience to conquer the [rival] immigrants by out-working them, outwitting them, and out-bargaining them in order to gain back the spirit of hard work as well as the white supremacist position of the founding fathers." This unusual interpretation of the play seems to ignore the fact that Lotta, not Elliott, is the play's central character, and she advocates working with and learning from immigrant farmers while promoting the marriage of Tonie to the Italian Victor DeLucchi.

S184   McGovern, Edythe M. "Sophie Treadwell." *American Women Writers: a Critical Reference Guide from Colonial Times to the Present.* Vol. 4. New York: Frederick Ungar, 1982: 256-58.
        Biographical entry with some large omissions and minor inaccuracies.

S185   Parent, Jennifer. "Arthur Hopkins' Production of Sophie Treadwell's *Machinal.*" *The Drama Review* **26.**1 (1982): 87-100.

An overview of the stylistic approach used for the Broadway production. Parent's scene-by-scene analysis of the staging, however, includes mostly plot summary and replication of published stage directions. Includes seven Vandamm production photos.

S186   Wynn, Nancy Edith. "Sophie Treadwell: the Career of a Twentieth-Century American Feminist Playwright." Diss. City U of New York, 1982.

The most detailed biographical and critical study of Treadwell to date. Wynn assisted in the organization of the initial collection of Treadwell's papers at UALSC, and kept some materials in her possession for years afterward. She therefore makes use of scrapbooks, letters and diaries to which Heck-Rabi (S167) did not have access. Wynn evaluates almost all of Treadwell's plays in light of her evolving career, and concludes that Treadwell's personality and feminism kept her from succeeding in the theatre. Many dates and interpretations cited in the study need confirmation for there are numerous inaccuracies.

1983

S187   Loney, Glenn. *Twentieth Century Theatre.* 2 vols. New York: Facts on File Publications, 1983.

Offers salient information on Treadwell's Broadway productions.

1984

S188   Bordman, Gerald. *"Machinal." The Oxford Companion to American Theatre.* New York: Oxford UP, 1984: 452.

Brief entry on *Machinal's* characteristics and initial producing artists. Bordman repeats the mistake of some early New York drama critics by claiming that Richard Roe was played by Hal K. Dawson, a stage name for Clark Gable.

S189   Dasgupta, Gautam. "Sophie Treadwell." *McGraw-Hill Encyclopedia of World Drama*. Ed. Stanley Hochman. Vol. 5. New York: McGraw-Hill, 1984, 40-41.
        Very short entry which offers sketchy descriptions of Treadwell's Broadway plays.

S190   Shipley, Joseph T. "*Machinal*." *The Crown Guide to the World's Great Plays*. Rev. ed. New York: Crown, 1984: 779-82.
        Provides a plot summary and overview of the critical responses to the play in New York, London and Moscow.

                                    1985

S191   Barlow, Judith E. "Introduction." *Plays by American Women, 1900-1930*. New York: Applause Theatre Book Publishers, 1985: ix-xxxiii.
        New edition of S177.

S192   Leiter, Samuel L., ed. *The Encyclopedia of the New York Stage, 1920-1930*. 2 vols. Westport [Ct.]: Greenwood, 1985.
        Plot summaries, production information and excerpts from reviews for Treadwell's productions of this period.

S193   Slide, Anthony, ed. *Selected Theatre Criticism. Vol. II: 1920-1930*. Metuchen [N.J.]: Scarecrow: 1985: 139-41.
        Excerpts reviews of *Machinal* by Benchley (R071) and Clark (R075).

                                    1987

S194   Chinoy, Helen Krich. "Art Versus Business: the Role of Women in American Theatre." *Women in American Theatre*. Eds. Helen Krich Chinoy and Linda Walsh Jenkins. Rev. ed. New York: Theatre Communications Group, 1987: 7.
        Revised edition of S178.

S195   Heck-Rabi, Louise. "Sophie Treadwell: Agent for Change." *Women in American Theatre*. Eds. Helen Krich Chinoy and Linda Walsh Jenkins. Rev. ed. New York: Theatre Communications Group, 1987: 157-62.
        Revised edition of S179.

S196   Hennigan, Shirlee. "Women Directors--the Early Years." *Women in American Theatre*. Eds. Helen Krich Chinoy and Linda Walsh Jenkins. Rev. ed. New York: Theatre Communications Group, 1987: 203-06.

Mentions Treadwell in a list of early twentieth-century women playwrights who also directed their own work.

1989

S197   Heck-Rabi, Louise. "Sophie Treadwell." *Notable Women in the American Theatre: a Biographical Dictionary*. Eds. Alice M. Robinson, Vera Mowry Roberts and Milly S. Barranger. New York: Greenwood, 1989: 875-79.

A detailed biographical and career overview. Heck-Rabi suggests that Treadwell's "volatile temperament, her frankness, and assertiveness" harmed her career as a playwright. The entry contains close to a dozen inaccurate or misleading statements, ranging from incorrect dates of Treadwell's trips to and from Europe during World War I to misspellings of names for *Loney Lee*, George Stillwell, Judith Barlow, Nancy Wynn, and Ishbel Ross. Treadwell's lawsuit against Barrymore also never went to court, as Heck-Rabi suggests.

S198   Leiter, Samuel, ed. *The Encyclopedia of the New York Stage, 1930-1940*. New York: Greenwood, 1989.

Brief plot summaries, production details and critical excerpts for *Lone Valley* and *Plumes in the Dust*.

S199   "*Machinal* is Canceled." *New York Times* 23 Oct. 1989.

The Equity Library Theatre's production of *Machinal*, due to open November 2, has been cancelled because of "financial problems."

S200   Worrall, Nick. *Modernism to Realism on the Soviet Stage: Tairov--Vakhtangov--Okhlopkov*. Cambridge: Cambridge UP, 1989: 57-58.

Useful analysis of Tairov's production of *Machinal* within the context of his other theatrical work in the 1920s and '30s, including other plays from the Western repertoire. Includes descriptions of settings and staging moments.

1990-1996

1990

S201   Bywaters, Barbara L. "Marriage, Madness, and Murder in Sophie
        Treadwell's *Machinal.*" *Modern American Drama: the
        Female Canon.* Ed. June Schlueter. Rutherford [N.J.]:
        Fairleigh Dickinson UP, 1990: 97-110.
        Although critics have often dismissed the work "as
        a derivative drama of social criticism" about modern
        mechanization, *Machinal* should more correctly be viewed
        within "a female tradition of literature that dissects the
        restrictive institution of marriage and its effects on women."

S202   Collins, Glenn. "Play Proves its Point in Obscurity." *New York
        Times* 7 Nov. 1990: C15, C17.
        This profile of *Machinal* director Michael Grief
        includes conceptual and staging details from the New York
        Shakespeare Festival's revival.

S203   Darling, Lynn. "Finding a Miracle in *Machinal.*" *New York Newsday*
        13 Nov. 1990, sec. 2: 3, 13.
        Actress Jodie Markell recounts her difficulties in
        getting *Machinal* revived. Producers felt the play was too
        old, the subject too dark, the cast too large. Markell
        identified with the innocence of Helen, not her victimization.

S204   Marcuson, Lewis R. *The Stage Immigrant: the Irish, Italians, and
        Jews in American Drama, 1920-1960.* European Immigrants
        and American Society Series. New York: Garland, 1990.
        Describes Treadwell's sympathetic characterization
        of Joe DeLucchi in *Hope for a Harvest,* and compares the
        play with both Sidney Howard's *The Knew What They
        Wanted* and Hy Kraft's *Cafe Crown.*

S205   "Royalties from *Machinal.*" *New York Times* 26 Oct. 1990: C2.
        The recent revival of *Machinal* is generating "more
        than $1,000 a week" in production royalties to be used for
        the education and care of Native American children, as
        specified in Treadwell's will.

S206   Stevens, Andrea. "Life as a Machine." *New York Times* 14 Oct. 1990, sec. 2: 26.
        Short biographical article on Treadwell on the eve of the premiere of *Machinal*'s revival. Stevens notes that the life of the play's central character was "the very opposite of its author's." Includes a little reproduced photograph of Treadwell by UPI/Bettman.

1991

S207   Brockett, Oscar G. and Robert Findlay. *Century of Innovation.* 2nd ed. Boston: Allyn & Bacon, 1991: 300.
        Revised edition of S163.

S208   Germany, Lisa. *Harwell Hamilton Harris.* Austin: U Texas P, 1991: 52, 212.
        Treadwell was one of architect Harris's "most interesting clients." Harwell designed a home for Treadwell in Beverly Hills, but it was never built.

S209   Miller, Jordan Y. and Winifred L. Frazer. *American Drama Between the Wars: a Critical History.* Twayne's Critical History of American Drama. Boston: Twayne, 1991: 25.
        Brief mention of *Machinal*, a "startling expressionist play."

S210   Scott, David Alan. "Undiscovered Treasure: An Actor's Search Brings *Machinal* to Life." *American Theatre* Jan. 1991: 36-37.
        Describes Jodie Markell's persistent efforts to stage *Machinal* in New York, efforts which resulted in a workshop production seen by an impressed Joseph Papp. Markell believes Treadwell's dialogue and dramatic techniques prefigured Clifford Odets and Tennessee Williams.

S211   Wynn, Nancy. "Sophie Treadwell: Author of *Machinal.*" *Journal of American Drama and Theatre* 3.1 (1991): 29-47.
        Wynn examines early manuscripts of *Machinal* to show that Treadwell was largely responsible for conceiving of the play's unique manner of staging, something often attributed to either Hopkins or Jones. Wynn also excerpts descriptions from the acting manuscript at the New York Public Library of the play's final lighting effect.

1992

S212   Bzowski, Frances Diodato, comp. *American Women Playwrights,*
        1900-1930. Westport [Ct.]: Greenwood, 1992.
             Includes an entry on Treadwell listing her complete
        plays and dates, their location in manuscript form and
        biographical sources. Contains several minor errors.

S213   Leiter, Samuel L., ed. *The Encyclopedia of the New York Stage,*
        1940-1950. Westport [Ct.]: Greenwood, 1992.
             Provides a brief plot summary, production details
        and critical excerpts for *Hope for a Harvest.*

S214   Strand, Ginger Gail. "American Stages: Representation and the News
        Drama." Diss. Princeton U, 1992: 103-48.
             In a dissertation examining plays based on news
        stories, Strand includes a chapter on *Machinal* which pursues
        the question: "can a woman's experience be represented in the
        masculine language of journalism?" Strand's comparisons of
        the play with *The Adding Machine* are much more detailed
        here than in the abridged version published in *Theatre*
        Journal (S215). The chapter also offers a comparison of the
        play with Glaspell's *Trifles.* Strand states that Treadwell was
        covering the Snyder trial for the *San Francisco Bulletin,*
        something which seems unlikely since Treadwell wrote
        nothing else for the *Bulletin* after her move to New York
        over a decade earlier.

S215   Strand, Ginger. "Treadwell's Neologism: *Machinal." Theatre Journal*
        44 (1992): 163-75.
             At times applying the theories of Roland Barthes,
        Hèlène Cixous and Michel Foucault, Strand insightfully uses
        "the relationships between event, news story, and play to
        stage the process through which event becomes representation
        and a woman's experience is obscured, as legal and
        journalistic forces transform it to narrative." The cover of the
        issue includes a production photo from the 1990 revival.

S216   Willis, John, ed. *Theatre World. 1990-1991 Season.* New York:
        Applause Theatre Book Publishers, 1992: 93.
             Reprints the cast list and includes a production photo
        from the 1990 revival of *Machinal.*

1993

S217   Barlow, Judith E. "Introduction." *Machinal*. London: Nick Hern
        Books, 1993: vii-ix.
                Repeats much of the standard information known
        about Treadwell's work as a playwright and journalist.
        Suggests that the revival of interest in *Machinal* is due in part
        to the fact that the play's "universe is uncomfortably like our
        own."

S218   Geis, Deborah R. *Postmodern Theatric(k)s: Monologue in
        Contemporary American Drama*. Ann Arbor: U Michigan P,
        1993: 12.
                Likens Treadwell's device of the "interior
        monologue" to that of the soliloquy. The technique draws
        "acute attention to the *theatrical* nature of the dramatic
        event."

S219   Gore-Langton, Robert. "The Enigma Behind the Broadway Hit."
        London Daily Telegraph 15 Oct. 1993.
                Biographical profile of Treadwell, "one of those
        fascinating people whose life was full of adventure but about
        whom little was ever recorded." *Machinal* is "a minor
        classic." Reprints the photo of Ruth Snyder's execution
        which ran in the *New York Daily News*.

S220   Gritten, David. "Backstage Genius." *Telegraph Magazine* [London]
        16 Oct. 1993: 28-35.
                This profile of designers and production personnel
        for the Royal National Theatre's production of *Machinal*
        provides insights into the staging choices employed.

S221   Hagerty, Donald J. *Desert Dreams: the Art and Life of Maynard
        Dixon*. Layton [Utah]: Peregrine Smith, 1993: 62, 89, 251,
        257.
                Contains information on Treadwell's relationship
        with painter Maynard Dixon.

S222   Huberman, Jeffrey H., Brant L. Pope and James Ludwig. *The
        Theatrical Imagination*. Ft. Worth: Harcourt Brace
        Jovanovich, 1993: 448-51.
                Reprints S210.

S223   Tilles, Denise. "Tyro Talents: David Gallo." *TCI* Feb. 1993: 20.
        Set designer Gallo briefly discusses his award-
        winning design for *Machinal* in 1990.

S224   Wainscott, Ronald H. "Commercialism Glorified and Vilified: 1920s
        Theatre and the Business World." *The American Stage:
        Social and Economic Issues from the Colonial Period to the
        Present.* Eds. Ron Engle and Tice L. Miller. New York:
        Cambridge UP, 1993: 175-89.
        Brief mention of *Machinal* as an example of an
        "expressionistic journey play" of the 1920s which portrayed
        "the business world as a great deadener."

                                    1994

S225   Beal, Suzanne Elaine. "'Mama Teach Me That French': Mothers and
        Daughters in Twentieth Century Plays by Women
        Playwrights." Diss. U Maryland-College Park, 1994.
        Discusses the mother-daughter relationships in
        Machinal in a chapter on "The New Woman." *Machinal*,
        while sharing similarites with Glaspell's *The Verge*, differs
        from that play in that it explores constrictions by social class
        as well as gender.

S226   Handley, Ann. "*Machinal* Comes Out of the Closet." *Boston Sunday
        Globe* 20 Feb. 1994.
        In a preview of the production of *Machinal* by a
        student drama group at Tufts University, director Bruce
        Shapiro talks about his interpretation of the play as a veiled
        lesbian drama. Shapiro repeats many of the assertions made
        in his program notes for the production (S231), but also adds
        that the choice of the name Richard Roe, a common legal
        alias, proves the character is actually a woman is disguise.
        He neglects to offer other, more obvious possible
        interpretations for Treadwell's use of the alias.

S227   Jones, Jennifer. "In Defense of Woman: Sophie Treadwell's
        Machinal." *Modern Drama* 37 (1994): 485-96.
        Jones responds to the frequent assertion that
        Machinal was only loosely based on Ruth Snyder by
        examining many similarities between the infamous case and
        Treadwell's subsequent play. "I believe," Jones writes, "that

Machinal is the testimony, disallowed by the court of law, that Treadwell wished to introduce into the court of public opinion."

S228   Nordern, Barbara. "Journey Without Maps." *Everywoman* [London] Dec. 1993/Jan. 1994.
Profile of actress Fiona Shaw during her performances at the Royal National Theatre in *Machinal*. This play was only the second written by a woman to be produced in the RNT's "main house." Shaw's hope is that the play will be recognized as "a major 20th century classic." Includes a production photo.

S229   Peter, John. "A Hard Act to Follow." *The Sunday Times* [London] 2 Jan. 1994, sec. 7: 27.
In revisiting the time-honored debate over the supremacy of text or spectacle in theatre, Peter concludes that Ian MacNeil's monumental designs actually enhanced Treadwell's script of *Machinal*.

S230   Sawelson-Gorse, Naomi Helen. "Marcel Duchamp's 'Silent Guard': a Critical Study of Louise and Walter Arensberg." Diss. U California-Santa Barbara, 1994.
Examines Treadwell's involvement with noted art patrons, the Arensbergs, and their intellectual and artistic circle of friends. Notes Treadwell's involvement as assistant director for a film financed by Walter Arensberg in 1918, probably Leonce Perret's *Lafayette, We Come*.

S231   Shapiro, Bruce G. "*Machinal* Annotations." *Prologue* [Tufts University, Balch Arena Theater] 49.2 (1994): n.p.
Shapiro argues that *Machinal* is a veiled lesbian drama based more after the 1920s murder case of Velma West than Ruth Snyder. In these notes designed to accompany a production of the play at Tufts University (S226), Shapiro often takes material out of context to prove his point that the "machine" symbol of the play "represents heterosexuality and its concomitant idea of American family life, the patriarchy." He cites such vague symbols in the play as "darkness, the moon, and especially the kiss shared by the Young Woman and her lover" as proof of the play's hidden message of lesbianism. He cites Treadwell's twenty years' companionship with Lola Fries as evidence of her lesbian

leanings, without mentioning that Fries was often hired as Treadwell's housekeeper. Furthermore, he pieces together an undocumented quote by Treadwell about the play, which despite its appearance in print as a single stagement, actually derives from two sources dated over twenty years apart. In short, while Shapiro offers a unique interpretation of the play and Treadwell's life, his methodology is so shoddy as to cast doubt on any of his claims.

S232   Sierz, Aleks. "Polishing the Kitchen Sink." *New Statesman & Society* 11 Mar. 1994.
          Discusses the Royal National Theatre production of *Machinal* as part of a trend in the 1990s to use "a vast expressionist design to soup up a slightly arthritic play."

S233   Stickland, Louise. "*Machinal*'s National Exposé." *Live!* [London] Jan. 1994: 42+.
          Focuses on the production details behind the Royal National Theatre's revival of *Machinal*, including many vivid descriptions of staging moments. Includes a production photo of the scene in Roe's apartment, with the set's eight-ton steel grid ceiling looming over the actors.

                                    1995

S234   Dickey, Jerry. "Sophie Treadwell vs. John Barrymore: Playwrights, Plagiarism and Power in the Broadway Theatre of the 1920s." *Theatre History Studies* 15 (1995): 67-86.
          Detailed historical account of the events leading up to Treadwell's lawsuit against John Barrymore. The incident is discussed within the larger context of theatrical plagiarism of the 1920s and the formation of the Dramatists Guild. Includes photos of Treadwell, Barrymore, Michael Strange and Henry Hull in *Plumes in the Dust*.

S235   Shafer, Yvonne. *American Women Playwrights, 1900-1950*. New York: Peter Lang, 1995: 255-70.
          In a chapter devoted to Treadwell, Shafer provides an overview of significant plays and critical responses to productions. Shafer concludes that although she was not always commercially successful, Treadwell "drew attention to the serious problems of women in American society" and was

unafraid to experiment with structure and subject matter.

S236   Steed, Tonia. "Sophie Treadwell." *American Playwrights, 1880-1945: a Research and Production Sourcebook.* Ed. William W. Demastes. Westport [Ct.]: Greenwood, 1995: 427-36.
        Useful overview of Treadwell's major plays and thematic concerns. Provides brief biographical information, as well as summary statements from critical reviews and selective primary and secondary bibliographies. Most of the commentary appears to be drawn from Heck-Rabi (S167) and Wynn (S186).

S237   Watt, Stephen and Gary A. Richardson. Introduction to *Machinal.* *American Drama: Colonial to Contemporary.* Ft. Worth: Harcourt Brace & Co., 1995: 362-64.
        This introduction to the play primarily summarizes Barlow (S217), Heck-Rabi (S167) and Strand (S215). It also excerpts reviews by Dolan (R351), Atkinson (R069) and Rich (R344).

1996

S238   Brockett, Oscar G. *The Essential Theatre.* 6th ed. Ft. Worth: Harcourt Brace College Publishers, 1996: 190.
        This brief sidebar on "Sophie Treadwell's *Machinal*" reflects the growing acceptance of this play into the critical canon following its noteworthy 1990 and 1993 revivals.

Forthcoming

S239   Dickey, Jerry. "The 'Real Lives' of Sophie Treadwell: Expressionism and the Feminist Aesthetic in *Machinal* and *For Saxophone*." *Speaking the Other Self: American Women Writers.* Ed. Jeanne Campbell Reesman. Athens: U Georgia P, in press.
        Examines unpublished manuscripts of the two plays which suggest that Treadwell was consciously attempting to devise a uniquely feminist aesthetic in the theatre.

S240   Dickey, Jerry. "Sophie Treadwell's Summer with Boleslavsky and
         Lectures for the American Laboratory Theatre." *Art, Glitter,
         and Glitz*. Eds. Arthur Gerwitz and James J. Kolb. Westport
         [Ct.]: Greenwood, forthcoming.
                 Traces Treadwell's training with Boleslavsky in
         relation to her development as a playwright.

S241   Fox, Ann M. "Open Houses: American Women Playwrights, Media
         Culture and Broadway Success, 1906-1948." Diss. Indiana U,
         in progress.
                 Includes a comparison of Treadwell's use of the
         female outcast in her staged plays with portrayals of "fallen
         women" and working women in other popular culture
         sources.

PRODUCTIONS AND CREDITS

The following is a list of significant productions of Treadwell's plays. The extensive listing for *Machinal* should help correct the oft-cited belief that the play was totally forgotten prior to the 1960 and 1990 New York revivals. Depending upon available information, cast lists, artistic personnel, premiere dates and length of run are provided. With the exception of premiere productions, I have excluded college or university performances. A list of reviews cited in the Secondary Bibliography appears at the end of each listing.

P1 GRINGO

P1.1   *Gringo*. Comedy Theatre, New York. Opened 12 December 1922. 35 Performances. Produced and staged by Guthrie McClintic.
   Leornard Light--Richard Barbee
   Bessie Chivers--Edna Hibberd
   Paco--Leornard Doyle
   Myra Light--Edna Walton
   Chivers--Frederick Perry
   Tito, el Tuerto--José Ruben
   Concha--Olin Feld
   Stephen Trent--Arthur Albertson
   Pepe--Harry Hahn
   Tonio--J. Andrew Johnson
   Eduardo--Harold McKee
   José De Le Cruz--Jorge Anez
   Carlo--Aleides Bricena
   Vincentes--Manuel Valdispino
   Herculano--Justiniano Rosales

Aurelio--Manuel Carillo
Alvarez--Jefferson Heath
Reviews: R002, R003, R004, R005, R006, R007, R008, R009, R010, R011,
R012, R013, R014, R015, R016, R017, R018, R019, R020, R024,
R025.

P2 HIGHWAY

P2.1   *Highway*. Playbox Theatre, Pasadena. 16-23 April 1944.
Zepha-- Eula Mae Rivette/Kitty Whaley
Truckdriver--Phin Holder
Mrs. Walter Clark--Lee Arnold/Helen Inkster
John Bigwell--Onslow Stevens
Charles Meadows--Nels Fitzgerald
James Billings--Paul Maxey
Pedro--Darryl Antrim
Auto Salesman--Robert Cowell
Rich Monighan--Gene Waggle
Roy--Robert Cowell
A Driller--John Low
A Tool Dresser--Darryl Antrim
Manuela--Jean Osborn/Rosemary Danterive
Mrs. John Bigwell--Ysobel Momsen/Helen Hansen
Pop--Culbertson Myers

P2.2   *Highway*. Newtown Players, Newtown, Connecticut. August 1948.
Staged by Sophie Treadwell and Arthur Hopkins.
Review: R300.

P2.3   *Highway*. Telecast on U.S. Steel Hour. 17 February 1954. Produced
by the Theatre Guild.

P3 HOPE FOR A HARVEST

P3.1   *Hope for a Harvest*. The Guild Theatre, New York. Opened 26
November 1941. 38 Performances. Produced by the Theatre Guild. Staged
by Lester Vail. Supervised by Lawrence Langner and Theresa Helburn.
Settings by Watson Barratt.
Mrs. Matilda Martin--Helen Carew
Antoinette Martin--Judy Parrish
Elliott Martin--Fredric March

Carlotta Thatcher--Florence Eldridge
Nelson Powell--John Morny
Victor de Lucchi--Arthur Franz
Billy Barnes--Shelley Hull
Bertha Barnes--Edith King
Joe de Lucchi--Alan Reed
A Woman--Doro Merande

Reviews: R233, R234, R235, R236, R237, R239, R242, R243, R247, R251,
R252, R253, R256, R260, R262, R266, R268, R269, R270, R271,
R272, R274, R278, R281, R283, R284, R285, R291, R292, R293,
R294, R295, R296, R297, R298, R299.

The production, with the same cast, previewed in the Theatre Guild
subscription cities of New Haven (4-5 April 1941), Boston (7-19 April),
Washington, D.C. (21-26 April), Pittsburgh (28 April-3 May), Baltimore (5-10
May), Bridgeport, Connecticut (8 November) and Philadelphia (10-22
November).

Reviews: R238, R240, R241, R244, R245, R246, R248, R249, R250, R254,
R255, R257, R258, R259, R261, R263, R264, R265, R267, R273,
R275, R276, R277, R279, R280, R282, R286, R287, R288, R289,
R290.

P3.2   *Hope for a Harvest.* Radio broadcast on the Treasury Hour's "Millions
for Defense." 23 December 1941.

P3.3   *Hope for a Harvest.* Televised on U.S. Steel Hour. 10 November
1953. Produced by the Theatre Guild. Script adaptation by Norman Lessing.
Production supervised by John Haggott. Directed by Alex Segal. Sets by
Albert Hershong. Cast included:
Elliott Martin--Robert Preston
Carlotta Thatcher--Faye Emerson
Joe de Lucchi--Dino Di Luca
Victor de Lucchi--John Cassavetes
Tonie--Daryl Grimes

Reviews: R301, R302.

P4 THE ISLAND

P4.1   *The Island.* Edmond Town Hall, Newtown, Connecticut. 11 August
1932. 2 Performances. Presented by the New York Company.
Loretta Anderson--Irene Homer
Felton Rine--Hunter Gardner

Reed Eliot--Philip Ober
Olof--Rex Coover
Mrs. Anderson--Margaret Dalton
Anderson--Frank Camp
Captain Lambert--J. Ascher Smith
Laura Poole--Natalie Schafer
Reviews: R176, R180.

P5 LADIES LEAVE

P5.1   *Ladies Leave*. Charles Hopkins Theater, New York. Opened 1
October 1929. 15 Performances. Produced and staged by Charles Hopkins.
Designed by Robert Edmond Jones. Miss Daly's and Mrs. Doucet's gowns by
Tappé. Maids' dresses by Saks, Fifth Avenue.
Hannah--Lucille Ferry
Dr. Arpad Jeffer--Charles Trowbridge
J. Burnham Powers--Walter Connolly
Zizi Powers--Blyth Daly
Philip Havens--Henry Hull
Irma Barry White--Catharine Calhoun Doucet
A Masseur--William Stern
Jessie--Vera Mellish
Barbara--Katharine Lyons
Hilda--Athene Taylor
Reviews: R131, R132, R133, R134, R135, R136, R137, R138, R139, R140,
R141, R142, R143, R144, R145, R146, R147, R148, R149, R150.

P6 LONE VALLEY

P6.1   *Bound*. Lakewood Theatre, Skowhegan, Maine. Opened 20 June
1927, for a one week run. Produced by Crosby Gaige. Directed by Howard
Lindsay. Scenery designed by Charles Perkins. [The play tried out under the
title *Better to Marry*, which was later changed to *Bound*.]
Henry Allen--Harold Vermilyea
John Hanson--Wright Kramer
Lottie Grainger--Laura Carpenter
George Grainger--John Daly Murphy
May Martin--Ellen Dorr
Harry Lyman--Brandon Peters
Ella Grainger--Lorna Elliott
Review: R059.

P6.2   *Wild Honey.* Ford's Theatre, Baltimore. Opened 17 October 1927. Produced by Crosby Gaige. Directed by Sophie Treadwell. Settings by Robert Edmond Jones.

> Henry--Harold Vermilyea
> Lottie--Arline Blackburn
> Lasly--William Jeffrey
> Grainger--Augustin Duncan
> May--Ellen Dorr
> Lyman--Raymond Van Sickle
> Ella--Effie Shannon

Reviews: R058, R060, R061, R062, R063, R064, R065.

P6.3   *Lone Valley.* Broadway Theatre, Nyack, New York. Opened 29 June 1932. 3 Performances. Presented by The Rockland Producing Company, Inc. Directed by Luther Greene and Sophie Treadwell. Settings designed by Louis Bromberg.

> Joe--Elisha Cook, Jr.
> Lottie--Ami di Cerami
> Lasly--L'Estrange Millman
> Grainger--Arthur Morris
> Mary--Irene Homer
> Lyman--Eric North
> Ella--Edmonia Nolley

Reviews: R177, R178, R179.

P6.4   *Lone Valley.* Plymouth Theatre, New York. Opened 8 March 1933. 3 Performances. Produced and directed by Sophie Treadwell. Settings by Raymond Sovey.

> Joe--Alan Baxter
> Lottie--Mab Maynard
> Lasly--Ian Wolfe
> Grainger--Charles Kennedy
> Mary--Marguerite Borough
> Ella--Virginia Tracy
> Lyman--Oliver Barbour

Reviews: R181, R182, R183, R184, R185, R186, R187, R189, R190, R191, R192, R193, R194, R195.

P7 *THE LOVE LADY*

P7.1   *Claws.* Lenox Little Theatre. 31 December 1918. 1 Performance. Offered by Sophie Treadwell.

Allisa--Emily Calloway
Miss Nancy ("Nana") Trumbull--Alethea Luce
Zachary Alton--Herbert Bradshaw
Mme. Alla Xares--Sophie Treadwell
Eulalie--Beatrice Wood
Constant--René de la Chapelle
William Beck--Halbert Brown

P7.2   *The Love Lady.* Heckscher Theatre, New York. Opened 12 January
1925. 6 Private Performances. Settings by Cleon Throckmorton.
Nanette ("Nana") Trumbull--Mariette Hyde
Zachary Alton--John Taylor
Katherine Trumbull--Joana Roos
Rita Alvarez--Ana Montes [Sophie Treadwell]
Alvin Kent--Robert Le Sueur
William Barnes--N. St. Clair Hales
Eulalie--Andrée Corday
Constant--Edward LaRoche

P8 *MACHINAL*

P8.1   *Machinal.* Plymouth Theatre, New York. Opened 7 September 1928.
91 Performances. Produced and directed by Arthur Hopkins. Settings by
Robert Edmond Jones. Occasional music by Frank Harling. Special lighting
by George Schaff.
A Young Woman--Zita Johann
A Telephone Girl--Millicent Green
A Stenographer--Grace Atwell
A Filing Clerk--Leopold Badia
An Adding Clerk--Conway Washburn
A Mother--Jean Adair
A Husband--George Stillwell
A Bellboy--Otto Frederick
A Nurse--Nancy Allan
A Doctor--Monroe Childs
A Young Man--Hal K. Dawson
A Girl--Zenaide Ziegfeld
A Man--Jess Sidney
A Boy--Clyde Stork
A Man [Richard Roe]--Clark Gable
Another Man--Hugh M. Hite
A Waiter--John Hanley

A Judge--Tom Waters
A Lawyer for the Defense--John Connery
A Lawyer for the Prosecution--James MacDonald
A Court Reporter--Otto Frederick
A Bailiff--John Hanley
A Reporter--Conway Washburn
Second Reporter--Hugh M. Hite
Third Reporter--Hal K. Dawson
A Jailer--John Hanley
A Matron--Mrs. Chas. Willard
A Priest--Charles Kennedy
A Jury, Dancers, Guards

Reviews: R066, R068, R069, R070, R071, R072, R073, R074, R075, R076, R077, R078, R079, R080, R081, R082, R083, R084, R085, R087, R088, R089, R090, R091, R092, R093, R094, R095, R096, R097, R098, R099, R101, R102, R103, R104, R105, R106, R107, R108, R109, R110, R111, R112, R113, R114, R115, R116, R117, R118, R119, R120, R121, R122, R123, R124, R125, R126, R127, R128, R129, R130.

The production previewed at the Shubert Theatre, New Haven, Connecticut, the week of 3 September 1928.
Reviews: R067, R086, R100.

P8.2   *Machinal*. Berkeley Playhouse Association, California. Opened 25 October 1929. 6 Performances. Directed by Everett Glass. Settings by Lloyd Stanford.

A Young Woman--Ruth Langelier
A Telephone Girl--Levonne Geist
A Filing Clerk--Adolph Benjamin
An Adding Clerk--Douglas G. McPhee
A Mother--Adelaide Blanchard
A Husband--George Sawyer
A Nurse--Jayne Hoffman
A Doctor--Pat Curren
A Young Man--Bernard Covit
A Girl--Lois Atterbury
A Man--James Wallis
Another Man--Edwin Rosenberry
A Waiter--Warren Phelps
A Judge--Otis Marston
A Lawyer for the Defense--Louis Piccirillo
A Lawyer for the Prosecution--Malcolm McGregor

A Court Reporter--George Creary
A Bailiff--Earl Hewitt
A Reporter--Bernard Covit
Another Reporter--Elvord Maleville
A Jailer--Victor Schoch
A Matron--Florence Mullins
A Priest--Robert Scott
Review: R151.

P8.3   *The Life Machine.* Produced privately at the Arts Theatre Club, London. Opened 15 July 1931. 6 Private Performances. Later transferred to the Garrick Theatre, after being licensed by the Lord Chamberlain. 178 Performances. Produced by Henry Oscar.
    Adding Clerk--Holland Bennett
    Filing Clerk--Don Gemmell
    Stenographer--Dorita Curtis-Hayward
    Telephone Girl--Doris Gilmore
    George H. Jones--David Horne
    Young Woman--Mary Grew
    Mother--Winifred Evans
    Doctor--Drelincourt Odlum
    Policeman--George Tempest
    Man [Richard Roe]--Colin Keith-Johnston
    Priest--E.A. Walker
Reviews: R152, R153, R154, R155, R156, R157, R158, R159, R160, R161, R162, R163, R167, R168, R169, R170, R171, R173.

P8.4   *Machinal.* Kamerny Theatre, Moscow. Opened May 1933. Performed in the Kamerny repertoire for two years. Adapted by Sergei Bertensson. Directed by Alexander Tairov. Sets by Vadim Ryndin. Original music by L. Polovinkin. With Alice Koonen as the Young Woman. Reviews: R188, R196, R197.

P8.5   *Ellen Jones.* Studio theatre of the Vakhtangov Theatre, Moscow. Fall 1933. Directed by Reuben Simonov.
Review: R197.

P8.6   *Maszyna [The Machine].* Produced in Warsaw, Poland, under the aegis of Leon Schiller. Opened 18 January 1934. Translated by Ewa Kuncewicz, who also appeared as the Young Woman.
Review: R333.

P8.7 *Machinal.* NBC Radio. Broadcast on "Arthur Hopkins Presents." 7 June 1944. With Zita Johann.

P8.8 *Machinal.* Theatre Arts Colony Players. Sequoia Club, San Francisco. December 1947-January 1948. Produced by Marie Darrack. Directed by Leon Forbes.

P8.9 *Machinal.* The President Theatre, New York. Opened 25 January 1950. One week run. Presented by Erwin Piscator's Dramatic Workshop and Technical Institute. Directed by Margrit Wyler.

P8.10 *Machinal.* NBC-TV. Televised on the Robert Montgomery Show. 25 January 1954. Adapted by Irving Gaynor Neiman. Directed by Perry Lafferty. With Joan Loaring (Young Woman) and Malcolm Lee Beggs (George H. Jones).
Review: R303.

P8.11 *Machinal.* Center Theatre, Los Angeles. Opened 11 April 1958. Presented by Quadrivium Productions. Directed by Joseph Sargent. Lighting by Howard Vaughn. With Mary Carver (Young Woman), Sid Clute (George H. Jones), Peggy Rae (Mother), John Duke (Richard Roe), Delia Salvi (Telephone Operator), Frank McCulley, Richard Voerg, Allan Emerson, Gene Terry, Vincent Griego, and Grace Hughes.
Reviews: R304, R305.

P8.12 *Machinal.* Produced by Whitewood Property Owners Association, near Nyack, New York [1958-59]. Directed by Zita Johann. Gowns by Clare Potter. The cast was composed of students who were studying acting with Johann, who resided at the time in Nyack. Johann, however, played the Young Woman.

P8.13 *Machinal.* Gate Theatre, New York. Opened 7 April 1960. 79 Performances. Produced by Richard Karp and John Eyre, in association with Max K. Lerner and Morton Siegal. Directed by Gene Frankel. Setting by Ballou. Lighting by Lee Watson. Choreography by Sophie Maslow. Sound created by H. Arthur Gilbert. Music by Ezra Laderman.
> Sceneshifter 1--Mark Ryder
> Sceneshifter 2--Gene Gebauer
> Sceneshifter 3--Beatrice Seckler
> Sceneshifter 4--Carol Bender
> Typist--Florence Anglin
> File Clerk--Sidney Kay
> Computor--Russell Bailey

Telephone Operator--Renee Taylor
George H. Jones--Vincent Gardenia
Helen Jones--Dolores Sutton
Mother--Florence Stanley
A Young Girl--Eve Lawrence
Card Players--Richard Mansfield, Paul Gloss
Tenement Woman 1--Juanita Torrence
Tenement Woman 2--Linda Seff
Tenement Woman 3--Ann Blackstone
Her Husband--Rod Bolbin
Nurse--Florence Anglin
Doctor--Charles Caron
Harry Smith--Rod Colbin
Richard Roe--Gerald O'Loughlin
Lover of Amontillado--Houghton Jones
His Young Partner--Richard Mansfield
Woman in Trouble--Linda Seff
Her Partner--Morton Siegal
Bailiff--Russell Bailey
Judge--Houghton Jones
Matron--Florence Anglin
Prosecutor--Art Smith
Defense Attorney--William Macy
Reporters--Ann Blackstone, Rod Colbin, Paul Gloss
Priest--Charles Caron
Prison Singer--Juanita Torrence
Barber 1--J. Thomas Degidon
Barber 2--Richard Mansfield
Reviews: R316, R317, R318, R319, R320, R321, R322, R324, R325, R326, R327, R328, R329, R330.

P8.14 *Machinal.* ABC-TV. Broadcast 14 August 1960. Directed by Philip Saville. With Joanna Dunham (Young Woman), Donald Pleasance (George H. Jones), and Gary Cockerell (Richard Roe).

P8.15 *Machinal.* Encompass Theatre, New York. Opened 6 April 1978. Presented initially as a staged reading.

P8.16 *Machinal.* New York Theatre Ensemble, under the auspices of NYTE's Women's Program. Opened 9 April 1981. Directed by Robin Pollock. Lighting by Tony Fristachi. Set and sound design by Robin Pollock.
Telephone Girl--Ann Benjamin
Helen Jones--Cathy Combs

Mother--Gloria Harper
Harry Smith, et al.--Bruce Higgison
Priest, et al.--John Imro
Lover--Mark David Jacobson
George H. Jones--Martin Krever
Prosecuting Attorney, et al.--Tom Kulesha
Stenographer II, et al.--Susan Mitchell
Defense Attorney, et al.--John Moraitis
Doctor, et al.--Mike Person
Stenographer I, et al.--Kit Wiener

Machinal was performed on the second half of a double-bill with Susan Glaspell's *Trifles*.

P8.17 *Machinal*. San Francisco Repertory. May-June 1983. Directed by Michelle Truffaut. Costumes by Pamela Masun-Brune. Sets by Fred Hartman. Sound Design by Bob Henry. Cast included:
Helen--Cynthia Wands
George H. Jones--Tom Dahlgren
Doctor/Man at Bar/Judge--Donald Hudson
Mother--Wana Dowell
Reviews: R334, R335.

P8.18 *Machinal*. Lifeline Theatre, Chicago. February-March 1988. Directed by Mark Lancaster.
Reviews: R336, R337.

P8.19 *Machinal*. Public Theatre/LuEsther Hall, New York. Opened 2 October 1990. 47 Performances and 24 Previews. Produced by Joseph Papp and the New York Shakespeare Festival. Directed by Michael Greif. Set design by David Gallo. Costume design by Sharon Lynch. Lighting design by Kenneth Posner. Original music and sound by John Gromada. Associate Producer Jason Steven Cohen.
Announcer/Bellboy/Waiter/Defense Attorney/Jailer--Timothy Britten
Parker
Adding Clerk/Prosecuting Attorney/First Barber--Ralph Marrero
Filing Clerk/Neighbor/Boy at Speakeasy Table #3/Reporter--Omar
Carter
Stenographer/Neighbor/Nurse/Final Speakeasy Woman/
Reporter--Linda Marie Larson
Telephone Girl/Neighbor/Court Senographer--Kristine Nielsen
Husband--John Seitz
Young Woman--Jodie Markell
Mother--Marge Redmond

Singer/Neighbor--Darby Rowe
Doctor/Salesman at Speakeasy Table #1/Neighbor/Reporter/
Second Barber--Christopher Fields
Lover--William Fichtner
Man at Speakeasy Table #3/Priest/Neighbor--Rocco Sisto
Man at Speakeasy Table #2/Neighbor/Bailiff/Reporter/Guard--Gareth
Williams
Judge/Final Speakeasy Man/Convict--Michael Mandell
Reviews: R338, R339, R340, R341, R342, R343, R344, R345, R346, R347,
R348, R351.

A workshop production of *Machinal*, featuring Jodie Markell and directed by
Michael Grief was originally produced by Naked Angels/Full Count in
December 1989 for a two week run.

P8.20   *Machinal*. Theatre Oobleck, Chicago. July-August 1991. Produced
by A Fly's Eye Production. Directed by Barbara Thorne. With George
Czarnecki as George H. Jones and Patti Hanson as the Mother.
Review: R349.

P8.21   *Machinal*. CityStage Ensemble, Theatre-at Jack's, Denver. March-
April 1992. Directed by Dan Heister. Sets by Hal Terrance. With Vicki
Gruda (Helen), Kurt Soderstrom (telephone operator/patron in gay bar/George
H. Jones), Rebekah Buric (Richard Roe), Terry Burnsed and David Quinn
(attorneys).
Review: R350.

P8.22   *Machinal*. Lyttleton Theatre, London. Opened 15 October 1993.
Produced by the Royal National Theatre. Directed by Stephen Daldry. Settings
by Ian MacNeil. Costumes by Clare Mitchell. Lighting by Rick Fisher. Music
by Stephen Warbeck. Movement by Quinny Sacks.
Adding Clerk/Judge/Barber 1--Bill Wallis
Filing Clerk/First Reporter--James Duke
Stenographer/Nurse/Matron--Lynn Farleigh
Telephone Girl--Matilda Ziegler
George H. Jones--John Woodvine
Young Woman--Fiona Shaw
Mother--June Watson
Garbage Man/Bailiff/First Guard--Alec Wallis
Woman--Yvonne Nicholson
Boy/Bellboy/Boy at Bar--Timothy Matthews
Young Man/Third Reporter--David Bark-Jones

Girl--Juliette Gruber
Woman/Woman at Bar--Rachel Power
Man/Man at Bar/Second Reporter--Michael Brogan
Wife--Cate Hamer
Husband/Man--Michael Bott
Singer--Sara Griffiths
Doctor/Court Reporter/Second Guard--Christopher Rozycki
First Man/Man [Richard Roe]--Ciaran Hinds
Second Man/Prosecution Lawyer--Colin Stinton
Man at Bar/Defense Lawyer--Roger Sloman
Man Behind Bar/Singer--Marcus Heath
Girl--Harriet Harrison
Clerk/Barber 2--David Holdaway
Priest--Allan Mitchell
Jailer--Paul Benzing
Other parts played by members of the company and stage technicians
of the Royal National Theatre.
Reviews: R353, R354, R355, R356, R357, R358, R359, R360, R361, R362,
R363, R364, R365, R366, R367, R368, R369, R370, R371, R372,
R373, R374, R375, R376, R377, R378, R379, R380, R381, R382,
R383, R384, R385, R386.

P8.23 *Machinal*. Eclipse Theatre Company, Chicago. December 1993.
Directed by Susan Leigh. Movement Coach Stephen Gray. Cast included
Casey Cooper as the Young Woman.
Review: R352.

P8.24 *Machinal*. Actors Theater of San Francisco. June-July 1994. Co-
directed by Chris Phillips and Catherine Castellanos. Set design by Michele
Tedeschi. Costumes by Denise Pieracci. Lighting by Deric Gerlach. Cast
included:

Helen--Nadja Kennedy
Mother--Joan Reynolds
Priest--Bryan Coleman
Telephone Operator--Darci Adams
Richard Roe--Henry Garrett
Office Manager--Edith Bryson
Filing Clerk--Kevin Heverin
Nurse--Luisa Adrianzen
Doctor--Finn Curtin
Husband/Older Man in Speakeasy--B. David James
Young Man in Speakeasy--Marcelo Griess
Reviews: R387, R388, R389.

P9 *O NIGHTINGALE*

P9.1   *Loney Lee.* Broadway tryout production: played Atlantic City, New Jersey, the first week of November 1923; played Hartford, Connecticut at the Parson's Theatre, beginning 12 November 1923. Produced by George C. Tyler. With Helen Hayes as Appolonia Lee, Thais Magrane as Mme. Vera Istomina, and Hamilton Revelle as the Marquis.
Reviews: R021, R022, R023, R026, R027, R028.

P9.2   *O Nightingale.* 49th Street Theatre, New York. Opened 15 April 1925. 29 Performances. Co-produced by Sophie Treadwell and Mary Kirkpatrick. Directed by John Kirkpatrick. Settings by Cleon Throckmorton. Miss Allen's and Miss Daube's gowns by H. Wells Hall. Miss Eliot's gown by Helen Pons.

 Richard Warrington--Lyonel Watts
 Mme. Vera Istomina--Constance Eliot [Sophie Treadwell]
 Dot Norton--Suzanne Willa
 Appolonia Lee--Martha-Bryan Allen
 Le Marquis de Severac--Ernest Lawford
 A Waiter--Marcel Lemans
 Lawrence Gormont--Fred Irving Lewis
 Flora St. John--Harda Daube

Reviews: R029, R030, R031, R032, R033, R034, R035, R036, R037, R038,
    R039, R040, R041, R042, R043, R044, R045, R046, R047, R048,
    R049, R050, R051, R052, R053, R054, R055, R056, R057.

P10 *PLUMES IN THE DUST*

P10.1   *Plumes in the Dust.* 46th Street Theatre, New York. Opened 6 November 1936. 11 Performances. Produced and directed by Arthur Hopkins. Production Design by Woodman Thompson.

 Mrs. Frances Allan--Fredrica Slemons
 Miranda--Laura Bowman
 Lizzie--Artie Belle McGinty
 John Allan--Charles Kennedy
 Rosalie Poe--Barbara Fulton
 Edgar Allan Poe--Henry Hull
 Moncure Harrison--Don Shelton
 Elmira Shelton--Ruth Yorke
 Mrs. Maria Clemm--Mary Morris
 Virginia Clemm--Amelia Romano

Miss McNab--Iris Whitney
John P. Kennedy--Earl Fleishman
Anne Lynch--Eleanor Goodrich
Sarah Anne Lewis--Hedwig Schoch
Mr. Lewis--Maruice Lavigne
N.P. Willis--William C. Jackson
Elizabeth Ellet--Gertrude Coghlan
Margaret Fuller--Portia Morrow
Frances S. Osgood--Dorothea Petgen
Dr. Griswold--Donald Willson
Mrs. Sutherland--Ada Potter
Lou--Pauline Myers
Dr. Snodgrass--Palmer Ward
An Attendant--Bernard Kisner
Dr. Moran--Edwin Cushman
Nurse--Juliet Fremont
Reviews: R198, R199, R200, R201, R203, R204, R205, R206, R207, R208,
R210, R211, R212, R213, R214, R215, R217, R220, R221, R222,
R224, R226, R228, R229, R230, R231, R232.

The production received tryout performances at the McCarter Theatre, Princeton
University, 24 October 1936; The National Theatre, Washington, D.C.
beginning 26 October 1936; and Ford's Theater, Baltimore, fall 1936.
Reviews: R202, R209, R216, R218, R219, R223, R225, R227.

P11 *SYMPATHY*

P11.1 *An Unwritten Chapter.* Pantages Theater, San Francisco. Opened 31
January 1915 for a one-week run. Staged by John J. Cluxton.
The Man--Frederick Snook
His Man--Ato Kiwata
Jean Traig--Herself
The play was performed on a vaudeville bill with the Pantages Theater
orchestra, comic jugglers with dogs, and a variety duo.
Review: R001.

P12 *WOMAN WITH LILIES*

P12.1 *Now He Doesn't Want to Play.* University of Arizona Department of
Drama, Tucson. Opened 25 July 1967. 5 Performances. Directed by Peter R.
Marroney. Set Design by Channing S. Smith. Costumes Helen W. Currie.

Annabel--Liz Kneeland
Cragg--M. David Storti
Dona Dora--Lita Felix
Lupe--Sylvia Ruiz
Herculano--Ernesto Polo
Juanito--Alberto Moore
Carmen--Diane Vidal
Bliss--William Reese
Peg--Lois Miller Tipling
Lodger--Russ Andaloro, Jr.
Taxi Driver--Timothy Gargiulo
Reviews: R331, R332.

AUTHOR INDEX

This index lists all critics and scholars included in the Secondary Bibliography. The references are keyed to the catalogue numbers assigned each entry.

SUBJECT INDEX

This index provides page references as well as references keyed to the primary ("A" = non-fiction) and secondary ("R" = reviews; "S" = books, articles, and sections) bibliographies.

About the Author

JERRY DICKEY is Associate Professor and Director of Graduate Studies in the Department of Theatre Arts at the University of Arizona. He has presented papers on Sophie Treadwell at numerous conferences and has published widely in such journals as *Theatre Journal, Theatre Topics,* and *New England Theatre Journal.* He is a Past-Chair of the Theatre History Focus Group of the Association for Theatre in Higher Education.

ISBN 0-313-29388-0

90000>

EAN

9 780313 293887

HARDCOVER BAR CODE